# CRIME

## and the

# PENAL SYSTEM

## A TEXTBOOK OF CRIMINOLOGY

BY

HOWARD JONES, B.Sc.(Econ.), Ph.D.

LECTURER IN SOCIAL STUDIES, UNIVERSITY COLLEGE OF LEICESTER

UNIVERSITY TUTORIAL PRESS LTD

CLIFTON HOUSE, EUSTON ROAD, LONDON, N.W.1

*Published* 1956

PRINTED IN GREAT BRITAIN BY UNIVERSITY TUTORIAL PRESS LTD, FOXTON
NEAR CAMBRIDGE

# PREFACE

In this book the causes and treatment of crime, together with methods of prevention and penal reform, are dealt with from the English standpoint—American and Continental experience, however, being drawn upon where necessary. It is hoped that the book will be of value, not only to students reading the subject of Sociology or training in social work, but will also serve as a guide to modern ideas in this field for those actively engaged in some form of social service, or otherwise interested in these problems.

Acknowledgments have been made in references at the end of each chapter to the many authorities whose works have been cited. If any to whom acknowledgments are due have been omitted, it will have been by inadvertence, and I ask their indulgence.

I should also like to thank various friends who have helped me by reading and commenting upon particular chapters: Mr Frank Dawtry, General Secretary, National Association of Probation Officers, who read through Chapters XIII and XIV; Mr Gordon Rose, M.A., Lecturer in Social Administration in the University of Manchester, for reading Chapter XV; and Mr K. M. Fogg, Principal Probation Officer, City of Leicester, for reading Chapter XVIII. They must not, however, be held responsible for anything that has been said in these chapters.

Finally, I cannot sufficiently emphasise my gratitude to my teacher and friend, Dr Hermann Mannheim, for inspiration, encouragement, and many kindnesses. To his actual work in the field of Criminology, not only this book, but also English Criminology and the cause of penal reform in this country, owe a tremendous debt.

H. J.

# CONTENTS

# CRIME AND THE PENAL SYSTEM

## A TEXTBOOK OF CRIMINOLOGY

## CHAPTER I

### THE SCIENCE OF CRIMINOLOGY

Crime is costly, and has reached such dimensions as to constitute a real threat to our way of life. According to one post-war estimate, one person in every nine becomes delinquent at some time in his life.[1] It is natural that we should be perturbed by figures such as these, but perturbation alone will not help us. For any improvement in the situation we must ultimately rely upon advances in our understanding of the problem. This is the function of criminology, as *the science that studies the social phenomenon of crime, its causes, and the measures which society directs against it.*

Some may feel that the claim of criminology to be called a science is very much open to question; its methods, like those of other social sciences, are often highly subjective, and it has been able so far to establish no scientific laws that can claim general validity.

### Criminology and Ethics

Above all, it is a reformist study, seeking to effect changes either in individuals or in society itself. How can a science be "reformist"? It has been a basic principle of science right back to Aristotle that a science is concerned with "what is" and not with "what ought to be". The science should aim at "ethical neutrality".[2]

But even in the natural sciences, where the banishment of normative concepts has gone so far, the trend nowadays is steadily towards recognising the social responsibility of the scientist. Knowledge for its own sake may keep unsullied the traditional scientific virtues, but it is a rather abstract and uninspiring motive for scientific work compared to the possibility of helping to build a better life for one's fellows. The growth of concern among scientists about their social role is well illustrated by the controversies about atomic energy and the atomic bomb, in which so many of them have joined in the years since Hiroshima and Nagasaki.

This "social concern" has been the mainspring of criminology from the very beginning. The earliest workers in the field, John

Howard, Elizabeth Fry, Mary Carpenter, were all drawn into it by their desire to alleviate suffering, or possibly quite often to "pluck brands from the burning". A similar spirit is very much alive among modern criminologists, and if it were not so, their science would lose its *raison d'être*.

This is not simply a historical accident. The regard paid in all the social sciences to reformist considerations is due to the fact that (unlike the physical sciences) their subject-matter, being man, is an end in himself. We have no right to use him merely as a means towards the attainment of knowledge "for its own sake", but only towards the attainment of knowledge for *his* sake.

As soon, however, as a science begins to concern itself with practical applications, many ethical issues arise. There is more involved here than the initial admission that criminology is an applied science directed towards the solution of the very practical problem of crime. We are also required to ask ourselves whether this or that practical application is a proper way to treat human beings. The criminologist, for instance, cannot avoid passing judgment upon the humaneness or otherwise of penal methods, as well as upon their effectiveness for the purpose of reducing crime. There are certain generally accepted decencies in our culture which also enter into the framework of ends which criminologists have set themselves.

So great is our present-day moral uncertainty that even these basic decencies have not gone entirely unchallenged, especially in totalitarian countries. However, mercy and humanity, and ideas like these, still stand, like rocks amid the cross-currents and whirlpools of contemporary morality, eroded a little perhaps, but still firm.

Moral judgments must, of course, also enter into the calculations of the criminologist as objects of study. To exclude them would be an impossible limitation, for the ethical beliefs of individuals play a decisive part in the aetiology of crime, and in the reaction of the community to it. The sort of questions which are likely to be asked are: To what extent does crime result from atypical moral development in individual criminals, and how may this be prevented? or, To what extent does a penal code result from a widely felt moral revulsion against the criminal rather than from a desire to reform him? Both of these questions could have a determinable answer, and might have significance for the understanding of crime.

At the same time, it must be admitted that the traditional scientific viewpoint is fundamentally sound. Any encroachment of ethics upon the process of analysis itself would impair the usefulness of criminology as a science, and perhaps prevent it from achieving its reformist aims. If a science is to make any progress at all in the understanding of nature, its practitioners must embark upon their examination of the facts of the real world free from any preconceived ethical notions.

## What is Crime?

In particular, in criminology, it is important to arrive at an objective definition of the word "crime". Now careful and exact definition is in any case a first requirement of science. Many scientific controversies, especially in the social sciences, owe their origin to verbal confusions. For example, two authorities may disagree because, although they do not realise it, they are really discussing different things. Thus most laymen believe they know what "crime" means, but among criminologists there is no such certainty. Different authorities use the term in different senses, and as a result come to different conclusions about it.

But the ethical issue also emerges sharply. Is crime to be defined as a "breach of the established criminal law", or is it to be used to refer to behaviour which is adjudged good or bad according to some ethical criterion, irrespective of whether the law is also broken? Where the latter point of view is adopted, it is implied that there are universal and permanently valid rules of conduct, standing above and beyond the criminal law, and by contrast with which the law is imperfect and vacillating—relative always to time and place. In short, that behaviour can be good or bad *in itself*.

This idea of the supremacy of the moral law over the laws of the state is always arising. In England we have long been accustomed to the conscientious objector—against vaccination, religious education in school, military service, and so on. It is the sort of claim which the Churches have always made—for the permanent truth of their doctrines as compared with the shifting and imperfect laws made by man.

There can be no doubt that the criminal law is relative, both to time and place. Thus, what is forbidden by the law changes from year to year, and is impressively transformed over longer periods, or at times of social upheaval such as war or revolution. In the eighteenth century, the death penalty was imposed for all sorts of trivial acts: appearing disguised on the public highway, shooting rabbits, "stealing anything privily from a person". And while murder was treated with great tolerance, it was a capital offence to slit a person's nose. Hurwitz[3] points out that such offences as blasphemy, swearing, adultery, and homosexuality, were once crimes according to Danish law, but are no longer so. The numerous new crimes created by the exigencies of both World Wars show that the relativity of the criminal law can be observed over short periods as well as long.

Similar striking differences in the penal code occur between different countries, even countries with the same general heritage of culture. Thus homosexuality between adult men, which is such a serious offence in England, is ignored in France and parts of Scandinavia. Differences multiply as one crosses cultural boundaries: bigamy is an offence in the West, but in some Arab countries and in many primitive communities, polygamy is an established social institution.

Can such a fluctuating and indefinite thing, as the criminal law is here shown to be, form the subject of scientific enquiry, or give rise to general and permanently valid scientific laws? Surely it would be better to identify behaviour according to its inherent nature than to rely upon the superficial and arbitrary categories of the criminal law.

## Natural Crime

In his concept of "natural crime", R. Garafalo has sought to achieve this without the sacrifice of objective standards.[4] Natural crimes, as he understands them, are acts which do violence to certain essential characteristics of human nature and human social life. They include behaviour which runs counter to the natural human sentiments of compassion and honesty, or which are harmful to the community. Unfortunately the objectivity of these standards is only apparent. For as modern anthropologists are showing, human nature is infinitely variable in its expression, and in the social institutions which it creates for itself. The idea of a constant human nature provides no peg on which to hang a more stable concept of crime.

Much the same applies to attempts to apply other sociological criteria, such as Mannheim's idea of crime as "anti-social behaviour".[5] On closer inspection, all these so-called objective criteria prove to be ethical judgments in disguise. One is forced in the end to return to the naked choice between a legal definition of crime and a purely subjective definition in terms of the essential "rightness" or "wrongness" of particular acts.

The latter could be maintained successfully by arguing that the moral law is divinely ordained, and no doubt many will take their stand on this religious platform. However, empirical study lends it absolutely no support. Vast changes have occurred in our Christian ethics over the centuries. The Ten Commandments would no longer be accepted as an adequate ethical code even by many Christians, and the lending of money at interest, which was stigmatised as usury and forbidden by the medieval Church, is a major and indispensable prop of contemporary capitalist society. Religious attitudes towards some issues, for example, towards the use of birth control, have changed within living memory.

In the Middle Ages, when the Church provided the main driving force in society, it might have been possible (in Europe at least) to have depended upon some ethical test, for at that time the current Church ethic was largely unchallenged. But in those days the law itself was dominated by the ethic of the Church, and might just as readily have been utilised. The breakdown of the stable and internally consistent legal code of the Middle Ages is a reflection of the disintegration of the medieval moral code. Our present legal contradictions faithfully reflect our disagreements about ultimate ends.

Nowadays general agreement about what constitutes "right" behaviour becomes unobtainable as soon as one moves far beyond the "basic decencies" already mentioned. The socialist, who takes an egalitarian view of property rights, is unlikely to be as disturbed by offences against the law of property as the staunch supporter of capitalism. The Catholic's hostility to the divorce laws or to contraception is not shared by all his Protestant fellow-countrymen. Then there is the explosive impact of totalitarian ethics in the last thirty years. This has called in question many of our most cherished moral principles. We face what Karl Mannheim has vividly called a "crisis of values" in our society.[6] As will be seen later, this moral predicament of ours makes its own contribution to the causation of crime.

The criminal law has at least this advantage over any ethical test: even though it does fluctuate, it is objectively determinable at any given time and place, and the changes which take place in it can be easily traced. Morality, on the other hand, has become an individual matter, and although (to the present writer) this represents moral progress, it does end in a kind of anarchy in which much is elusive and uncertain, and from which few agreed principles emerge. On this ground alone, the ethical criterion must be rejected. In addition there are all the dangers of confusion and misunderstanding which are likely to arise if a word which has become established in one sense is used in another.

## White Collar Crime

The difficulties into which we are led by non-legal definitions of crime may be illustrated by reference to E. H. Sutherland's theory of "white collar crime".[7] According to Sutherland, there is much crime in America which escapes punishment. Some of it is crime in the sense of a breach of the "established criminal law", but the criminals go scot-free because they are rich and powerful, and so can bribe the police, or even sometimes the judges, or bring political influence to bear to secure their immunity. Some of it, being breaches by business men of administrative laws and commercial regulations, is dealt with by administrative tribunals instead of by the criminal courts, and is not therefore recorded as crime. The inevitable omission of these two types of offence in research based upon recorded crime, is bound, says Sutherland, to cause us to obtain an incomplete and unbalanced picture of the problem.

Much "white collar crime", however, is not a breach of any kind of law, or even of the spirit of the law. It includes such things as falsehood in advertising or in company prospectuses, the manipulation of the property markets, or even the sale of securities which are about to fall in value on the stock-market, in order to avoid loss.

However reprehensible one may feel behaviour of this kind to be, it only confuses an already complex situation to call it crime. It is clearly behaviour which Sutherland considers should be prohibited and punished by the criminal law, and many will strongly agree with him. Others, however, may disagree. Especially in America, many would still subscribe to Cobden's dictum that there is nothing immoral in endeavouring to buy in the cheapest market and sell in the dearest, and that, indeed, the welfare of society depends upon the skill with which this is done. It embodies the basic morality of contemporary capitalism, which our commercial law expresses in the maxim *Caveat emptor*. Sutherland, as a moralist, is entitled to condemn such behaviour, and to seek to have it made illegal, but until he has achieved this, he is not entitled to call it crime.

It is no answer to say, as does Sutherland, that "legal definitions should not confine the work of the criminologist and he should be free to push across the barriers of legal definitions whenever he sees behaviour outside the legal field which resembles the behaviour

within".[8]  No legal definition of crime would restrict the investigations of the criminologist: it would still remain open to him to
study any social phenomena outside the field of crime which might
illumine problems within that field.  For instance, if, as Sutherland
maintains, the activities of the white-collar "criminaloids" cause a
general lowering of standards of honesty, then they are important
as possible causes of crime; but it is as possible causal factors that
they must be studied, and not as crime.

The fact that some are, and some are not, willing to carry their
machinations as far as a breach of the law, suggests that there may
even be a crucial difference involved, which is of the very essence of
crime, as distinct from anti-social or dishonest behaviour within the
law.  Most of us behave in a dishonest or anti-social way at times,
but where a breach of the law is concerned we feel it to be a much
larger step.  Many motives seem to be involved in our reluctance
to take this step—the fear of being disgraced or punished, or the
feeling that to break the law would be a serious wrong.  None of
these deter the criminal.  The distinction may well prove to lie at
the heart of the whole problem.

To the Englishman, many of the practices which Sutherland
attacks seem very familiar.  We also have the advertiser who
claims that his patent medicine will cure all the ills of humanity,
but we would no more describe him as a criminal than we would
the shopkeeper who puts all his best apples at the front of the
window.  What shocks us at least as much is the corruption in
political and legal circles in America, which allows organised
criminals to continue their operations unchecked.  The revelations
of Senator Kefauver's committee on this subject have made it clear
that drastic and urgent house-cleaning is necessary.[9]  This aspect
of "white-collar criminality" cries out for more attention from the
American criminologist, and it is at least concerned with crime
proper.

Administrative offences are a different matter, and if very
numerous could transform the picture of crime drawn from police
and court records.  Unfortunately it is almost impossible to obtain
data about them of a sort which would be useful in research; it
would, for example, be a herculean task to separate those administrative offences which are really crimes from those which are merely
technical, and the question of criteria would arise all the time.  It
is possible that this category of offence, in peace-time at least, is not
of very great importance in this country, but in time of war a
definition based solely upon the criminal law might be very

inadequate.  Breaches of war-time regulations might then add substantially to what is already a formidable total of unreported and
undetected crime.[10]

One can hardly avoid the conclusion that Sutherland, in
stretching the meaning of the word "criminal" to include those who
are engaged in unfair and dishonest practices in business, is trying,
whether consciously or not, to cast on them the slur which this
word carries with it.  His sense of justice is outraged by their
activities, and he has set out to use the weapon of opprobrium to
make up for the omissions of the criminal code.  But in so doing,
he plunges a situation which is eminently suitable for objective
study into a maelstrom of ethical and verbal controversies.  More
serious still, he is displaying a moralistic attitude towards his subject
of study which begs the whole question of causation.  For if the
"criminaloid" (or the criminal for that matter) is blamable, it
means that the cause of his anti-social behaviour is to be found
largely in his own defects of will.

## Personal Responsibility and Criminal Behaviour

This raises the whole question of how the criminologist deals
with the thorny problem of personal responsibility for crime.
There are, in fact, two senses in which the word "responsibility" is
used in criminology.  There is first of all the legal sense; the
extent to which the law itself holds the individual responsible for
his actions.  All countries accept the principle of diminished
responsibility in certain circumstances, or for certain classes such
as the young or the insane.[11]

The second usage of the term brings to the fore again the
importance of separating ethical judgments from scientific study in
criminology.  To impute personal responsibility implies here that
the criminal is himself to blame for his crimes.  If this is true, the
patient search for causal factors is a waste of time.  The cause of
crime is known; it lies deep in the moral nature of the individual
delinquent himself.  This does not even lead to a psychology of
crime, for a psychological theory would imply that there were
mental factors at work within him which made him a criminal, and
such a position would be incompatible with real personal responsibility.  The concept of personal responsibility is inevitably a
religious one, tied up with the ideas of free will and conscience,
and with the doctrine of sin.

It is not possible here to join in the age-old dispute about
"free will" and "determinism".  All one can say is that the

criminologist eschews question-begging moral judgments, and seeks by empirical study to determine what causal factors exist. His approach is that of the ethical agnostic.

It is not always easy to maintain such detachment. The crimes themselves are often horrifying enough to arouse much indignation, and, in addition, we all seem to need a scapegoat on to whom we can project our own hatred and feelings of guilt. Also the general social attitude towards the criminal is so unambiguously moralistic and punitive, that we are under strong social pressure to follow suit. Nevertheless, the only attitude which will meet the requirements of scientific method is to see crime as the result of certain natural causes, and to make no distinction on ethical grounds between it and other social happenings, say the self-sacrificing services of a Father Damien, or the benefactions of a Nuffield.

## Subdivisions of Criminology

There remains for consideration the internal anatomy of the science—the subdivisions into which it is divided. Many different professions are now engaged in the study or the treatment of crime. Radzinowicz and Turner give twenty-four subdivisions of "criminal science", all of which are in use from time to time.[11] As these writers themselves point out, there is much danger in such "atomisation", and they recommend instead that as far as criminology proper is concerned only two subdivisions should be recognised. Criminal biology would be concerned with the study of the personality of the criminal, and the role of his personality in causing his delinquencies, while criminal sociology would study the social factors in the aetiology of crime. It is possible to classify all the other more specialised fields of study under one or the other of these general headings.

However, even this modest scheme has its difficulties, and they stem from the same roots as the defects of the more "atomistic" systems of classification. The chief danger in specialisation in any science is that the specialist will become so absorbed in his own narrow field that he loses sight of the overall picture. This has been especially true of criminology in recent years. The psychologist, for example, or the social ecologist, glimpses a part of the truth about crime, and believes he has the whole answer. It is now vital for further development that the watertight divisions between the different specialisms in criminology should be broken down.

Specialist work will, and certainly should, continue. It is a far cry, for instance, from the empirical study of gang-life in a great city to the highly technical medical work now in progress on glandular dysfunction or the electrical activity of the brain, and yet both are necessary at the present stage of development in criminology. At the same time, the specialist must be a criminologist, able to take a synoptic view of the science, even though he does not understand the more technical aspects of the work of some of his colleagues in other branches. Radzinowicz rightly states that the human personality must be understood as a whole, and not as a collection of traits (physical, intellectual, psychiatric, etc.), each with its own specialist.[12] It is equally true that the crimogenic situation must be seen as a whole, with contributions from both the personality and the environment. To subdivide criminology in the way proposed is to imply that personality and sociological studies can be pursued independently, and to encourage the reaching of narrowly independent conclusions. In a science which is already as specialised and as narrow in range as criminology, there is no room for subsidiary sciences, but plenty of opportunity for its practitioners to secure an overall grasp of the subject.

This, despite the fact that the present writer would extend the range of criminology as ordinarily conceived. It is usual, though by no means a universal practice, to make a distinction between criminology and penology. Criminology is said to be concerned with the causes of crime, and penology with its treatment. But in the definition of criminology adopted above, treatment and prevention are included as well as causation.

Penology as a term is certainly out of date in present circumstances. The emphasis in criminological circles nowadays, is increasingly being placed upon the curative and reformative rather than the punitive approach to the criminal. The words "penal system" may still be appropriate as a description of current correctional methods, but the criminologist, aiming at a reduction in the amount of crime, may feel impelled to criticise those methods for that very reason. This accounts for the replacement of the word penology by "criminal policy" in the writings of some authorities.[13]

However, criminal policy is itself a misleading title. It has an empirical ring about it which suggests the practitioner rather than the scientist. Thus Hurwitz describes it as a kind of applied criminology.[14] Such an attitude does not do justice to the fundamental work which is now being undertaken. This includes the sociological analysis of the prison community, thorough investigations of the results of particular kinds of treatment, and studies of prophylactic methods, both in the training of children, and in the organisation of community life.

At the same time, Hurwitz's description points to the underlying unity which exists between aetiological studies and remedial ones. The latter clearly cannot avoid being affected by what is known about the nature and causes of crime; and as we proceed with treatment, the operative causal factors begin to emerge. The extent to which they are becoming interwoven is illustrated by a current tendency for the investigation of both causation and treatment to be combined in a single remedial attack upon some manifestation of the problem of crime, say in some heavily delinquent neighbourhood.[15] What we have in fact, in criminology, is a single science, in which aetiological studies and studies of treatment and prevention are united as full and equal partners.

But what, after all, makes a science? A science, it has been said, is concerned with the study of the natural universe, but artists, for example, or poets, all explore the world around them in their own way. A science, then, must be identified either by the kind of conclusions it is able to reach about the universe it studies, or by the methods of investigation it adopts. In the earlier stages of its development, every science is forced to base its pretensions largely upon its methods of study. This is the case with criminology. It is therefore to the methods of investigation adopted by criminologists that we must now turn, in order to judge whether, in view of the kind of problem they have to tackle, the strictures which have been passed upon them are justified.

## NOTES TO CHAPTER I

1. Trenaman, J., and Emmett, H. B., in *Howard Journal*, **8**: 1, 1949-50, pp. 49 ff.

2. Max Weber's phrase. See his essays on "The Methodology of the Social Sciences", ed. E. A. Shils and H. A. Finch, 1949.

3. Hurwitz, S., *Criminology*, 1942, p. 20.

4. Garafalo, R., *Criminology*, 1914, pp. 40 ff.

5. Mannheim, H., *Criminal Justice and Social Reconstruction*, 1946, p. 5.

6. Mannheim, K., *Diagnosis of Our Time*, 1943.

7. Sutherland, E. H., *White Collar Crime*, 1949. Also his paper: "Is 'White Collar Crime' Crime?" *Am. Sociol. Review*, **10**, pp. 132-9.

8. Sutherland, E. H., *Principles of Criminology*, 1947, p. 24.

9. Kefauver, E., *Crime in America*, 1952.

10. See Chapter II below, pp. 16 ff.

11. Radzinowicz, L., and Turner, J. W. C., *Modern Approach to Criminal Law*, 1945, p. 14.

12. *Ibid.*, p. 17.

13. *Ibid.*, pp. 21 ff. Hurwitz, *op. cit.*, pp. 13 ff.

14. *Ibid.*

15. The Bristol Social Project, under the direction of Dr J. C. Spencer, is a current example of this sort of approach. See p. 258 below.

# CHAPTER II

## METHODS OF INVESTIGATION

The criminologist is not immune from the natural human craving for certainty. So like other social scientists he looks enviously at the methods of investigation which the physical scientist is able to use, with all the possibilities they offer of measurement, objectivity in observation, and the staging of really crucial experiments.[1]

However, although such standards do provide a yardstick against which the scientific adequacy of the methods of criminology may be measured, it must in the end be recognised that they have only a limited application to studies like this. Human motives, for example, are often deeply hidden, so that even the individual himself hardly realises that he has such feelings or wishes within him. The observer must infer them from external behaviour or derive them in personal contact (in interviews, for example) by some mysterious inter-personal alchemy that we must, for want of real understanding of its nature, call intuition. And causal factors are inextricably interwoven one with another, modifying each other in the process.

As for experiment, our very proper respect for human beings as persons precludes our using and manipulating them, like guinea-pigs or puppets, in the interests of science. In recent years, there has been a tendency in the direction of experimentation in social science, but it has brought with it, as its justification, the obligation to help the subjects of the experiment to solve their problems through the experimental measures adopted. This is very different from the *experimentum crucis* of the natural scientist, in which all possible causal factors except one must be held constant, so that any results observed from the experiment can be safely attributed to the one variable factor. Even without the added complication of therapeutic action, however, the factors involved in any given social situation seem to be far too complex for any really controlled experimentation to take place.

### Statistical Methods

The use of statistical methods has been developed as a solution, by those who lay stress upon the importance of evolving a methodology comparable with that of natural science. Shying at the subtlety and intricacy of the causal matrix, they may turn for refuge to a calculation of the degree of association between the general trends shown in the annual criminal statistics and in, say, the national figures of unemployment. Or the statistically minded criminologist may investigate in a numerical way the extent to which criminals are certain kinds of people, or have been subjected to certain kinds of experience.

Such expedients can, of course, tell us nothing about the substance of the causal process at all. All that one can decide as a result of such an enquiry is that the two quantities do go together to a significant extent. What their relationship is, in a qualitative sense, still has to be determined by a process of risky and largely subjective inference.

But it must not be concluded that the use of statistics is merely an evasion of the real problem, to which we must return willy-nilly in order to arrive at a solution. What has happened has been that from a problem which would otherwise have been intractable except on a purely subjective basis, the more objective and measurable part has been abstracted, and its implications thoroughly explored. The irreducible subjective core may then be tackled in the comfortable knowledge that the background work is sound according to the best canons of the exact sciences. The precision and reliability of criminology cannot but benefit by such a procedure.

The danger is in assuming that the statistical relationship is also thus established as a causal one, and it is a very real danger, for the statistically minded investigator is often reluctant to venture out from the security of an objectively demonstrated correlation. He may well argue that he prefers facts which can be objectively demonstrated, to unproven speculations; but if he limits himself to what his statistical studies can actually *prove*, he will add very little to our understanding of the problem of crime. Only too often, however, he will go further and read a causal meaning into his figures which they do not justify. Scientific method demands that one shall not skate lightly over assumptions and unproven inferences in this way. Only so can they be prevented from getting out of hand.

The subjective element in the process of interpretation must not be overstressed. Often the conclusions reached are those to which common sense or the general body of knowledge in the science would inevitably lead. There is also the possibility of confirming one's own interpretation by those of other investigators in similar circumstances. At the same time, for a sound general methodology it is important to distinguish it from any process of objective proof.

## Research into Treatment

What has been said above applies with equal force to both aetiological studies and research into treatment. Commonly in the latter, a form of treatment is adjudged good or bad according to whether those who have been subjected to it relapse into crime again afterwards. This is a rough guide, but if it is accepted unconditionally we may be biasing our results strongly in favour of the method of treatment concerned. For quite apart from the possibility that some who have in fact committed crimes after discharge may not have been caught, so that the appearance of improvement in these cases is illusory, the improvements actually established may have had nothing to do with the formal treatment at all.

There is, for example, no certainty that these "reformed characters" would have committed further offences even if they had not received treatment. This is a particular hazard in studies of the milder forms of treatment, such as probation, where first-offenders are most likely to be involved. The mere experience of arrest and arraignment in court may already have brought the offender to his senses before his period of probation commenced.

Then there is the influence of maturation to be borne in mind. Where an offender has been under treatment for a period of years, his "reformation" may simply be due to the fact that he has grown up. Sheldon and Eleanor Glueck laid some emphasis upon this factor in their studies of the after-careers of former inmates of the Massachussets Reformatory.[2] Or it may be due to some incidental and unrecognised aspect of his experience while under treatment, *e.g.* friendships made with other prisoners, or his wife's having a baby while he was in prison. Success achieved through unacknowledged factors like these, cannot be used to justify a form of treatment.

Such pitfalls may be avoided if we are prepared to study the dynamics of treatment at close quarters. We could then watch the reaction of offenders to the treatment measures applied, and try to discern any consequent changes in their behaviour and characters. But such a subjective process also has its dangers.[3]

## Control Groups

The problem of providing a crucial test under controlled conditions, to replace the experiments of the natural scientist, still remains. It has been met to some extent by the use of control groups. Thus if one set out to test the importance of a certain kind of environment as a cause of delinquency, one could compare the incidence of delinquency in a sample of children brought up in that environment with a sample brought up in a different setting but being in all other respects similar to the first group. Statistical measures, such as "t" or "chi-squared", could then be applied to the figures obtained to see if the difference between the two groups was large enough to mean something, *i.e.* too large to be reasonably attributable to chance. As before, of course, the causal significance of the results obtained remains open to interpretation.

The control group is a way of sorting out from a large number of possible observations, the comparison which most adequately isolates the factors to be studied. Much obviously depends upon whether the two samples are otherwise alike. If there are relevant differences, apart from the specific difference which is under investigation, then the comparison is no longer crucial. It is here that many control-group studies appear to be defective. It is very difficult indeed to match individuals and groups for all the subtle qualities which may be relevant in an investigation of this sort, and often, as a result, such disturbing elements remain, and are not adequately taken into account in drawing conclusions from the study. At the same time it must be recognised that, so long as their limitations are borne in mind, control-group methods are of tremendous value in many branches of criminological enquiry.

## Ecological Methods

Other criminologists have applied statistical methods in quite a different way. They have plotted the addresses of criminals, the centres of gang activity, or the places where crimes have been committed, on a map, and have then sought to account for the differences in distribution between different areas.[4] Clearly the crude differences between different areas have little significance; they must be expressed as a rate—a proportion of the number at risk. For example, a neighbourhood with few children might, for that reason alone, tend to have an exceptionally low incidence of juvenile crime. This requirement tends to limit the application of these "ecological" or "cartographic" methods in Britain, for it is only for census years that local details of the distribution of the population are available. And even the census does not give figures divided into age groups for the smaller neighbourhood areas, such as the wards of a city.

## Official Statistics of Crime

It will already be apparent that the annual volume of Criminal Statistics published by the Home Office, provides a wealth of ready-to-hand material for the criminologist. The figures are presented under two main headings: "Crimes known to the police" and "Number of persons dealt with". They are cross-classified according to the way in which they are finally disposed of (imprisonment, fine, etc.), and also according to age and sex. And in addition to the crime-figures for the current year, comparative figures for other years are also given. Any enquiry into such matters as the general trend of crime in the country, or the trends in particular kinds of crime, or into such questions as the peak-age for crime, is bound to draw heavily upon this material.

There are obvious differences between "crimes known to the police" and "persons dealt with". The police may know of a crime, but may not have detected the criminal, or may have been unable to secure a conviction. Or an offender guilty of many crimes may be dealt with by a single conviction, the others being, in the legal phrase, "taken into account". The police figures do, therefore, seem to provide the best measure of the amount of crime which has actually occurred.

The police statistics, however, have been themselves assailed. They are bound, of course, to be defective if members of the public who know of crimes do not report them, and this does happen on a vast scale. The employer usually dismisses his dishonest employee and says no more about it. Many cases of assault get no further than an exchange of invective over the garden wall. It has even been asserted that the family setting within which it occurs often prevents a serious offence like incest from reaching the ears of the police.[5] The police statistics are bound, therefore, for such reasons as this, to underestimate the amount of crime which has in fact been committed, and there is little that the police can do about it.

But some serious sources of error may be attributable to the police themselves. Dr Mannheim points out that there is a real temptation for the local force to keep the figure of "crime known" at the lowest possible level, in order to forestall any criticism which might follow a large balance of crimes over convictions.[6] In the same way, the individual policeman may feel reluctant to follow through a complaint if he has had no success in dealing with it. There is no suggestion that the police would deliberately suppress the facts about crimes which they are certain have taken place, but often there is an element of doubt in the situation. It may be doubtful, for example, whether some article reported as stolen has really been stolen or has merely been lost or mislaid. In such circumstances, the police might be inclined to adopt the more optimistic view.

The position is made even more confusing by the lack of uniformity between different forces. Thus one force may be much less tolerant of street bookmaking or prostitution than another, or bring in children for all sorts of offences which other police forces would handle in some other less formal way. Such variations tend to vitiate comparisons between crime figures for different areas. The Home Office have striven hard to secure a greater degree of uniformity by the issue of detailed instructions upon the procedure to be followed,[7] but he would be a brave and rather imprudent man who would say that the divergencies are not still very substantial.

All these defects have their effect not only upon the value of police statistics as a means of determining the amount of crime in a given year, but also upon comparisons over a period. As the policy of the police or the attitude of the public changes, so does the proportion of the total crime which finds its way into the Criminal Statistics. Changes in the law also have their effect upon trends over a period; for example, a reduction in the penalty for an offence, or the fact that a charge which previously meant an action at Quarter Sessions or the Assizes can now be brought summarily before the frequently held and more informal Petty Sessions. Much of the increase in recorded juvenile offences after 1933 has been attributed to the Children's Act of that year, which provided a more lenient procedure for dealing with delinquent children.

Even the gradual improvements which have been effected in the method of recording crime play their part in distorting trends over a period of years, for the earlier figures must underestimate the position more than the more recent ones. One such improvement was the abolition of the Suspected Stolen Book in the Metropolitan Police Area in 1932. This forced the police to record as actual crimes a much larger proportion of the total reported to them, and the amount of crime recorded, therefore, increased from 26,000 in 1931 to 83,000 in 1932. "It has been estimated that if the 1931 returns had been compiled on the principle now adopted, the figure would have been approximately 79,000",[8] making an increase of only 5 per cent. in place of 300 per cent.

It was thought at one time that these objections against the police statistics were conclusive, and that in spite of the patent

2

defects of the court figures, they were the more reliable. It can readily be seen that there is a fallacy here, for if the police statistics are unsatisfactory, the court statistics, which must be derived from police action, must be equally so and, in addition, embody errors accumulated at the subsequent stages of trial and conviction. The generally accepted view nowadays is that stated by Sellin in the following general rule: "The value of a crime-rate for index purposes decreases as the distance from the crime itself in terms of procedure increases."[9] For each further procedural stage interposed between the crime and the recording of it, brings with it its own sources of error.

The heading of "Persons dealt with", however, has its own particular application where it is the characteristics of persons rather than offences which are under examination, *e.g.* the number of separate offenders, the sex ratio, or the numbers in each age group. For, of course, none of these facts can be known until offences have been detected and tried.

International comparisons of criminal statistics are even more hazardous, for in addition to the difficulties already mentioned, the classifications used in different countries vary widely, so that the numbers under each heading are rarely comparable. In a federal country like the U.S.A. this sort of difficulty arises even in comparing figures between different constituent states.[10] In many countries the official Criminal Statistics are far less complete than in this country. Few of them give details of "crimes known to the police"; even in America these figures are only available for certain cities.[11]

## Case-study Methods

The alternative to the statistical approach is the intensive study of individual cases. This may take the form of direct observation over a period, as in Thrasher's studies of adolescent gangs in Chicago[12] or in the first-hand observations of the treatment process already referred to. On the other hand, the period of observation may be shorter, consisting of perhaps one or two specially arranged interviews. These are supplemented by a study of the offender's history. Facts about his family life and his social experience are collected from a variety of sources—from himself, members of his family, his schoolmaster, and so on, with the idea of tracing the route by which he has become what he is. Healy with his *The Individual Delinquent*[13] was a pioneer in the use of the criminological case history.

These methods owe their origin in the main to psychologists and psychiatrists engaged in clinical treatment, who necessarily base their therapeutic work on an intimate relationship with their patients, and an attempt at a sympathetic and largely intuitive understanding of their problems. It may be that this is the only way in which real understanding of an offender may be achieved, but it is bound to be a rather uncertain and capricious one. It depends so much upon the clinical skill and experience of the investigator, and leaves the door wide open to the entry of subjective bias in all its disguises.

Various devices have been adopted to introduce an element of objectivity into the situation. Several workers may collaborate on a case and thus serve as a check upon each other. Standardised psychological tests can sometimes be used to provide objective evidence about an offender's personality or attitudes. There is also often scope for combining the clinical with the statistical approach, by, for example, the rigorous testing of any of the clinician's conclusions which are suitable for this, or conversely by the more intensive exploration of hypotheses suggested by statistical studies.

Closely connected with the problem of objectivity is that of neutrality. A person who is being interviewed reacts to his interviewer in all sorts of ways. The interviewer's attitude may show itself without his knowledge in that edge to his voice, the tiny but telling pause, or even in a rather excessive warmth and geniality, and the person being interviewed will be quick to draw either comfort or discouragement from it. It has been argued, by such writers as Susan Isaacs[14] and Norman Polansky,[15] that even if the investigator is truly neutral in his attitude, the subject will tend to interpret this as a sign of approval of whatever he is doing or saying. An observer must be prepared to see some element which is due to himself in any human situation which he observes, and to discount part of what he witnesses accordingly. The difficulty of being truly neutral, and the danger of thus having some effect upon the situation without being aware of it, has led some research workers to suggest that it would be safer to adopt a definite attitude, the therapeutic attitude, towards your subject.[16] Your motives would then be quite clear, the reaction of the person you are studying would be intelligible, and your approach would be one which is likely to call forth his co-operation.

In so far as case-studies in criminology have been a by-product of clinical work, research has necessarily been combined with a therapeutic approach, but in some recent experimental work, as will be seen below, it has become an essential methodological principle.

### Criminal Life Stories

Very similar to the case history is the criminal life story, of which C. R. Shaw's books, *Natural History of a Delinquent Career* (1931) and *The Jackroller* (1930), are celebrated examples.[17]   In these the criminal tells the story of his own life, describing and trying to account for his own descent into crime.   Accounts by prisoners of their prison experience fall within the same class.[18]

It could, of course, be most revealing to see the problem through the eyes of the offender himself, but only if he is both perceptive and frank.   Unfortunately, and this is really only to be expected, he is very likely to be neither.   We all try to justify ourselves if we can, to blame others for our misdeeds or to attribute them to unavoidable circumstances.   In a situation in which so much must be obscure and doubtful, subjective bias of this sort can have free rein.   This of course quite apart from the question of simple truthfulness, which must arise in dealing with criminals.   Nevertheless, if care is taken to check statements which can be checked, and if the consistency of the narrative itself is carefully examined, if in fact the safeguards used by Shaw himself are adopted, a personal document of this sort has its value.[19]   After all, even if the facts are not exactly as stated, it is probably very significant that the criminal does see them thus or needs to falsify them in this way.

### Experimental Methods

Apart from a certain amount of relevant work by the Lewinist school (especially the celebrated Lippitt and White study of children's groups), little attempt has been made to carry out controlled experimentation in criminology.[20]   Indeed, it may be misleading to call them experiments; a better name may be participant case-studies.

The difficulties of real control are probably insuperable.   It usually involves, as in the Lippitt and White study, the setting up of an artificial situation for study, in order to reduce the numerous and complex factors involved to manageable proportions.   Quite apart from the frequently prohibitive cost of doing this, there is no guarantee that the results obtained will be applicable to real-life conditions.

Then there is the moral issue already referred to which tells against many kinds of experiment with human beings.   The therapeutic experiment meets the moral objection, but administers the final *coup-de-grâce* to controlled experimentation, for therapeutic measures can hardly be standardised, or confined within limits primarily determined by considerations of scientific method.

At the same time, some of the values of the strict experimental method may be secured in these more informal studies. It is possible to test a hypothesis, even though the interpretation of the results is often at a subjective case-study level. And the person engaged in treatment has all the advantages of that intimate understanding of those he is studying which also goes with the case-study method. However, the requirement that treatment and research shall be carried out by the same persons does raise in question the calibre of our treatment staffs. Certainly, a different and better training will be required, if our prison officers, for example, are to carry such a dual responsibility, but in so far as they do really begin to understand the problems of the men under them, they will perform their reformative task the better.[21]

## NOTES TO CHAPTER II

1. Even in the physical sciences, crucial experiments are probably rarer than our methodological purists would like to think.

2. Glueck, S. and E. T., *After-conduct of Discharged Offenders*, 1945, Chapter VIII. See p. 108 below.

3. See pp. 18-20 below.

4. The classical studies are: Shaw, C. R., *Delinquency Areas*, and Shaw, C. R., and McKay, H. D., *Juvenile Delinquency and Urban Areas*, 1942; but the method has since been used very extensively by others. See Chapter VI.

5. *Report of the Department Committee on Sexual Offences against Young Persons*, Cmd. 2561, 1926, pp. 13-14.

6. Mannheim, H., *Social Aspects of Crime in England Between the Wars*, 1940, pp. 36 ff. The first three chapters of this book are a scholarly and penetrating examination of the whole question of English Criminal Statistics.

7. See *Instructions for the Preparation of Statistics Relating to Crime*, issued by the Home Office (latest edition, 1949).

8. *Report of the Commissioner of the Metropolitan Police*, 1932. Cmd. 4294, 1933, p. 17.

9. Sellin, T., "Basis of a Crime Index", *Journal of Criminal Law and Criminology*, **22**, 1931, p. 346.

10. Cressey, D. R., "Criminological Research and the Definition of Crimes", *American Journal of Sociology*, **56**, 3, 1951, pp. 546 ff. On the general problem of international comparisons see Grunhut, M., *Journal of the Royal Statistical Society*, **114**, 1951, pp. 154-6.

11. Grunhut, *ibid.*, pp. 154-5.

12. Thrasher, F. M., *The Gang*, 1937.

13. Healy, W., *The Individual Delinquent*, 1915.

14. Isaacs, S., *Social Development in Young Children*, 1933, pp. 419 ff.

15. Polansky, N., *et al.*, "Problems of Interpersonal Relations in Research on Groups", *Human Relations*, **2**: 1, 1949, pp. 281 ff.

16. Among modern social research groups in this country, the Tavistock Institute of Human Relations has adopted "no research without therapy" as a working principle. For a discussion of many related issues see *Delinquency—*

*the Case for Operational Research*, the report of a Conference on the Scientific Study of Juvenile Delinquency, held at the Royal Institution, London, in 1949.

17. Other books of this type include Chic Conwell's *The Professional Thief* (ed. E. H. Sutherland), 1927, and Benney Mark, *Low Company*, 1936.

18. There is an extensive literature.    See the various books cited in Chapters XIII and XIV.

19. Burgess, E. W., Preface to Shaw, C. R., *Natural History of a Delinquent Career*, 1951.    For a thorough examination of the utility of this sort of evidence, see Gottschalk, L., Kluckhohn, C., and Angell, R., *The Use of Personal Documents in History, Anthropology and Sociology* (American Social Science Research Council, Bulletin 53), 1945.

20. Lippitt, R., and White, R. K., "Social Climate of Children's Groups" in Barker, R. G., Kounin, J., and White, H. F. (eds.), *Child Behaviour and Development*, 1943, pp. 485 ff.    Those interested in the possibility of controlled experimentation in the social sciences should also read Lewin, K., "Field Theory and Experiment in Social Psychology", *American Journal of Sociology*, **44**, 1939, pp. 868 ff.

21. A rigorous criticism of the methods used in criminological research will be found in Michael, J., and Adler, M. J., *Crime, Law and Social Science*, 1933.

# CHAPTER III

## CONSTITUTIONAL EXPLANATIONS OF CRIME

Of all the approaches to the study of crime, none is more dampening to the enthusiasm of the eager reformer than this one. For to say that criminality is a constitutional matter means that it is a part of the essential nature of the offender, and cannot be changed. The efforts of priest, judge, and social worker, alike are wasted on him, for he is a "born" criminal, and therefore incorrigible. Often this fatalism goes further, and it is contended that his criminal tendencies are inherited. The family stock from which he has sprung is irremediably tainted, and must be eliminated by sterilisation, in order to protect society from its depredations.

### Crime and Physique

The apostle of this pessimistic creed is undoubtedly the famous Italian criminologist Lombroso, whose book *L'Uomo Delinquente*, first published in 1876, founded the so-called Anthropological School in criminology. According to Lombroso, criminality is inborn, being due to a degeneration of the stock. This often shows itself in epilepsy, and always in certain physical characteristics, as well as in criminal behaviour.

He based this theory upon the physical measurement of large numbers of criminals. The "degenerative stigmata" found included a small cranium, receding forehead, projecting ears, a luxuriant growth of hair on the head but no beard, a thin upper lip, and various actual defects of physique. The "criminal type", claimed Lombroso, could be recognised by the possession of at least five of these stigmata. In later editions of his book, as he extended his researches over more and more cases, he modified his views, and admitted that in perhaps two criminals out of three, environmental factors may be important, but it is with his earlier, more austere theory that his name is most associated.

Lombroso's theory has been attacked on many grounds, but chiefly because his researches did not provide for control groups, constituted from the non-criminal population. How, argue his critics, is it possible to prove that certain physical characteristics are particularly associated with the "criminal type" unless you ascertain how prevalent they are among non-criminals? Nor does it follow that if criminality and these so-called "stigmata" do go together, that the former must be inborn. There is the possibility that the criminals are reacting to the effect which their physical peculiarities have upon their lives and their relationships with people. Thus the anti-social "epileptic personality" may be seen as an understandable reaction to the frustrations and misery which the epileptic has to suffer in our society.[1] It is also difficult to understand how some of the physical characteristics upon which Lombroso relies can be described as degenerative. They are certainly not typical of any known primitive human type.

Dr Charles Goring, an English prison doctor, was responsible for the most damaging attack upon the central thesis of the Lombrosian school.[2] Bearing in mind the criticisms of Lombroso's research method, Goring carried out a study of some 3,000 British convicts, comparing them with controls from the normal population; and concluded that there was absolutely no evidence of the existence of a "physical criminal type". Goring's demonstration has been accepted as fairly conclusive by most authorities. A subsequent attempt at the vindication of Lombroso by the American, Hooton, made very little impression. The samples he studied were unrepresentative, and were also too small for safe conclusions to be drawn from them about criminals in general.[3]

All in all, there seems to be very little left of the ambitious Lombrosian theory of criminal degeneration. But this must not be allowed to conceal the very real contribution which Lombroso made in other respects, to the scientific study of the problem. He and his students, Ferri and Garafalo,[4] attacked the current orthodoxy that crime was a moral, not a scientific, matter, and established the approach to it in terms of natural causation which lies at the root of modern criminological method. He also directed attention to the characteristics of the criminal himself, and thus was the forerunner of some of the most fruitful of subsequent researches. It is for these reasons that, although the specific theories of Lombroso have fallen into disrepute, he is often called the founder of modern criminology.

GORING'S VIEWS. Goring did not confine himself to refuting Lombroso, but put forward certain positive conclusions of his own, and these ironically enough led direct to a theory of inborn criminality as rigid as that of Lombroso himself. Although Goring denied the existence of specific physical stigmata, he decided, on the strength of his own investigations, that the criminal was both physically and intellectually inferior to the normal person, and that both this inferiority and his criminal tendencies were inherited.

His views of the physical inferiority of the criminal have not been confirmed by later work, with some minor exceptions.[5] Norwood East (also a prison medical officer) found no evidence of general physical inferiority among the 4,000 adolescent offenders who he studied,[6] and Sheldon, after examining 200 young Americans, most of them delinquent, has come to a diametrically opposite conclusion. He found the most common physical trait to be "mesomorphism", in which there is "a relative predominance of muscle, bone and connective tissue".[7] In any case, it is a moot point whether inferiority of physique, where found, is better considered as a cause or as an effect—of poverty, malnutrition, or slum-life, etc.

TEMPERAMENT TYPES AND CRIME. But the general theme is by no means exhausted. Recent developments have stemmed from the work of Kretschmer, a psychiatrist who developed a theory of a relationship between physique and temperament.[8] He divided the population into four physical types. The thinner, taller, more angular type he called the "asthenic"; the "rounded" type he called the "pyknic"; those with well-developed musculature and skeleton, the "athletic"; and those with marked physical anomalies, the "dysplastic". He claimed that while the pyknic physique is associated with the warm, sociable, but rather "up-one-day-down-the-next" type of personality (the "cyclothymic" temperament), the other physical types are more apt to be of the detached, inturned, meditative type of temperament (the "schizothymic" type). This famous theory is considered to be of great prognostic and diagnostic value in psychiatry.

By comparing his own estimate of the proportions of the various physical types in the general population with studies which have been made of the physical types found among criminals, Kretschmer found that pyknics were less likely to become criminal than any of the others. Willemse followed this up with an investigation of the type of offence committed by different constitution types, and found that the type of temperament according to Kretschmer's scheme did appear to explain the form which criminality took.[9]

However, it had been obvious all along that most of us are neither exclusively asthenic or pyknic, athletic or dysplastic, but are mixtures of the various types in varying proportions. In the latest work along these lines by the American, W. A. Sheldon, this fact has been taken amply into account.[10] He uses a different terminology from Kretschmer, but a very similar basis of classification, his endomorphic, mesomorphic, and ectomorphic components corresponding very approximately to the pyknic, athletic, and asthenic types respectively.

Where he does depart decisively from Kretschmer is in treating these as components rather than as types of physique, and in giving a quantitative value to the amount of any such component which an individual possesses. The strength of each component is expressed on a seven-point rating scale, the number 1 implying that it is absent, and the 7 that it is possessed to an extreme degree. The ratings for all three components are then brought together to form a sort of index of physical type. Thus the "7-1-1 is the most extreme endomorph, the 1-7-1 is the most extreme mesomorph, and 1-1-7 is the most extreme ectomorph". Most of us, of course, would find our place on values nearer the middle of the scales.

Sheldon applied this scheme to the study of 200 young Bostonians, most of them delinquent, and came to the conclusion that the typical criminal displayed a high rate of mesomorphy, average endomorphy, and a very low rating for ectomorphy.

Sutherland reported very unfavourably on this investigation, criticising the sample used as unrepresentative and the method of scoring as highly subjective, and pointing out that there seemed to be no specific relationship between type of physiques and type of offence.[11] Nevertheless, the results of a recent major study of juvenile delinquency by S. and E. Glueck do on the whole support Sheldon's conclusions, and this is formidable support indeed. If his methodology was a little slapdash, theirs was impeccable. They based their conclusions on a study of no fewer than 500 delinquents and 500 non-delinquent controls. They were able to reconcile their conclusions about physical type with psychological and social elements, and weave them all into an intelligible pattern of causation.[12] Then there is the general acceptance of Kretschmer's work by clinicians, which bears testimony to the value of this sort of approach. If the scientifically minded enquirer can avoid being repelled by Sheldon's eccentric and even frivolous way of writing, he may well feel that the latter's fundamental proposition "That behaviour is a function of structure" is reasonable, and could be expected to lead where Sheldon has followed it.

Another contemporary formulation of this same proposition is to the effect that human personality is largely determined by the activity of the endocrine glands, and that crime may therefore be merely a matter of unbalance in the operation of the gonads, the thyroid, the pituitary, and the rest. There is little doubt that such an unbalance sometimes has the most remarkable effects upon human beings. Congenital underactivity of the thyroid, for example, produces the stunted and mentally defective cretin, and abnormalities in the gonads or the cortex of the adrenals may create an effeminate man or a bearded, masculine woman.[31]

Nevertheless, the sweeping claims made for the endocrinological approach to crime have still to be established; at present they take the form of unproven, and rather extravagant speculations.[14] They have led to one important practical application: in certain countries persistent sex offenders may be castrated. But although this has been found to achieve its aim in abolishing the offender's sex drive, it is suspect as both an irrevocable and possibly unnecessary step, and as contrary to religious and humanitarian sentiment.[15]

ELECTRO-ENCEPHALOGRAPHIC STUDIES. Another formulation of Sheldon's proposition is based upon studies of the electrical activity of the brain, made possible by the invention of the electro-encephalograph (E.E.G.), a delicate recording instrument.[16] Many E.E.G. studies of criminals have been made, but the work of Hill and of Grey Walter is probably representative.[17]

Hill and Watterson claimed that 65 per cent. of a group of "aggressive psychopaths" and 32 per cent. of "inadequate psychopaths",[18] as compared with 15 per cent. of normal controls, showed an unusual cerebral rhythm of a sort which would normally be displayed by much younger persons. It was suggested that this might indicate some form of cerebral immaturity.[19] Sessions Hodge and Grey Walter found a similar predominance of the slower rhythms in their E.E.G. studies of 100 delinquent boys admitted to a British approved school in early 1950. Eighty-four per cent. of this sample showed some E.E.G. abnormality, most of them (68 per cent. of the total) displaying the slow "delta" rhythm of three cycles per second. The delta rhythm was found to be connected with an immature, dependent sort of personality.[20]

Hill, Stafford-Clark, and Taylor reported to the Royal Commission on Capital Punishment on ninety-four cases of murderers on whom E.E.G. studies had been carried out. Forty-four were found to have abnormal records. As shown in Fig. 1, E.E.G. abnormalities were found in only a minority of the cases of incidental killing or clearly motivated murder, but in a majority of the apparently motiveless murders, sex murders, and cases of insanity.[21]

The parallel here between "abnormal" murder and abnormal E.E.G. is most suggestive.

However, leaders in this field deprecate any hasty conclusions about the inherited, or unalterably constitutional nature of such features of brain physiology as the E.E.G. Educational and environmental factors also probably play a part.[22]

BODY-MIND RELATIONSHIP. We have travelled a long way in the study of the physical factor since Lombroso first propounded his theory of criminal stigmata. In the physical types of Kretschmer and Sheldon we are dealing not with discrete physical traits, but with syndromes, groups of traits which do commonly seem to occur together, and which have a clear connection with types of human

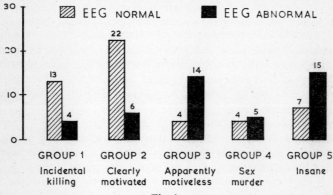

Fig. 1.

personality. In endocrinology and electro-encephalography we are able to examine the mechanism of human functioning at close quarters. At the same time we must not assume too much. These physiological facts are more tangible, but are not therefore more fundamental than their psychological correlates. The body-mind relationship is more complicated than that. On the contrary there is evidence that our personalities and psychological experience may sometimes be the more fundamental, the physical manifestation being secondary to them. This is true, for example, in cases of psychosomatic illness.

In the light of such considerations as these, we may wish to question the common assumption that if only we can establish a connection of some sort between physique and criminality, criminality is thereby proved to be constitutional. Just as the physical symptoms of the hysteric may be removed by psycho-therapy, so may, not only crime, but perhaps even (if they exist) the physical correlates of criminality.

By comparison with these controversial theories, the modest but established role of certain organic illnesses must seem tame. The connection between epilepsy and crime was noted even before Lombroso called attention to it. Apart from the secondary effects of what is called the "epileptic personality", the epileptic may commit offences during a period of mental confusion after the fit has ended. But some neurologists go further than this, and contend that certain forms of violent outburst may be "epileptic equivalents", substitutes for fits, and may even occur to people who have never had actual epileptic fits at all.[23]

It is also generally accepted that if the neurological illness known as *encephalitis lethargica* (sleeping sickness) is contracted in childhood, one of the symptoms is usually difficult or delinquent behaviour. Medical science knows no way of treating this form of disturbance, but happily we have had no epidemic since the 1920s, and new cases are almost non-existent.

## Role of Intelligence

So much for the relationship between crime and physique. Controversy continues to rage about the other points made by Goring: that criminality is hereditary, and is closely connected with feeblemindedness. The latter has its main protagonist in H. H. Goddard, who stated: "It is no longer to be denied that the greatest single cause of delinquency and crime is low-grade mentality, much of it within the limits of feeblemindedness".[24] It is not difficult to see how the connection between subnormal intellect and crime might arise. The feebleminded person tends to be easily led. His failure to get on in school or to keep a job may upset his social adjustment in all sorts of ways. He may very well find difficulty in understanding, and learning how to cope with, the complexities of modern social life.

There are, however, certain special difficulties to be faced in research on the intelligence of offenders. First as to the sample. If, as many criminologists believe, the more intelligent offenders are more likely to avoid arrest and conviction, then any study of convicted offenders is bound to understate the intelligence of criminals in general.

Then there are the many pitfalls in the actual process of measuring intelligence. Intelligence tests are often said to be imperfect as measuring instruments, being affected by such extraneous factors as anxiety or lack of concentration, or by the cultural or educational background of the subject.[25]    Consequently both the delinquent behaviour and the low test result may be due to common emotional factors, or to a poor home.

Or it may be that the delinquency was itself really the primary factor, and the offender's apparent subnormality was caused by his truanting, or refusing to work in school.  It is clear that although the value of intelligence tests has been many times confirmed by the use which has been made of them in clinical and other circles, they are not the infallible and objective instruments which some still seem to imply they are.

Much depends upon the skill of the tester, and where more than one tester is involved, there is some danger of the results being affected by differences in skill, and in methods of scoring the test. In a recent British study it is suggested that the wide differences in intelligence between delinquents and non-delinquents, found in earlier studies such as that of Goddard, is due to the inadequacies both of the tests used and the techniques adopted in administering them.  As tests and testing skill have improved, the differences found have gradually diminished.[26]  The group tests which have been devised for mass testing, and which are therefore very likely to be used in large-scale studies, are considered much more likely to err than the individual type of test.[27]

The evidence on the part which low intelligence plays in criminality is conflicting.  Against Goring, and against the conclusions of Goddard that 50 per cent. of the prisoners he studied were feebleminded, there is Sutherland's survey of 350 different investigations of the problem up to 1929.  Wide variations were found in the methods of scoring intelligence tests used by different investigators.  After allowances had been made for this, and for the fact that the criminal samples were confined to those who could be caught and convicted, Sutherland decided that the distribution of intelligence test scores was very similar to that in the population at large.[28]

Other similar surveys of the literature suggest that lack of intelligence plays some part, but that it has by no means the overwhelming importance ascribed to it by Goddard and Goring. Zeleny[29] estimates the preponderance of mental deficiency among criminals as compared with the general population to be in the proportion of 1·2 to 1, and C. F. Chassell finds positive correlation coefficients between morality and intelligence, but only of between

0·1 and 0·39.[30]   Gittins, in a study of 1,000 juvenile delinquents passing through a British approved school, obtained an average intelligence quotient of 89·5, as compared with the recognised norm of 100.[31]

For further light it is particularly revealing to examine the amount of criminality which is connected with different degrees of intellectual subnormality.   Most investigations show that the delinquent belongs to the higher grades of subnormality rather than the lower. Ferguson studied 293 boys discharged from a special school for dull children, and concluded: "None of the sixteen boys of I.Q. below fifty were convicted in the courts.   Above that figure, the incidence of conviction and frequency of repeated conviction tended to increase as the level of intelligence quotient increased".[32] The following figures, taken from Trenaman's study of 400 delinquent soldiers,[33] show the same trend:—

TABLE I

PERCENTAGES OF DELINQUENT AND NORMAL SOLDIERS (AGED EIGHTEEN YEARS) GRADED BY THE MATRIX TEST INTO INTELLIGENCE GROUPS

|  | Bright | Above Ave. | Average + | Average − | Below Ave. | Dull |
|---|---|---|---|---|---|---|
| Delinquents        ..        .. | 7 | 19 | 21 | 26 | 21 | 6 |
| Normal Army  Population | 11·5 | 22·4 | 22·8 | 20·8 | 17·3 | 5·2 |

If these figures are plotted on a graph (see Fig. 2), it can be seen that the peak, or modal group, is upper-average for non-delinquents and lower-average for delinquents.   The percentage in the lowest group, in the case of the delinquents, is little more than in the controls.   As it is usual to confine the term "mental defective" to the very dull,[34] the problem of crime cannot really be said to be a problem of mental deficiency, but of the more mildly handicapped.

Another point of the greatest importance which emerges from all these enquiries is that the delinquents always include a wide range of intelligence.   While some are mentally defective, others belong to the highest intellectual grades.   Statements above modal groups, or the average intelligence quotient, tend to obscure this important fact.

The picture is in fact no simple "black and white".   Intelligent persons also commit crimes, and some dull persons commit crimes, while others do not.   These anomalies occur surely because, as clinical case-studies clearly show, more is involved than intellectual

ability.[35]    Much depends upon the sub-normal individual's temperament also.    If he is emotionally unstable as well as dull he is very
likely to get into trouble, as Burt pointed out thirty years ago.[36]
If he is of a more placid and acquiescent type, then he may well
escape.    Then there is his environment; he will find it much more
difficult to achieve a satisfactory social adjustment if he suffers from
environmental handicaps such as an unsatisfactory home life, or
has a very complicated environment to cope with.[37]

A further question is whether particular levels of intelligence are
connected with particular types of offence.    Investigations in this
country have been inconclusive.    Thus Ferguson, in the study
already mentioned, found that the dull juvenile offender in his

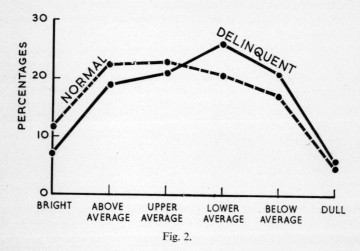

Fig. 2.

sample was more likely to have committed theft or sex crimes than
housebreaking.[38]    Norwood East, also, found a connection between
lower ranges of intelligence and sex offences among adolescent boys
in Borstal,[39] and Milner, among adult criminals.[40]    Bagot, however,
in an investigation of juvenile delinquents in Liverpool discovered
no clear pattern of this sort.[41]

In America, both Fox[42] and Merrill[43] reported that intelligence
was obviously a factor in determining the type of crime.    The
former found that the more intelligent committed offences like
robbery, forgery, and the theft of cars, and the less intelligent,
assault and homicide, rape and perjury.    Common sense would
lead one to expect something of this sort.    In spite of the deceptive

veneer of sharpness and sophistication which some subnormal persons present to the world, it seems reasonable to expect that certain kinds of offence would be beyond their capacity, and that the more intelligent person, for his part, would gravitate towards the type of offence in which he could take advantage of his intellectual assets.

## Inheritance of Criminal Tendencies

Goring's other principal thesis was that criminal tendencies were hereditary. It is clear, however, that he came to this conclusion on the evidence before him largely because he failed to understand that the importance of the family environment in shaping behaviour is in emotional relationships and in its general atmosphere. Delinquent children do not simply copy the offences of their parents, and to show that such direct "contagion" does not take place is no proof that the home environment has no influence. Goring was also led astray by his belief that the mental deficiency he found among his sample could be assumed to be inherited. Although it seems safe now to assume that much mental deficiency is inherited, it is known that some is acquired, as a result, for example, of disease or birth injuries. The amount of acquired mental deficiency is sometimes said to be as much as one-half of the total.[44]

All attempts to exhibit conclusively that there is an hereditary element in crime are hedged about with difficulties. It is not sufficient to show that crime runs in families, for parental example and training could very easily perpetuate criminal habits in children, generation after generation. There is also the question of what is supposed to be inherited. Is it an actual tendency to criminal behaviour, or some other factor, such as lack of intelligence, which leads to crime secondarily? If the latter, how does one account for the exceptions who do not become delinquent?

DEGENERATE FAMILIES. The most vulnerable of all these attempts are the accounts of "degenerate families", such as the Jukeses,[45] and the Kallikaks.[46] The patriarch of the Jukes brood was born between 1720 and 1740, and by 1874 his descendants totalled 709. Of these, 180 had received pauper relief of some kind, and 140 were criminals. There were 7 murderers, 60 thieves, 50 prostitutes, and 40 were known to have had venereal disease. Startling as these figures seem, however, the actual percentage of criminal members according to the most recent study of the Jukes family was only 6 per cent.,[47] and this is less than recent estimates of the crime rate in the general population, which, for example, a post-war British estimate places at one in every nine.[48]   The accuracy of the data is also open to challenge, for it extends over a long period, and one for which reliable documentary material would be difficult to come by.   Finally, it cannot be repeated too often that proof of the "family incidence" of crime is no proof that it is inherited.

This latter consideration inevitably casts its shadow also over the many statistical studies of the incidence of criminal behaviour in families.[49]   Some of the investigators have been aware of this, and have tried to develop techniques which would separate the influence of "hereditary taint" from that of parental example and training. Thus Kuttner[50] compared the incidence of criminality among step-children of habitual offenders with that of "own" children. Although the crime rate was high in both cases, it was much higher among the latter than the former.   But only the very naivest would accept the implication that because an "own" child and a step-child are brought up by the same parents, the effects of family environment have been effectively standardised.

TWIN STUDIES.   The "twin method", in its turn, has been hailed as the final solution to this difficulty, and it does merit the most careful examination, if only to demonstrate how intractable the whole problem is.   This method relies upon the fact that "identical twins", being formed from the division of a single egg-cell into two immediately after fertilisation, may be assumed to have an exactly similar inheritance.   If, then, identical twins show a great degree of concordance with regard to criminality than non-identical twins of a single sex (in whom, of course, inheritance is not exactly similar), this may be put down to the influence of inheritance.

This was the argument of Lange in his book *Crime as Destiny*, published in 1929.   He studied the histories of thirteen pairs of identical and seventeen pairs of fraternal twins, one of each pair having been convicted of offences.   He found that the second twin had also been convicted in ten of the identical pairs, but in only two of the fraternal pairs.   This he felt, adequately demonstrated the predominance of the hereditary element.

Other studies along the same lines followed, and showed similar though rather less striking differences between the two groups. Thus Rosanoff found twenty-five criminally concordant pairs in thirty-seven pairs of identical twins, and five concordant pairs in twenty-three pairs of fraternal twins.[51]   If the results of five well-known twin studies[52] are totalled, seventy of the 120 pairs of identical twins are found to be concordant (67·3 per cent.), but only thirty-seven of 112 pairs of fraternal twins (33 per cent.).[53]

But these twin studies do not provide the conclusive proof which is sought. Although it has been claimed that identical twins can be diagnosed with a fair degree of certainty in after-life, some authorities are doubtful about this.[54] It is also by no means easy to secure full information about the criminal records of individuals; people are naturally reticent about such matters. It is to Lange's failure to trace all the examples of criminality among his fraternal twins that Stumpfl attributes the exceptionally high rate of concordance which he obtained.[55] Twin studies must also necessarily be very small in scale, for identical twins are themselves few and far between. This means, as in the studies cited, that the transfer of only a few cases from one category to another would make all the difference to the results.

And apart from these objections, there is a methodological difficulty of some substance: the unstated assumption that the environment of identical twins is no more similar than that of fraternal twins. This is most unlikely. The very similarity in appearance of the identical twins will tend to make people react to them in a similar way. They will be constantly mistaken for each other. The close bond which often exists between them, seems often also to make them actually seek a similar environment. They often like to do the same things, to join the same organisations, and to be with the same people. It would be surprising if this did not result in some assimilation of their behaviour and ideas.

Only the intensive study of individual cases can tell us what role environmental factors do play, and cases in which only one of a pair of identical twins has been in trouble provide us with special opportunities for finding out. Stumpfl describes several cases of this sort.[56] Their histories give unmistakable evidence of similar temperamental qualities and patterns of behaviour in early life, but in the course of development these are moulded in the one into a criminal, and in the other into a law-abiding form.

Another case is reported by Wheelan, in the study of which all the resources of modern neurology and psychology were brought to bear.[57] The twins began to develop along different lines before they reached the age of ten. Information about their early environment was not available in sufficient detail to show whether they were being treated differently, but it was noted that one twin soon became the dominant partner. "This slight initial difference might produce an habitual difference in attitude and behaviour, which would grow out of their intimate association together. Each twin was part of the environment of the other, and a part which differed increasingly as their paths began to diverge."[58] In the end, while one made a happy marriage and settled down into a job and a stable way of life, the other married a girl who was already delinquent, and from whom he was soon separated, was discharged from the Army with a deplorable record, as "psychopathic", attempted to murder his brother and to commit suicide, and has been constantly in and out of prison.

E.E.G. studies appear to confirm the constitutional similarity of the twins, both displaying epileptic types of reaction. Their very similar intelligence test-scores tended to the same conclusion. However, it is in the various tests of character and personality that the effect of experience is to be seen. While the criminal twin emerges as markedly neurotic, the responses of the other are normal. It is perhaps worth while observing that in two recent major studies of twins (neither, however, being specially concerned with criminality) it was noted that one twin usually emerged as the leader,[59] and that in one of these enquiries (that of Eliot Slater) it was found, as in the present study, that the dominant twin developed less satisfactorily than his brother.

In the end we are faced with a paradox. Twin studies have been proffered as proof of the decisive role of inheritance in the causation of crime, but all that they do conclusively prove is that environment must always be reckoned with. This emerges not only from the case-histories, but also from the statistical studies, for if heredity alone were concerned, concordance in criminality between identical twins would have to be 100 per cent., for their inheritance is assumed to be identical.

## The Psychopathic Personality

Much loose thinking about these problems is connected with the concept of the "psychopathic personality". This is the clinician's own contribution to the theory of the criminal constitution. Certain lifelong social misfits whom he finds he cannot reach by any sort of remedial treatment, and whose misdemeanours cannot be traced to some recognised social or psychiatric cause, are assumed to be constitutionally inferior, and this is usually taken to mean morally inferior. At one time the term "moral insanity" (coined by Prichard in 1835)[60] was used, but the idea of an inborn deficiency analogous to mental deficiency gradually superseded that of disease which the word "insanity" had implied. Mercier [61] introduced the term "moral imbecile" to describe cases of this sort, and this name was actually incorporated in the British Mental Deficiency Act of 1913.

Psychopathic personality is the latest appellation. Neither sane nor insane, the psychopath is said to be congenitally incapable of making a satisfactory adjustment to normal social life. He may be aggressive and violent, or merely inadequate. He may be criminal, or merely feckless. In spite of his apparent stupidity in persisting in profitless courses of action, he may often be of high intelligence. His behaviour may lead him either to the prison cell or the mental hospital, but in either case very little can be done for him.

Henderson, who divides psychopaths into aggressive, inadequate, and creative types, considers that the causes may be of many different kinds, sometimes being predominantly hereditary, and sometimes predominantly environmental. Often complicated neurological abnormalities are involved.[62] "In all of these instances the conduct of the individual may be so seriously interfered with as to render him unable to adapt to society."[63] This is very similar to the view of Eliot Slater, who, however, lays more stress upon the hereditary element. "With few exceptions," he writes, "the psychopathic personality is the result of a combination of hereditarily determined tendencies, which in other combinations might have led to normality or even to a superior type of personality."[64]

Many different types of personality, brought about by many different kinds of cause, are thus called psychopathic. Often the word seems to have been used as a sort of waste-paper basket into which all those cases which fall into no other established category can be deposited. Even more, it seems sometimes to be used to explain away the therapist's failure to understand and to cure his patient. The types of individuals who are described by the term vary widely between investigators, and it is often difficult to see any common element in those grouped together under it. Thus some even seem to include classical cases of neurosis or insanity. Sweeping and unjustifiable generalisations about the innateness of psychopathy are made. And the whole trend of the theory is towards a highly undesirable fatalism, which is inimical both to further aetiological study or experiments in treatment.[65]

But in spite of all this, there almost certainly is an element of truth in the conception. There are cases which seem especially difficult to treat successfully, and they appear to display certain common symptoms. And these types of case are to be seen (though often with a heterogeneous collection of bed-fellows) in the diagnostic schemes of most writers on the subject. It is becoming clear that a widely acceptable definition of psychopathy could centre around the following points:—

(a) Failure to adjust to the demands of society from the earliest years.

(b) Inability to learn by experience.

(c) No sign of guilt or shame when "found out".

(d) Inability to make personal relationships with other people, except the most shallow and fleeting.

Case-studies, complemented by careful statistical controls, have been carried out by John Bowlby and others, and confirm the existence of such a condition. At the same time, Bowlby,[66] Bender,[67] and the others, with refreshing impartiality, have begun to tear down much of the tottering edifice which their predecessors had built up. They reject the idea of a constitutional and inborn inferiority, and instead present the case for psychopathy as a form of psychological illness, due to emotional deprivations in infancy. This theory will be discussed in more detail in the next chapter.

## NOTES TO CHAPTER III

1. See also Trenaman, J., *Out of Step*, 1952, pp. 41-2.

2. Goring, C., *The English Convict*, 1913.

3. Hooton, E. A., *Crime and the Man*, 1939. Also his, *The American Criminal: an Anthropological Study*, 1939.

4. Ferri, E., *Criminal Sociology*, 1917. Garafalo, R., *Criminology*, 1914. The term "criminology" is said to have been invented by Garafalo. Ferri, as the title of his book indicates, attributed much more importance to social factors than did Lombroso. He was also responsible for the famous Ferri "progetto", a model criminal code for Italy, which, however, was never adopted. In this, the ideas of criminal responsibility and of punishment for crime were completely abandoned.

5. Trenaman's report on Army offenders showed them to be generally inferior to the normal Army intake as regards both height and weight. (Trenaman, J., *Out of Step*, 1952, Chapter VII.) Some physical inferiority was also found by Ferguson among Glasgow juvenile delinquents, though the latter points out that the physical differences between delinquents and non-delinquents was not as wide as for social and environmental factors. (Ferguson, T., *The Young Delinquent in his Social Setting*, 1952, pp. 115-19.)

6. East, W. Norwood, *Adolescent Criminal*, 1942, pp. 167 ff.

7. Sheldon, W. A., *Varieties of Delinquent Youth*, 1949.

8. Kretschmer, E., *Physique and Character*, 1925.

9. Willemse, W. A., *Constitution Types in Delinquency*, 1932.

10. *Op. cit.*

11. Sutherland, E. H., in *Am. Sociol. Review*, **16**, 1951, pp. 10-13.

12. Glueck, S. and E. T., *Unravelling Juvenile Delinquency*, 1950. See especially Chapters XV and XXI, and Appendix C. The Gluecks will shortly

be publishing a more detailed study of the anthropometric data collected in this study.

13. Hoskins, R. G., *Endocrinology*, 1941. A brief account of the functions of the various endocrine organs will also be found in Mottram, V. H., *Physical Basis of Personality*, 1946, Chapter 8.

14. See, for instance, Schlapp, M. G., and Smith, E. H., *The New Criminology*, 1928.

15. See below, Chapter XX.

16. A comprehensive account of the whole subject will be found in Hill, D., and Parr, G., *Electro-encephalography*, 1950.

17. The work of other investigators will be found listed in the *Minutes of Evidence, Royal Commission on Capital Punishment*, 1949, p. 299 and pp. 303-4.

18. The classification into aggressive and inadequate types is due to D. K. Henderson—see end of this chapter.

19. Hill, D., and Watterson, D., "Electro-encephalographic Studies of Psychopathic Personalities", *J. Neurol. Psychiat.*, **5**, 1942, pp. 47 ff.

20. Hodge, R. Sessions, and Walter, W. Grey, "Juvenile Delinquency: an Electro-physiological, Psychological and Social Study", *Brit. J. of Delinquency*, **3**: 3, 1952, pp. 155 ff.

21. See the evidence of Hill, Stafford-Clark, and Taylor—*Minutes of Evidence*, *loc. cit.*, pp. 300-5.

22. Sessions Hodge and Grey Walter, *loc. cit.*, pp. 167-9.

23. Henderson, D. K., and Gillespie, R. D., *Textbook of Psychiatry*, 1950, pp. 556-60.

24. Goddard, H. H., *Human Efficiency and Levels of Intelligence*, 1920, p. 74.

25. Blackburn, J., "Influence of the Social Environment on Intelligence Test Scores"; Woodward, M., "Role of Low Intelligence in Delinquency", *Brit. J. of Delinquency*, **4**: 4, 1955, pp. 281 ff.

26. Woodward, *ibid*.

27. An examination of the relative virtues of individual and group tests will be found in the *Report of the Consultative Committee on Psychological Tests of Educable Capacity* (Board of Education), 1924, pp. 90-1.

28. Sutherland, E. H., Chapter XV in Young, Kimball (ed.), *Social Attitudes*, 1931, pp. 357-75.

29. Zeleny, L. D., "Feeble-mindedness and Criminal Conduct", *Am. J. Sociol.*, **38**, 1933, pp. 564-76.

30. Cited Sutherland, E. H., *Principles of Criminology*, 1947, p. 105.

31. Gittins, J., *Approved School Boys*, 1952, p. 59.

32. *Op. cit.*, p. 93.

33. *Op. cit.*, p. 60.

34. The term is usually applied to those with an intelligence quotient of less than about 70.

35. See, for instance, the cases quoted in Weber, H., "The 'Borderline Defective' Delinquent", *Brit. J. of Delinquency*, **3**: 3, 1953, pp. 173 ff.

36. Burt, Cyril, *Young Delinquent*, 1925, p. 308.

37. Woodward, *loc. cit.*; also below, pp. 92 ff.

38. *Op. cit.*, pp. 113-14.

39. *Op. cit.*, pp. 226 ff. and p. 310.

40. Milner, K. O., "Delinquent Types of Mentally Defective Persons", *J. Mental Sci.*, **95**, 1949, pp. 842-59.

41. Bagot, J. H., *Juvenile Delinquency*, 1941, p. 51.

42. Fox, V., *J. Criminal Law and Criminology*, **37**, 1946, pp. 141 ff.

43. Merrill, M. A., *Problems of Child Delinquency*, 1947.

44. Barnes, H. E., and Teeters, N. K., *New Horizons in Criminology*, 1945, p. 179. The proportions obtained by Penrose from a study of 1,000 patients in a mental deficiency institution are probably more reliable, *i.e.* 29 per cent. due entirely to heredity, 9 per cent. entirely to environmental factors, and the

remainder to both kinds of factors in combination [see Radzinowicz, L., and Turner, J. W. C. (eds.), *Mental Abnormality and Crime*, 1944, p. 96].

45. Dugdale, R., *The Jukes*, 1877.

46. Goddard, H. H., *The Kallikaks*, 1912.

47. See Hurwitz, S., *Criminology*, 1952, p. 61.

48. Trenaman, J., and Emmett, H. B., in *Howard Journal*, **8**: 1, 1949-50, pp. 49 ff.

49. For example, Burt, *op. cit.*, p. 52, who found criminality in the families of 54 per cent. of his delinquents, as compared with only 17 per cent. of his controls.

50. Quoted Hurwitz, *op. cit.*, pp. 77-9.

51. Rosanoff, *et al.*, *J. Criminal Law and Criminology*, **24**, 1934, pp. 923-34.

52. Those of Lange, Rosanoff, Stumpfl (see below), Legras (1932), and Kranz (1936).

53. Quoted Barnes and Teeters, *op. cit.*, p. 172.

54. For an example of the kind of evidence relied upon, see Wheelan, L., "Aggressive Psychopathy in one of a pair of Uniovular Twins", *Brit. J. of Delinquency*, **2**: 2, 1951, pp. 132-3.

55. Stumpfl, F., *Die Ursprünge des Verbrechens dargestellt am Lebenslauf von Zwillingen*, 1936.

56. *Ibid.*

57. Wheelan, *loc. cit.*, pp. 130 ff.

58. *Ibid.*, p. 142.

59. Slater, Eliot, *Psychotic and Neurotic Illnesses in Twins* (Medical Research Council), 1953; Newman, H. H., Freeman, F. N., and Holzinger, K. J., *Twins: a Study of Heredity and Environment*, 1937.

60. Prichard, J. C., *A Treatise on Insanity*, 1837.

61. Mercier, C., "Moral Imbecility", *Practitioner*, **99**, 1917, pp. 300-11.

62. Henderson, D. K., *Psychopathic States*, 1939.

63. Henderson and Gillespie, *op. cit.* (1946 edn.), p. 384.

64. Quoted in East, W. Norwood, *Society and the Criminal*, 1949, p. 131.

65. Cleckley, H., *The Mask of Sanity*, 1941, for a discussion of such issues as these.

66. Bowlby, J., *Forty-four Juvenile Thieves*, 1946.

67. Bender, L., "Psychopathic Behaviour Disorders in Children", in Lindner, R. M., and Seliger, R. V. (eds.), *Handbook of Correctional Psychology*, 1946.

# CHAPTER IV

## PSYCHOLOGICAL THEORIES

There is a sense in which all crime may be said to be "psychological"; for an appropriate urge or intention must arise in the criminal's mind before he commits his offence. This, however, does not mean that all crime is due to psychological abnormality. The man in the street does not believe that it is, and he is probably right.[1] The psychological responses, in fact, often seem to be very normal responses to a highly abnormal environment.

Nevertheless, the personal response is still present as the peculiar contribution of the individual himself to his predicament, and accounts for the fact that some normal people do, and some do not, get into trouble under similar circumstances. There is a range of normality, and within this range many different types of personality may exist. Indeed, personality in all its ramifications is probably unique, and will react in its own unique way to the trials and temptations of life. But in such cases, the circumstances in which the individual has to live must still receive the lion's share of attention. It is they which are maladjusted and not he.[2]

### Psychological Abnormality and Crime

But there are other offenders who do owe their criminality to an abnormal mental state. No one would question this, for example, in cases of insanity (psychosis), or obvious neurosis. Among the psychoses, schizophrenia has been known to give rise to a variety of criminal acts: murder, rape, arson, theft, etc. The paranoid patient may attack those who, in his deluded state, he believes are plotting against him, as may the manic those who obstruct him in his ceaseless and feverish round of activity.

Similarly with the neuroses. In the course of a hysterical "fugue" (a state of "altered consciousness") the individual may commit many offences of which he has no recollection afterwards. The obsessional neurotic also may be forced by an irresistible inner compulsion to go on performing some act, which may well be an offence, such as stealing, sexual exhibitionism, or wandering. Then there are various sex offences which are clearly the product of a disordered mind.

All of these are forms of mental illness and are readily diagnosable as such. Even though the law may not always acknowledge it, such

41

offenders are no more responsible for their crime than is, say, the tubercular patient for the respiratory symptoms which go with his disease.[3]

## The Role of Temperament

There would probably be more controversy about the existence of psychological abnormality in certain other kinds of cases. Some such have already been considered as constitutional factors—lack of intelligence or temperamental type, for example. The former passes muster without any trouble; here is a clear case of a constitutional psychological abnormality which may lead to delinquency. But what of temperament: those features of the emotional life which are predominantly innate and provide the ground-plan for later emotional development? Not all would accept abnormal temperament as an explanation of criminal tendencies. The individual displays no obvious abnormal symptoms, but only appetites and tendencies which we ourselves also have but have managed to curb. Yet if the strength and direction of the basic emotional drives differ between individuals, this must be a very relevant consideration in explaining why they behave as they do. And some, because of their particular temperaments, may have more difficulty in running their lives on an even keel than the average person.

BURT'S THEORY. Something has already been said about temperamental factors in connection with the work of Kretschmer and Willemse. Here Burt's theory of "general emotionality" calls for special mention. Pointing out that the impulses with which we are endowed at birth vary in strength between individuals, Burt contends that many offences may be traced to either an excess or a deficiency of a particular instinctive drive. An excess of the submissive instinct is thus postulated to account for the tendency of many criminals to be weak-willed and easily-led. The impulse of fear is seen as the root-cause of stealth and cunning, lying and absconding. The callous type of offender is said to be deficient in the primitive emotion of love, and an excess of the instinct of grief to be the cause of suicide.[4]

This sort of explanation is open to obvious objections. How do we know that there is a simple imbalance of an inborn quality? The instinct-psychologists led by William McDougall[5] argue, by analogy with the theory of animal instincts, that human instincts may be presumed where there are patterns of behaviour which have a powerful drive behind them and which seem to be universal throughout the human species. Clinical psychologists, however, have noted that the emotions go through many vicissitudes in the course of development, and that if they do exist in differentiated forms at birth, they are, nevertheless, transformed by later experience.[6] Anthropologists have found that behaviour which the instinct-psychologists have described as instinctive does not exist in anything like the same form in other cultures than ours. The universality of those patterns of behaviour they argue, is confined to a particular culture-area, and can be explained as the result of the common mode of life which the people of such an area share.[7]

In taking this theory further, however, Burt propounds a view which is much less open to challenge. He claims to have demonstrated by statistical analysis, that behind all the specific instincts there is a general factor, a given level of "general emotionality" for each individual.[8] As a result, excess or deficiency in one impulse may bring with it a similar excess or deficiency in others. Those with a general excess, he calls the "unstable". They are explosive and unbalanced, unpredictable and inconsistent. The "temperamentally defective", on the other hand, are emotionally impoverished persons, possibly including what other writers have called schizoid types or introverts, as well as Bowlby's "affectionless" characters. This theory is more in line with the present view about the nature of the innate element in our emotional make up, as a sort of fixed reservoir of energy which can flow into various behavioural channels according to circumstances.

Burt compared 200 young delinquents with a control group of 400 non-delinquents, and found that general temperamental deficiency was present in 9·6 per cent. of his delinquent cases, but in only 1·0 per cent. of the controls; and instability in 34 per cent. of the delinquents, and in only 9·2 per cent. of the controls.[9] He concluded that "among all the innate psychological characteristics of the delinquents, a marked emotionality is one of the most frequent, as it is one of the most influential". It might be expected, as Burt himself remarks, that the unstable would be especially likely to get into trouble if they were also feebleminded, for they would then have more difficulty in finding outlets for their urgent impulses.

## Importance of Early Training

To say that all emotional difficulties of this sort are the result of an abnormal innate endowment, however, is going beyond the evidence. There is direct evidence of a clinical and observational character that many difficulties of this sort arise as a result of unwise handling in early childhood. In a small sample of fourteen cases Bowlby attributed emotional impoverishment to heredity in three cases, and to early family experiences in eleven.[10]

### The Psycho-analytic School

We owe our present understanding of the important part played by our infantile experience in our emotional development, to the psycho-analytical theories of Sigmund Freud and his followers. It is not intended here to give any full account of psycho-analysis as such, for it is now an enormous subject with a vast literature.[11] A few main principles can, however, be outlined.

The infant is conceived of as a young animal, with many selfish, violent, and anti-social wishes of an instinctual character. In the course of development he has to learn that these wishes cannot be realised in civilised human communities. In the main, he must learn these lessons in the course of his relationship with his parents. Some things they directly prohibit. Others he realises that they would not permit, though neither he nor they actually make an issue of them. He has to accommodate himself to this situation, and how well he does this depends largely upon how these necessary frustrations are imposed by his parents. For satisfactory development it is necessary that they impose them gradually and tolerantly, giving the child time to get his desires in hand, and also making it possible for him to find adequate substitutes which would give him similar satisfaction.

Difficulties arise where parents are very censorious, or when vital emotional needs have to be frustrated without hope of compensation, for then the child may well react by becoming aggressive and hostile. Or because these unacceptable wishes are "bad", and the child wishes to be "good", he tends to dissociate himself from them, to deny their existence, and even to blot out all memory of them from his mind. The psycho-analyst then says that they have passed into the "unconscious" or have been "repressed". Then, although the individual is no longer aware of their existence, they fester on, disturbing his adjustment in all sorts of ways.

A most important stage is reached when the child, instead of merely identifying the things which his parents permit and prohibit, with "good" and "bad" respectively, identifies himself personally with the parental code, so that this becomes his own code, part of himself, and operates even when his parents are not present. This is no less an event than the dawn of conscience or personal morality, as the psycho-analyst sees it. The parent's standards are said to be "introjected", and to form an organ within the mind, the super-ego, which roughly corresponds to what we call conscience. Much repression, according to Freud, takes place at the behest of the super-ego. Its very existence, of course, opens up the possibility of much conflict within the mind itself.

Freud himself sought to explain one particular kind of criminality in terms of this theory. We have all come across the individual whose wrong-doing is always found out, and who, in fact, seems to have taken precious little care to keep it secret. It often seems as though he were actually seeking punishment, though he himself would be the first to reject this idea if it were put to him. Freud argues that this is precisely what he is doing, but that his desire for punishment is unconscious, and so he could not be aware if it. Forbidden impulses have been repressed, but still remain active in the unconscious, and he has as a result an unconscious sense of guilt which causes him to seek punishment. The punishments which he receives for the offences which he actually commits, alleviate the guilt, about those which exist only in his own mind.[12]

WORK OF AICHHORN. Aichhorn, a Viennese psycho-analyst who was also a gifted worker with delinquent children, formulated the first systematic theory of crime from a psycho-analytical standpoint in his book *Wayward Youth* (1925). As others have done, Aichhorn saw the many parallels between the behaviour of the criminal and that of the infant who has not yet been socialised. He therefore contended that the most important cause of crime must be faulty methods of child training. If a child does not learn to give up or modify his instinctual demands, he will become a criminal, but he will only be prepared to make the necessary sacrifice if he feels that his parents love him. He will, as it were, give up these other satisfactions only in exchange for love. A parent may be at fault in giving too little love, but, argues Aichhorn, he may also give love too easily, so that the child does not have to earn it by renouncing his more primitive desires.

Alternatively parental attitudes may be inconsistent; so that renunciation is not always demanded, or the child can play off one parent against the other, getting from one the love which the other is withholding and thus again needing to make no adjustment on his own part. In addition, Aichhorn recognised two other apparently less important causes of criminality. One derives from the

Freudian view of conscience.   A child may "introject" the standards of criminal parents, and as a result his moral judgment will be seriously impaired.   The other is Aichhorn's sole concession to the idea of constitutional tendencies.   A child may sometimes, he feels, be constitutionally incapable of making the identifications with his parents which social adaptation demands.

Aichhorn is at pains to emphasise that although his theories postulate an abnormal form of psychological development, this is not the same as a neurotic condition.   The neurotic is at conflict within himself.   The moral side of his nature (represented by his super-ego) and the instinctual sides are at war with each other, and his neurotic symptom is a way, if a pathological one, of resolving that conflict.   The delinquent, on the other hand, is at war with society.   Also the neurotic finds his symptom painful, and is therefore only too ready to co-operate in treatment, while the delinquent enjoys his symptom, as it enables him to satisfy his instincts without let or hindrance.

## Critics of the Psycho-analysts

The onslaught on these ideas has come from several different directions.   There is first of all the general attack on psychoanalysis as a theory of human nature.   Its clinical method of investigation is criticised as unscientific, and many of its particular hypotheses are decried as "fantastic", "not in accordance with common sense", or "derived from the analysis of the mentally-ill and therefore not applicable to normal people".   Freud plausibly argued that much of this hostility to psycho-analysis was inevitable, and resulted from its concern with unconscious mental processes. Ideas and wishes which are repressed are so because the conscious mind dare not accept them.   When their existence is later postulated as part of a psycho-analytical theory, the same repressive mechanisms will make people continue to deny their existence.   This would apply, for example, to the untamed instinctual wishes which Aichhorn considered to account for much delinquency; if we have repressed these wishes in ourselves as the psycho-analysts would argue that we have, we shall continue to deny any theory of delinquency in which they play a part, for otherwise we should be implicitly accepting their existence, and disturbing our own mental adjustment.[13]

That part of psycho-analytical theory which is concerned with the super-ego suffers not only from this disadvantage, but also is bound to be opposed by those with strong religious convictions.   To the religious person, conscience is no mere infantile mental mechanism, but a divinely inspired arbiter, perhaps even the very voice of God. And the moral standards for which it stands are permanent and intrinsic virtues, and not merely those which one's parents happen to have believed in. But the evidence of clinical psychiatry is on the whole against both of these claims.

Even if one meets Aichhorn's theory on its own psycho-analytical premises, however, it can be criticised. A major contribution of the psycho-analysts to our understanding of human mental development has been its discovery that if we cannot realise an impulse in one form we tend to deflect it into some other channel, and to content ourselves with this as a substitute for the real thing. Such a deflection is usually sufficiently similar to the original desire to supply us with at least some satisfaction. This, as a solution to the eternal problem of social training with its concomitant frustrations, is obviously an alternative to repression, and if the new channels of expression are socially valuable ones (they are then called "sublimations"), real progress will have been made.[14] Thus the person with strong aggressive wishes may sublimate them by fighting against poverty as a philanthropist or a reformer, or against sin as a militant preacher.

On the other hand, the individual may find less acceptable means of securing substitute satisfactions, seeking to compensate himself for his affective deprivations by delinquent behaviour of one sort or another. The argument then would be that delinquency was due not simply to the failure to inhibit primitive desires; the infantile impulses had been restrained, but had then been redirected into the wrong channels. The possibility of this sort of compromise was not allowed for by Aichhorn, but it is one of the main themes of *New Light on Delinquency and its Treatment* by William Healy and Augusta F. Bronner,[15] who were much influenced by psycho-analytical ideas. This book has had a tremendous influence upon subsequent thinking. The debt owed to it by, for example, recent writers such as D. H. Stott,[16] is very obvious to any close student of their work.

## Healy and Bronner

One hundred and forty-three young offenders, mostly boys, were considered, from the point of view of their behaviour, their emotional condition, and their family background. No fewer than 131 were found to be suffering from "major emotional disturbances" —feeling rejected, frustrated or inadequate, troubled about rivalries or disharmonies within the family, or with other deeper-lying emotional conflicts, such as an unconscious sense of guilt, with the accompanying feeling of a need for punishment.

Of the total delinquent sample, 105 had non-delinquent brothers or sisters who were sufficiently similar to them to serve as controls. Many factors were bound to be common to both the delinquent and the non-delinquent sibling: the more material aspects of environment and family life, for instance. Attention was thus directed towards the less tangible factors and, in particular, the pattern of emotional relationship within the family, which might well differ for different siblings.

Now it is relatively easy to obtain a measure of the level of material welfare in a family, but a far more difficult thing to come to any conclusion about the quality of the personal relationships involved. Take a parent's love for a child, for example. This cannot be deduced from the fact that the child receives all or even more than it needs materially, for there is no doubt that parents who do not really love their children will often, out of a vague sense of guilt about this, tend to load them with material things. Real feelings are often unconscious and masked by compensatory attitudes such as this, so that neither the parent nor the child is consciously aware of what lies behind it all. And if *they* do not know, how is the investigator to find out? Only, it would seem, by a process of risky inference, or after prolonged clinical study in the course of which underlying motives can gradually be laid bare. However, Healy and Bronner essayed this task, and of the delinquents eighty-six were considered to be living in "apparently inimical" family situations, and nineteen in "apparently favourable" situations, as compared with seventy-five and thirty respectively for the non-delinquent controls.

The difference is a small one, but in itself very suggestive, and when the family circumstances were examined indirectly through an interpretation of the emotional reactions of the children, several, even of the nineteen delinquents who were in apparently favourable family situations, were found to have emotional troubles centring on their homes. Eight of the sibling pairs being twins (fraternal not identical), these were studied separately, as making for a closer control of genetic factors and of such factors as differences in age. Each pair of twins was subjected to a most detailed clinical comparison, and while this revealed the complex web of causes at work, it also brought out most vividly and convincingly the role played in every case by adverse family relationships and the resultant emotional disturbance.

A comparison of the degree of emotional adjustment achieved by the delinquents and their non-delinquent siblings showed the most remarkable contrast of all. Ninety-one per cent. of the delinquents evinced signs of emotional disturbance as compared with only 13 per cent. of the controls.

Healy and Bronner themselves sum up the results of this phase of the enquiry when they write: "The more objective data concerning the delinquent's life and the various social pressures upon him are rather easily knowable and may be important factors in the production of his delinquency. But it is clear that there are more fundamental considerations and that we must shift the emphasis of our studies and pay more attention to the emotional implications of human relationships ".[17] This is the first step in the new orientation which they offer.

The second step turns on the idea of sublimation. When some explanation was sought for the fact that seventy-five of the non-delinquents remained so in spite of the fact that they lived in "apparently unfavourable" family situations, it was found that while thirty-two owed it to their diffident and less demanding personalities, thirty of the remainder seemed to have found some special activity, in school, social life, or sport, for example, which absorbed them and gave them satisfaction.

Healy and Bronner claimed that delinquent acts also had a substitution value for the individuals who committed them. They could be seen as highly meaningful for the children, if related to the latter's specific emotional needs and deprivations. In some cases, the delinquency could be seen as an escape from the unpleasant emotional situation. In others it compensated for this. Sometimes it bolstered up the ego of a child who had strong feelings of inferiority (an explanation which clearly owes much to the idea of the "inferiority complex" as developed by Alfred Adler),[18] and sometimes it embodied attitudes of hostility and revenge. In some, the offences were committed with the unconscious motive of securing punishment. In any event, the delinquent act, it was contended, could best be understood as a redirection of frustrated instinctual urges.

It may sometimes be difficult for an onlooker to recognise it as such: the satisfaction obtained may be symbolical only, or of unconscious desires, which appear irrational to the outsider. But what really matters is the "subjective value, conscious or unconscious" which the delinquent behaviour has for the delinquent himself. So long as he finds it satisfying, it will be fulfilling its sublimatory function for him.

It is not difficult to find methodological flaws in *New Light on Delinquency*. The controls, for example, are not really adequate. It cannot for a moment be assumed that they eliminate genetic factors, even in the case of the twins. Nor was the material subjected, as it might have been, to statistical tests of its validity and significance. But that was not really the sort of study which Healy and Bronner were trying to carry out. Theirs was essentially an interpretative and qualitative approach. They were trying to trace the emergence and growth of delinquent trends, and to understand the role which delinquency plays in the child's mind, not to establish formal statistical correlations or to carry out a crucial experiment. And they frankly admitted that their sample was deliberately selected so as to include only the more serious offenders.

## Similar Theories

Many other psychologists have developed explanations of criminal behaviour which fit very well into this general formulation. The "inferiority complex" of Alfred Adler has already been referred to in this connection. Alexander's theory of the "neurotic character" is another such. It sees certain criminal acts as the playing-out in real life of an unconscious conflict, *i.e.* the reconciliation of an inner need with the demands of the ego and the super-ego, by means of criminal activity which attempts to satisfy both.[19] Other writers have explained specific types of offence as attempts to satisfy particular emotional needs. According to Bowlby, stealing is often a means whereby the deprived child tries to find some substitute for the parental love which he lacks.[20] Arson has been found, by Simmel and other psycho-analysts, to satisfy the sexual needs and aggressive impulses of many of those who commit it.[21]

A little more should perhaps be said about Stott's intensive study of 102 boys in a senior approved school. He found delinquency, in every one of his cases, to be a form of psychological breakdown; the delinquent seeking to escape from an emotional predicament, centring on his home, which has become unbearable to him. He may perhaps have suffered the loss of, or been deserted by, his parents, or be anxious about parental quarrels or ill-health. Or he may have been unwanted and unloved from infancy. In any case he reacts by adopting such a pattern of delinquent behaviour as will help him to cope with his feelings.

Thus some will rely upon the element of excitement in their delinquencies to take their minds off their troubles ("avoidance excitement"). Others, seeking reassurance, test out the love of their parents by misbehaving. Some try through their delinquencies to make themselves feel important, and thus to compensate for a sense of personal inferiority. In some cases, the motive is clearly hostility towards the parents, or an underlying wish to secure removal from home.

The similarity between these views and the views of Healy and Bronner is obvious. However, Stott gives even more predominance to the emotional factor than did the latter. While Healy and Bronner were prepared to admit the contribution made by the climate of moral ideas in the social environment of the children, Stott saw no reason to do this. There is in fact little doubt that he underestimated the value of environmental factors. For example, the delinquencies of Royston (one of the cases discussed by Stott), might much more reasonably have been ascribed to a family tradition of crime than to more subtle psychological factors.

The work suffers in general, however, from a tendency to over-simplification. Thus causal factors are seen as single, overwhelming incidents in a child's life, rather than (as is more likely to be the case) an accumulation of stresses, which build up delinquent character traits bit by bit. Moreover, all the insights which psycho-analysis has given us into the intricate nature of mental processes, has been abandoned in favour of a rather superficial, "descriptive" approach, in which, for example, the unconscious hardly plays a part at all. However, because he is not committed to any of the main schools of psychological thought, Stott is able to show us some aspects of the psychology of crime in a new and quite revealing light.

## Maternal Deprivation and the Affectionless Offender

Bowlby[22] was more interested in the particular problem of the persistent offender, the hard-boiled, apparently amoral type of person whom no sort of treatment seemed to reach, in fact, the psychopath. He carried out a detailed clinical study of forty-four young thieves, and compared them with a control group of a similar number of emotionally disturbed children who did not steal. He found that far more of the thieves (seventeen), than of the non-delinquents (two), had been separated from their mothers for a prolonged period during their earlier years.

He then examined the personality characteristics of the forty-four delinquents, and found a number of them to be of an "affectionless type". "Clinically such children appear emotionally withdrawn and isolated. They fail to develop libidinal ties with other children or with adults and consequently have no friendship worthy of the name. It is true that they are sometimes sociable in the superficial sense, but if this is scrutinised we find there are no feelings, no roots, in these relationships. This, I think, more than anything else, is the cause of their hard-boiledness. Parents and school-teachers complain that nothing they say or do has any effect on the child. If they thrash him he cries for a bit, but there is no emotional response to being out of favour, such as is normal to the ordinary child. It appears to be of no essential consequence to these lost souls whether they are in favour or not. Since they are unable to make genuine emotional relations, the conditions of a relationship at a given moment lacks all significance for them."[23]

This type of delinquent personality was found to be much more frequently associated with a break in the early mother-child relationship, than the other types, the proportions being 86 per cent. and 17 per cent. respectively. When the statistical measure, chi-squared, was applied to these figures, it was estimated that there was less than one chance in a hundred that the difference between the two groups was due to chance.

Various other factors which might have had causal significance were considered in the same way. They included heredity, as measured by the presence of mental ill-health in either of the parents; or unsatisfactory emotional attitudes towards the child on the part of either father or mother; and environmental stresses, in recent as against early childhood. None was found to have a statistically significant relationship with the affectionless personality, nor even with the group of delinquents as a whole. Bowlby, not unnaturally concluded that the affectionless type of delinquent personality was the result of early maternal deprivation.

There was plenty of evidence from the parents of these children to confirm this conclusion. Bowlby quotes several, who describe how a child, perhaps in hospital, gradually ceases to respond to his parents' visits, until he becomes at last completely detached and impersonal, and very difficult to handle.

Two theoretical questions remain for consideration. Why does early maternal deprivation lead to the development of the affectionless personality, and why should such a person become a persistent delinquent? Bowlby suggests that the abnormal personality development could occur in three ways. One of the results of

frustration and deprivation, especially in infancy, is rage and resentment, and so long as the child is angry with his mother he will not
establish a positive relationship with her. Or, of course, he may be
prevented from establishing such a relationship by the simple fact
of being separated from her for such a long period at the crucial
time. Finally, he may have been so frequently hurt and disappointed
by one change after another in his mother-figures (*e.g.* foster mothers,
nurses, etc.), that he decides, as it were, against making further close
ties of the same sort, and begins to build up his life on another more
impersonal basis.

His resistance to treatment, Bowlby explains as due to the fact
that there is a point, during the first five years of life, when human
beings as part of their normal development set about the building
up of personal relationships. If they fail to do this at the right time,
then it becomes very difficult, if not impossible, for them to achieve
it later. Only if they can be persuaded to relinquish their present
mode of adjustment, to go back to the emotional attitudes of that
period of infancy and start to grow again, can a cure be hoped
for. And this, anyhow, presupposes a personal relationship with
a therapist which can rarely be established with such detached
individuals.

Yet their desire for love is not completely extinguished. It has
been repressed, and often finds its outlet, Bowlby believes, in stealing.
The objects stolen become symbols for love in the child's unconscious, and stealing them is thus unconsciously the securing of love.
This transformation of emotional needs into delinquency is assisted
by the fact that as the child never establishes a strong, positive
relationship with his parents, he fails also to identify with them,
and to introject their standards to form a strong super-ego. In
other words, he is as conscienceless as the psychopath is often
alleged to be. Bowlby also suggests that the prostitute may have
been created in the same way. In prostitution there seems to be the
same combination of strong and untamed instinctual needs, and an
inability to establish permanent personal relationships.

Thorough as Bowlby's researches have been (many of the cases
were subjected to psychiatric study over a period of six months
or more), they do not have to stand alone. By a remarkable
coincidence, a number of workers in other countries were independently reaching the same conclusions at about the same time. In a
survey of the literature undertaken for the World Health Organisation,[24] Bowlby refers to the work of five Americans (Levy, Powdermaker, Lowrey, Bender, and Goldfarb), who, while differing from

him and from each other in minor details, agree on the main points arising. Here then is a well-attested theory of the development of psychopathy which provides a real alternative to the idea of an innate moral defect.

If, however, Bowlby is right when he contends that the condition is practically incurable, there is not so much difference on this score between the two approaches. The "maternal deprivation" hypothesis, on the other hand, does show how the condition may be prevented from occurring; in this respect at least, it is more hopeful than a view which postulates an innate deficiency. Also efforts at treatment may not be as futile as Bowlby feared.[25]

## Extent of Abnormality among Criminals

The psychological theories of crime are many and protean; here it has been possible only to trace the main lines of development —as the present writer sees them. But the various theories outlined above do, in total, provide a convincing explanation of much criminal behaviour. It would be only too easy to take the next step, and to assume that all criminality was the result of psychological abnormality.

This view has already been dismissed, though there is some difficulty in basing any judgment upon the data provided by the psychiatric examination of criminals. This is partly because the criminals available for such examination tend to be a highly selected sample: prison populations, for example, or persons selected for examination because some abnormality was suspected. The cases described by Healy and Bronner, and Bowlby, fall within the latter group.

There is also the difficulty of distinguishing between an abnormal, emotional disturbance, and the sort of conflict and insecurity from which we all suffer, and which is responsible perhaps for the light and shade of our personalities. D. H. Stott,[26] who found emotional troubles at the root of criminal behaviour in all his hundred consecutive approved school cases, seems to have fallen into this trap. No doubt the emotional difficulties did enter into the crimogenic complex in his cases, but why do such difficulties not always lead to crime, wherever they are found? Healy and Bronner found emotional disturbances in no fewer than 13 per cent. of their non-delinquents.[27] Even where these emotional stresses are excessive, they may just as readily lead to a neurosis as to anti-social behaviour. Bowlby does make a claim for maternal deprivation as an emotional factor making specifically for criminality, and his statistical demonstration of this appears reasonable—but not as an explanation of all crime. Bowlby's is convincing as a theory of a particular kind of persistent criminality, but there are other types of criminality, and probably even other types of persistent criminality.[28]

The proportions of criminals found to be psychologically disturbed range widely, therefore, from Stott's 100 per cent. (of approved school boys) to the 2 per cent. found in a study of 800 boys in L.C.C. remand homes, published in 1930.[29] In an investigation of serious criminality on the Danish island of Bornholm in 1944,[30] the proportion was put as high as 40 per cent., but this figure was predominantly made up of psychopaths or suspected psychopaths, and the diagnosis of psychopathy is notoriously imprecise,[31] as American figures show. About 10 per cent. of the criminals entering New York and Massachussets state prisons are diagnosed as psychopathic, but about 75 per cent. of those entering institutions in Illinois.[32] The percentage diagnosed as psychotic varies for different reports between 1 per cent. and 5 per cent.[33]

Before any really satisfactory estimate of the size of the problem can be made, much more agreement on diagnosis will have to be achieved. Even then no deductions can be drawn from the figures themselves until they have been compared with the figures for the distribution of mental disturbance in the population at large, and no firm estimate of this latter proportion is yet available.

## NOTES TO CHAPTER IV

1. See the data summarised at the end of this chapter.
2. Jones, Howard, "Group Sentiment and Delinquency", *Mental Health*, Nov. 1948. "The Social Malaise of Delinquency", *Howard Journal*, **8**: 1, 1949-50, pp. 45 ff.
3. For further information on psychiatric cases such as these, refer to the standard works, *e.g.* Henderson, D. K., and Gillespie, R. D., *Textbook of Psychiatry*, 1950.
4. Burt, Cyril, *Young Delinquent*, 1925, pp. 423 ff.
5. MacDougall, W., *Social Psychology*, 1908; *Outline of Psychology*, 1923; Shand, A. F., *Foundations of Character*, 1914.
6. See below, pp. 144-5.
7. Benedict, R., *Patterns of Culture*, 1935.
Mead, M., *Sex and Temperament in Three Primitive Societies*, 1935. A classical discussion of the whole question will be found in the "Symposium on Instincts", *Brit. J. of Educ. Psychol.*, **11**, 3; **12**, 1, 2, and 3; and **13**, 1.
8. Burt, *op. cit.*, pp. 506 ff.
9. *Ibid.*, Table XVIII, p. 514.
10. Bowlby, J., *Forty-four Juvenile Thieves*. There are no large-scale studies. Bowlby gives an account of such work as has been done in related fields in *Maternal Care and Mental Health*, 1951, Chapter III.
11. Fenichel, O., *Psycho-analytical Theory of Neurosis*, 1945, gives a survey of much of the literature up to its date of publication. See also Healy, W.,

*Theories and Structure of Psycho-analysis.* For a survey of more recent trends see Lorand, S., *Psycho-analysis Today,* 1948.

Of recent general works on the subject, Glover, E., *Psycho-analysis,* 1949, may be mentioned.

12. Freud, S., "Some character-types met with in psycho-analytic work" in *Collected Papers,* **11,** pp. 342-4.

13. This is the essence of the psycho-analytic theory of "resistance". See Freud, S., "Negation", *Collective Papers,* **5,** pp. 181 ff.

14. The concept of "sublimation" has been criticised as unscientific because it introduces a normative criterion, *i.e.* "social value" into psychology. (See Thouless, R. H., *General and Social Psychology,* 1951, p. 121.) The words "socially acceptable" would seem less exceptionable on this score.

15. Healy, W., and Bronner, A. F., *New Light on Delinquency and Its Treatment,* 1936.

16. Stott, D. H., *Delinquency and Human Nature,* 1950. See below, pp. 50-1.

17. Healy and Bronner, *op. cit.,* p. 120.

18. Adler, A., *Practice and Theory of Individual Psychology,* 1932.

19. Alexander, F., *International J. of Psycho-analysis,* **11,** 1930.

20. Bowlby, *Forty-four Juvenile Thieves, op. cit.*

21. Fenichel, *op. cit.,* pp. 371-2, and Simmel, E., "Incendiarism", in *Searchlights on Delinquency* (ed. K. R. Eissler), 1949, pp. 90 ff.

22. Bowlby, *op. cit.,* p. 49.

23. Bowlby, J., *Maternal Care and Mental Health,* 1951, p. 32.

24. *Ibid.,* p. 31.

25. For references to therapeutic work with psychopaths see note on p. 253 below.

26. *Op. cit.*

27. Healy and Bronner, *op. cit.,* p. 122.

28. See below, p. 94.

29. Report of the L.C.C. School Medical Officer for the year 1930.

30. Cited Hurwitz, S., *Criminology,* 1952, p. 198.

31. The definition of psychopathy has been discussed on pp. 36-8 above.

32. Sutherland, E. H., *Principles of Criminology,* 1947, p. 110.

33. *Ibid.,* p. 107.

# CHAPTER V

## SOME SOCIAL FACTORS

Many thinkers have treated crime as a symptom of some more fundamental sickness in our society. Notable among these have been the socialists. They contend that crime is due to Capitalism, with its basis of economic exploitation, and the acquisitive ethic which it fosters. Derived from the writings of Marx and Engels these ideas go back to the middle of the last century,[1] but have received their most thorough and carefully documented support from W. A. Bonger's *Criminality and Economic Conditions*, published in 1916.

### Capitalism and Criminality

Bonger marshalls a formidable array of arguments, authorities, and statistical tables, but his conclusions, nevertheless, are unconvincing. They relate to an over-simplified capitalism which has surely never existed except in the works of Marx and Engels or in some of the propaganda of the Soviet bloc. In this strange world of half-truths, it is possible for Bonger, without any appearance of incongruity, to lay part of the blame for prostitution on the fact that "the keeping of mistresses is a pastime for those who have been demoralised by a life of luxury and ease".[2] He shows the statistical connection between crime and such factors as poverty, lack of education, and alcoholism, but then must stretch his argument to breaking-point in an attempt to demonstrate that these factors in their turn are the inevitable result of a capitalist society, and would disappear under socialism. Alcoholism, for example, which is treated at some length, is seen as the solace of a downtrodden proletariat, and a convenient subject of expenditure for the capitalist, with more money than he knows how to use.[3]

What Bonger has failed to realise is that Capitalism is not a causal factor at all, but a construct, built up of many different factors. Only these more immediate precipitants can be subjected to scientific enquiry; for the rest one must rely as a rule upon speculation, or even on mere opinion. *Criminality and Economic Conditions* is itself the best proof of this. Much the same, of course, applies to other multiple-factor constructs, such as economic depression or war.[4]

Its second defect is one which it shares with other exclusively sociological approaches: it fails to explain how, in what should be an impartial group process, certain individuals do emerge as criminals, and others do not. In other words, it does not allow for the effect of individual peculiarities. Inconvenient as the unique individual may be, difficult though it may be to fit him neatly into our theories, we cannot escape the responsibility of studying him if we hope to understand our social problems. For if it is true that the individual does not exist apart from his group, it is equally true that the group only exists through its individual members.

Bonger lays some stress upon the ego-centric ethos of Capitalism,[5] and suggests that the selfishness thus engendered lies at the very root of criminal behaviour. He quotes anthropological support for his view that altruism may take its place in other, different kinds of society. Many primitive societies certainly do seem to give more scope to mutual aid, as against competition, than does ours, and to frown upon the accumulation of private property in excess of such day-to-day necessities as tools or weapons. This difference would seem relevant to the problem of crime, but the sort of evidence about crime in other cultures, which would show how relevant, still has to be collected. All that is known for certain is that crime does exist in these non-competitive communities.[6] The real issue is probably, how much, and what sort of crime.

## Poverty

Poverty as a causal factor is a very different matter. In studying the criminological effects of poverty, the criminologist has a more elementary (if still difficult) problem to tackle. Much work has been done on this subject, and along two main lines. Some investigators have asked themselves the direct question: how prevalent is poverty among offenders against the law? The others have sought to trace a relationship between crime and unemployment, either by comparing the relevant statistics or by examining the employment records of criminals.

CRIME AND THE POVERTY LINE. Burt[7] found that 56 per cent. of his young delinquents came from homes that were "poor or very poor", as compared with only 30 per cent. of the general population. However, he estimated that in only rather more than 3 per cent. was poverty the main source of the delinquency. A few years later, in the *New Survey of London Life and Labour*,[8] London streets were graded according to the economic position of their inhabitants, and all London offenders arrested for indictable offences during 1929 were then classified according to their place of residence. The following proportion of arrests in each grade of street were obtained:—

TABLE II

ARRESTS PER 10,000 OF POPULATION IN LONDON
STREETS OF DIFFERENT ECONOMIC GRADES IN
THE YEAR 1929

| Economic Grading | Arrests (per 10,000) |
| --- | --- |
| Lowest (degraded) .. .. | 41 |
| Still below poverty line .. | 30 |
| Mass of unskilled workers .. | 14 |
| Skilled workers .. .. | 11 |
| Middle-class and above .. | 6 |

Thus there was a criminal concentration of 35·5 per 10,000 in the impoverished neighbourhoods, and only of 10·3 per 10,000 in the rest. The steady and consistent increase in criminality throughout the grades as economic position worsens, is also worthy of note.

Similar studies have been carried out for other English cities. Bagot[9] analysed the details about family income given in probation officers' reports on juvenile cases in Liverpool in 1934 and 1936. Using standards worked out for the University of Liverpool's *Survey of Merseyside*, he found that in either year more than one-half of the offenders' families were below the poverty line, and a total of 85 per cent. were below the "human needs" standard, postulated as necessary for the "bare essentials of a civilised life". In the ordinary population, the corresponding proportions were 16 per cent. and 30 per cent. all told.

In America, Shaw and McKay,[10] as a result of their studies of high crime rate areas, came to the conclusion that such areas owed their anti-social nature primarily to the poverty of their inhabitants.

Almost alone, Healy, in all his various books, has tended to depreciate the importance of material factors such as poverty, as compared with emotional factors.[11] One explanation of the conclusions to which he came, may be the special nature of his samples as "clinical cases".

CRIMINALITY AMONG THE WEALTHY. Nevertheless, most poor people do manage to "keep straight", and there are many criminals in the higher strata of society.    Sutherland,[12] indeed, has issued a challenge to all research of this sort by his assertion that the numbers of the rich who are convicted would be far more if it were not for their influence, and the fact that many of them, as business men for example, commit offences which are dealt with nowadays by administrative action and not by the criminal courts.    Following Sutherland's pioneer work, there have been many studies which have shown how important "white-collar criminality" of this sort is in the United States, but it is doubtful if it has anything like as much significance in this country.

On the other hand, the youngster of good family who has delinquent tendencies, is hardly as likely to reach the courts as his less fortunate fellow.    Apart from social attitudes towards the "good home" as compared with the "bad", which must tend to make "cautions" or "second chances" more likely, there are so many expedients which the well-off family can adopt to help their miscreant offspring, from psychiatric treatment to placement in a private boarding school.    And misbehaviour must cause less irritation in a wealthy area of large, spaciously situated houses than in the terraces of Liverpool or the cramped back-to-back slum districts of Birmingham, and so be less speedily noticed or attract the attention of the police.    Nor can one overlook the fetish of "respectability" among the British middle-class.    They really do feel the disgrace if the child of a friend or a neighbour is brought before the court.    In the face of such an appalling possibility it is not surprising if they close their ranks.

If one considers the incidence of particular offences, it is probable that certain kinds of offences such as tax evasion, are actually more prevalent among the rich groups.    An American enquiry has shown that the theft of cars by juveniles in the States is commoner among the rich than the poor.[13]

POVERTY AS A CONCEPT.    The question of how poverty ought to be defined for purposes of research in criminology also gives rise to difficulties.    Is it to refer to sheer physical want, or to the "lack of the bare essentials of a civilised life"?[14]    A psychological analysis would seem to suggest that it should not be an objective standard at all, but depend upon what level of subsistence the individual is determined that he will maintain at any cost.

This may be partly a matter of individual needs or individual cupidity, but it may also be affected by more general influences. Thus what we demand as a standard of life seems to be affected by what we have been used to, and by what our friends and neighbours are at present able to enjoy. There is thus a widely diffused risk where standards of life are declining or unemployment increasing, but the effects of such changes are ameliorated a little if others are also seen to be suffering. For example, Mannheim quotes from George Orwell: "It is not only Alf. Smith who is out of work now. Bert Jones is out of work as well, and both of them have been 'out' for years. It makes a great deal of difference when things are the same for everybody ".[15]

It seems certain that the line should in any case be drawn higher than the level of actual physical need; for many the factor of poverty would be an effective crimogenic factor well above that level— though if one deals with the problem as an individual matter rather than as one of mass trends, it must be admitted that there are many who would advance to the very threshold of starvation rather than commit a crime. But for others, many of the so-called "conventional necessaries" would have to be included.

## Unemployment

There are many criminologists, however, de Greef among them, who believe that poverty (however we define it) at any particular time is a less important consideration than whether the family's economic position is improving or deteriorating.[16] This directs attention specifically to the question of unemployment. The most important British study is that of Mannheim.[17]

TABLE III

NUMBER OF MALE OFFENDERS FOUND GUILTY OF INDICTABLE OFFENCES PER 100,000 IN EACH AGE GROUP

| Year | Unemployment (per cent.) | 21 Years but Under 30 | 30 Years and Over | All Ages (10 and Over) |
|------|--------------------------|-----------------------|-------------------|------------------------|
| 1929 | 10·3 | 402 | 166 | 299 |
| 1930 | 15·8 | 409 | 169 | 314 |
| 1931 | 21·1 | 431 | 175 | 326 |
| 1932 | 21·9 | 485 | 180 | 254 |
| 1933 | 19·8 | 454 | 171 | 337 |
| 1934 | 16·6 | 444 | 171 | 351 |
| 1935 | 15·3 | 439 | 163 | 370 |
| 1936 | 12·9 | 446 | 168 | 383 |
| 1937 | 10·6 | 463 | 172 | 404 |
| 1938 | 12·6 | 487 | 173 | 407 |

Comparing the general trends of the unemployment figures in this country from 1900, with those for indictable offences, he found little similarity until 1932. There was then a considerable leap in convictions in spite of a steady improvement in the employment position, but this increase was largely confined to the under-twenty-ones, and if these were eliminated the two sets of figures were found to correspond fairly well.

If the figures of adult crime quoted by Mannheim are broken down according to the type of offence, it can be seen that there is an even closer relationship between trends in unemployment and in the main types of property crime. Offences against the person and sex offences, on the other hand, show a very different pattern:—

TABLE IV

NUMBER OF ADULT* OFFENDERS PER 100,000 OF POPULATION FOUND GUILTY OF VARIOUS INDICTABLE OFFENCES

| Year | Unemploy-ment (per cent.) | Larceny | Fraud and False Pretences | Breaking and Entering | Violence Against the Person | Sex |
|------|------|------|------|------|------|------|
| 1929 | 10·3 | 109·2 | 13·3 | 8·7 | 3·7 | 5·1 |
| 1930 | 15·8 | 113·9 | 14·0 | 10·3 | 3·9 | 5·0 |
| 1931 | 21·1 | 117·5 | 14·8 | 11·7 | 3·5 | 4·5 |
| 1932 | 21·9 | 124·8 | 16·2 | 14·9 | 3·4 | 4·6 |
| 1933 | 19·8 | 116·8 | 16·1 | 12·3 | 3·7 | 4·4 |
| 1934 | 16·6 | 110·2 | 15·6 | 10·8 | 3·9 | 4·9 |
| 1935 | 15·3 | 107·7 | 15·0 | 10·1 | 4·4 | 4·7 |
| 1936 | 12·9 | 111·3 | 14·9 | 10·0 | 4·3 | 5·0 |
| 1937 | 10·6 | 116·5 | 14·1 | 11·2 | 4·9 | 5·3 |
| 1938 | 12·6 | 117·3 | 15·3 | 13·1 | 4·7 | 5·9 |

* Adult here means over juvenile court age, e.g. sixteen and over until 1933, and seventeen and over from 1934 onwards.

The coefficients of correlation here between unemployment and property offences are positive; with Larceny, 0·56; Fraud and False Pretences, 0·5; and Breaking and Entering, 0·59. Even more significant are negative correlations with Violence Against the Person and Sex Crimes—of 0·76 in each case.

LOCAL UNEMPLOYMENT AND CRIME. A comparison by Mannheim of crime and unemployment in various cities of a similar size and character gave more doubtful results. It might have been anticipated that, say, a very high level of unemployment in one area would be reflected in a high rate of crime relative to the more prosperous areas, but this has been only partly borne out. For example, the comparison between Liverpool, Manchester, and Birmingham was remarkably consistent with this theory, while that between Leeds and Sheffield was quite inconsistent with it. The comparison between Cambridge, Chesterfield, and Merthyr Tydfil becomes consistent only if the juvenile figures alone are taken into account.

Mannheim rightly points out that the level of criminality in a particular place does in fact depend upon a variety of factors, many of them local in character, so that a very close correlation with unemployment fluctuations is hardly to be hoped for. Thus he accounts for the fact that South Shields has more indictable offences than Gateshead, although the latter has the larger population and also rather more unemployment, by the fact that South Shields is a better shopping centre than Gateshead. Residents in the latter place have to do much of their shopping in Newcastle, and this reduces the number of such offences as "larcenies from shops, vehicles, and meters". Even the very satisfactory relationship shown in the Liverpool-Manchester-Birmingham comparison cannot be taken at its face value, for the high crime rate of Liverpool must have been very much affected by the mixed racial and religious complexion of the population, and the existence of a large body of casual dock labour.[18]

The sceptic may scoff at such ambiguous material, and with some justification; but we face here the fundamental difficulty in social research—of demonstrating the intricately interwoven mechanism of a social process by objective, and therefore rather crude and superficial means. The more subjective type of evidence is much less equivocal. Mannheim quotes prison governors and others, who confidently confirm the relevance of unemployment to the problem, and most practical workers in the field will be able to cite cases which show its specific effect. On the statistical relationship between the two, however, Mannheim cautiously concludes that where both are high, then it is reasonable to assume that the unemployment has been decisive, but where a large amount of unemployment is not accompanied by high crime figures, then "certain factors are obviously at work which counterbalance its evil effects".[19]

EMPLOYMENT RECORDS OF OFFENDERS. The other method of investigation was adopted by Norwood East, in his examination of the employment records of no fewer than 4,000 Borstal boys.[20] While the general employment history of the delinquents was no worse than that of the general population, the amount of unemployment among them at the time they committed their offences was much higher than the average.[21]

Biased as such an institution population must be, it is a more representative sample than more localised American studies provide, for there local conditions of unemployment, etc., must affect the results. This fact is reflected in the very different percentages obtained in different American investigations. While Mary van Kleeck found 52 per cent. of 300 men committed to Sing Sing, the New York State Penitentiary, were out of work at the time of the offence, and obtained annual proportions varying from 26 per cent. to 38 per cent. over the period 1920-9,[22] Clemmer found that of 800 men committed to a large state prison, even in the depression years 1931-4, only 11 per cent. were unemployed when arrested, a proportion substantially lower than the national average of unemployment at this period.[23]

There is also, as Mannheim and others have pointed out, some danger in these enquiries in relying upon the unsupported word of prisoners about such a matter as employment, or even in depending on the evidence of the Employment Book.[24] To admit a poor work record is to risk being labelled lazy and feckless, or unstable, and this might affect not only one's sentence, but also one's chances of early licence.

### Non-material Aspects of Poverty and Unemployment

Common sense would suggest that poverty must make itself felt not only because of the material privation which results, but also because of other hazards to which the poor man is subjected because of his poverty: overcrowded home conditions, the family tensions generated by overcrowding and financial stringency, the lack of recreative and cultural opportunities, and the very real danger of contagion through residence in slum areas with a high crime rate.

Unemployment, likewise, is much more than an economic matter. A man's contentment and sense of worthwhileness are bound up with his having a job, and the man who is out of work for a long period may well become discouraged, and at last demoralised. Unemployment offers a special threat to the young. At a time of severe economic depression young people may have left school for years without ever having known what it was like to earn a living by steady work. The connection was clearly established in a national survey just before the war which showed highly significant differences between the unemployment figures of delinquents as compared with non-delinquents. Delinquents were also found to have changed jobs more frequently than the non-delinquent controls.[25]   A related issue is that of the "blind alley" job.   In such an occupation, the youngster may earn good money for a year or two, but is then thrown out on to the labour market without having acquired any useful skill or experience.

Less often recognised, perhaps, is the danger to juveniles which results from a surplus of employment opportunities—as, for example, after the recent war.   At such times, boys and girls can earn excessively high wages—until the bubble bursts, with catastrophic effects—and they can move from job to job so easily that they never establish sound work habits or a stable pattern of life.

## General Conclusions on the Causal Significance of Poverty and Unemployment

The results of these various studies are not at all clear-cut, but they offer some support for the view that the poorer members of the community are more likely to offend than the more comfortably-off. At the same time, the strictures of Sutherland must be borne in mind.   It may be that a larger proportion of the poorer offenders do find their way into the criminal statistics than of the richer. Also it is not easy to decide whether, in the studies described, an unfavourable economic position is a cause of criminality, or whether both are rooted in the same unsatisfactory traits of character.

### Religion

Poverty, even with all its secondary effects, is clearly not a sufficient explanation in itself.   The figures show too many exceptions for that, particularly the unemployment studies, and testify to the presence of other potent factors.   Some may be toxic influences, similar to poverty itself.   Others may be serving to reinforce the natural recuperative forces of the community, acting as it were as the antibodies of society, and it is then in their absence that crime begins to increase.   It is often argued that religion could play such a role, and that the rising tide of immorality and crime in the modern world is due to the declining influence of the Church and of religious belief.   There seems little prospect of our being able to test this view, for there is, of course, no way of ascertaining with any certainty how important and genuine people's religious beliefs are.

As a very inadequate substitute for this, church or Sunday school attendance are sometimes used as a criterion.   Among 548 school-leavers in Glasgow who had attended church regularly throughout a period of three years, the proportion convicted was 8·9 per cent. as against 14·9 per cent. among the 670 who did not

attend, or did so only irregularly.[26]   The difference was even more
marked if calculated only for boys with a poor social and family
environment, but substantially narrowed where the boy's background was good.   In America, Ernst found that regular church-
goers succeeded on probation more frequently than the rest.[27]

There is some evidence on the other side, the most frequently
quoted going back to 1926.   C. V. Dunn[28] enquired into the religious
affiliations of the inmates of twenty-seven prisons and nineteen
juvenile delinquency institutions in the United States.   Seventy-one
per cent. were connected with some church or other, as compared
with only 46·6 per cent. in the country as a whole.   It is difficult
to know how to evaluate this study.   If regular church attendance
is an unsatisfactory measure of religious belief, mere affiliation with
a church must be even more so.

The other studies cited are in little better case.   There is, for
instance, a very strong probability that those who attend church
have, on the whole, had a more satisfactory upbringing.   Such
differences as have been found may then be due to differences in the
quality of family life, and not to the influence of religion at all.   If,
however, the value of church attendance is recognised as established,
it may be due to membership of the Church as a social group, and
to the influence of that group's *mores* upon its individual members
rather than to ethical conviction.   This, if true, does not, of course,
derogate from the value of the Church as a preventive of crime.

Some criminologists have asked a further question: is there any
significant difference between the crime rates of different religious
denominations?   A remarkable degree of unanimity has been
achieved as to the answer, though the interpretation to be put upon
it is a very different matter.   In Germany,[29] Holland,[30] Britain,[31]
and America,[32] Roman Catholics have been found to have a higher
crime rate than Protestants; Jews (except in the British survey)
have a lower crime rate than either.

It is tempting to attribute the high rate among Catholics to the
practice of confession (as some criminologists have done) but more
pertinent factors are almost certainly the comparative poverty and
unsatisfactory environmental conditions of Catholic groups in the
countries studied.   As for the Jews, they are not only a religious
group, but also a community.   Mutual help among Jews is considerable, and Jewish social welfare agencies are numerous and
highly efficient.   It is only to be expected that such a concentrated
attack upon social ills will have some effect upon the amount of
crime.

## Literature and the Press

While some have thus seen in the absence of the restraining and moralising force of religion, the cause of our declining moral standards, others have attributed them to the positively corrupting effect of the great modern organs of mass communication—literature or the press, the radio or the cinema. The current attack on "horror comics" is only the latest skirmish in a long series of campaigns. Thus in 1947, a Departmental Committee was set up to study the effect of films on children;[33] some may remember the controversies about such radio plays as the "Dick Barton" or the "Just William" series; and so on.

There is at present no statutory censorship of literature or the press in this country. There is only a rather capricious censorship, imposed through the courts, which may declare a publication "obscene" if they find that it is "calculated to corrupt" those who read it. This has led to some strange decisions at times, for example, condemnation of established classics, such as the *Decameron* of Boccaccio. James Joyce's book *Ulysses*, now recognised as an important literary landmark, was banned by the British courts for several years.

Literary censorship of any sort is probably opprobrious; moral standards are highly personal, and in any case, real inner growth in individuals must depend upon freedom of choice. One may perhaps assume, in the absence of any real evidence to the contrary, that adults are not very likely to be depraved by what they read. In a total of 3,000 Danish cases, Le Maire found possible literary influence to be present in only two cases.[34]

With children the situation is a little different. They are more impressionable and suggestible than adults. They are less firmly "set" in their social adjustment. They have had less experience. There might be a case for protecting them against the possibly corrupting influence of unsavoury books or comics, though empirical evidence is lacking.

Censorship of the press is even more undesirable, in view of the political use to which such censorship has often been put. On the other hand, the press, especially in America, has received much of the blame for increasing criminality. The publicity which criminals receive is said to satisfy their desire for notoriety, and also to make them seem important and even possibly heroes to those who read about them. The publicity given to the crimes may "give people the idea", and teach them the techniques to be used, and also keep them abreast of the latest advances in detection procedures. The practising criminal may also be helped by being apprised of the progress made by the police in a particular case. On the credit side is the publicity which the newspapers give to the arrest and punishment of criminals who are caught. Here the press may be performing an important deterrent function.

There is again little of a factual nature to go on. Much seems to depend upon how crime news is presented. It could be presented in a way which was sympathetic to the criminal, and Sutherland quotes a remarkable example of how the attitude of readers may be affected by this.[35] A notorious criminal was at last arrested, but as a result of the way in which the newspapers had dealt with the case, a great crowd gathered to cheer him. The police were booed, and found themselves faced with a potentially very dangerous situation. On the other hand, a responsible press might become a real agency of crime prevention if only it could manage to steer a middle course between sensationalism and rather obvious, high-pressure propaganda of the "Crime does not Pay" type. As for allegations that rising crime rates in the U.S.A. could be blamed on the press, Frank Harris has shown that up to the 'thirties there had been no striking increase in the amount of space devoted to crime news in American papers.[36]

Restraint and self-discipline on the part of the newspapers themselves is the most obvious requirement. The British approach to this in the last year or two has been the setting-up of the Press Council. This consists entirely of representatives of the press—journalists and proprietors. It has no compulsory powers, but it can use publicity as its weapon. It considers complaints about the behaviours of a particular newspaper, and then issues a public statement, either vindicating or censuring the paper in question. It can hardly be claimed that the decisions made so far have had much effect upon the policies of the papers involved. If the press of this country really wishes to clean out its Augean stables, then it may have to consider severer sanctions, perhaps of an economic character. The public appetite seems merely to be whetted by any hint that such and such a newspaper is not "fit to read".

## The Cinema

The cinema is a more potent instrument of suggestion than the press. Life as portrayed on the screen has an immediacy, and carries with it an illusion of reality, which the printed word cannot achieve. It is so much easier to be completely "caught-up" by a film, identifying oneself breathlessly with the characters in it. It may then be very important that many films are concerned with crime and with sex, and many more falsify reality, placing, for example, an undue emphasis on wealth.[37] The morality of a film also is often very questionable—success of some sort is often the chief mark of the hero however that success may have been achieved.

On the whole, however, British workers in this field have not attached as much importance to the cinema as a crime-producing agency as have American authorities. Blumer and Hauser in the U.S.A.[38] claimed that "motion pictures were a factor of importance in the delinquent or criminal careers of about 10 per cent. of the male and 25 per cent. of the female offenders studied". Such a distinguished clinician as Burt, on the other hand, as a result of his intensive study of individual cases, attaches very little importance to the cinema. He found that the direct imitation of crimes portrayed on the screen was almost non-existent, and that the effect of their general atmosphere and their falsification of reality was probably confined to those already inclined to criminal behaviour.[39] Stott, in the hundred approved school youths whom he examined, found not a single case in which delinquency could be attributed to the films.[40]

From such clinical sources comes the further suggestion that the portrayal of crime on the screen may even operate so as to reduce actual criminality. It may sometimes provide a substitute satisfaction for those with anti-social tendencies which will make it unnecessary for them to "kick over the traces" in real life.[41]

The influence of the cinema on young people has been explored from a variety of angles by a group in the Birmingham area, working under the chairmanship of W. D. Wall.[42] They concluded that while more superficial patterns, such as hair-style, fashions in clothes, or style of dancing, were often copied from the films, only 3 per cent. of the hundreds of children studied, copied delinquent behaviour from the films—though they did often copy such patterns in their play. More fundamental effects upon the personality in the shape of emotional disturbance did sometimes follow erotic or "horror" films. The investigators reported also that the misrepresentation of life by the films was harmful: that children who had had no experience which taught them better did believe that what they saw on the screen was true.

Although, therefore, the direct inculcation of anti-social behaviour as a result of going to the cinema is slight, the indirect crimogenic effects, on children at least, may be more substantial. And even on adults, if their lives are very narrow and their experience very restricted, this powerful medium may cast its spell.

There is, it seems, every justification for the current classification of films according to the age of those who should be allowed to see them, and room for more conscientious enforcement of this classification by the exhibitors. As everybody is well aware, children, with the aid of only a little subterfuge, can usually manage to see an "A" film if they wish to, and sometimes "X" or "H" films also. On the whole, British Board of Film Censors (a form of self-censorship by the trade) does its job well. It is difficult to see what more they could do to safeguard the susceptible adult.

## Radio and Television

Radio and television, penetrating straight into the home, are perhaps the most compelling media of them all, but in spite of occasional criticisms, they seem to be fairly wholesome in their influence. There have not, for example, been any denunciations of British broadcast programmes to compare with the remark of Barnes and Teeters that in America "hundreds, perhaps thousands, of adolescent boys and girls are to a greater or lesser degree adversely affected by radio thrillers".[43] This is partly due to the status of the B.B.C. as a public body with a strong tradition of caution and responsibility. Like The Times it is a national institution and must take no chances with its reputation. Unlike The Times it is also publicly owned, and is likely to be heavily criticised, in Parliament or in the country, if it steps too far out of line. It remains to be seen whether the sponsored television stations to operate under the aegis of the Independent Television Authority will be able to resist the temptation to cash in on sensationalism, and to pander to the lowest common denominator among their viewers.

Perhaps the influence of these great engines of instruction and amusement upon crime has sometimes been exaggerated, but they do form part of the environment of the individual. They take their place with all the other multifarious forces which are playing upon him, and shaping his behaviour. They form part of the climate of ideas in our community, and if they are not counterbalanced by equally powerful forces, such as education or religion, will remain uncurbed at our peril. In such an event, in cases where the individual is particularly susceptible, such as feebleminded, naive, or maladjusted persons, or above all the child, whose mind is still being formed, they must take their toll.

## Alcohol

The importance of alcohol as a causal factor has long been acknowledged. Apart from offences directly connected with the liquor laws, drunkenness impairs the individual's judgment and control, and so makes him more likely to offend. There have been many attempts to determine how often this happens. Bonger quotes many of the researches[44] and more recently Stürup and Christiansen found that nearly one-quarter of the inmates of the Danish State Prison at Vridløselille were drunk when they committed their offences. The proportions of different offences varied, as might be expected: 73 per cent. for aggressive offences, about 30 per cent. for thieves, and 0 per cent. for embezzlers.[45] The emphasis upon the more impulsive type of crime is obvious.

The psychiatric study of chronic alcoholism, suggests that where there is a confirmed habit, the consequences are even more serious. It is then not merely a matter of a temporary loss of inhibitions. Radical personality changes begin to take place, which are effective even when the victim is not for the time being actually drunk.

Many questions still remain unanswered, of course. Thus it is unsafe to draw generalisations about the meaning of correlations between drunkenness and crime without taking into account the possibility that alcohol may not be an important cause, but itself largely an effect. Excessive consumption of alcohol and criminality may both be due to the same root cause, e.g. personal maladjustment, lack of intelligence, or poverty.

Drunkenness among adults also probably affects the amount of juvenile delinquency. It was at one time held that alcoholism in the parents led to some form of degeneracy in the offspring (e.g. mental deficiency), and thus to crime, but there is now little support for such a view. Norwood East does, however, canvass the possibility of a common and inherited psychopathy between drunkard parent and delinquent child.[46] But apart from such considerations, a drunkard father or mother is almost bound to have a harmful effect upon the stability and happiness of the family, and therefore upon the development of the children. Burt found drunkenness present in the families of 8·1 per cent. of his delinquents and in only 3 per cent. of the controls.[47] Norwood East, who, however, had no control figures obtained a rate for drunkard fathers among his Borstal boys of 39 per 1,000. Some family history of drunkenness, involving either father, mother, or other relative was present in 52 cases per 1,000.[48] These proportions are manifestly much lower than Burt's, and very little more than Burt obtained for non-delinquent controls, but these were soberer times.

Until very recently, general observation suggested that drunkenness as a social phenomenon was decreasing in importance in this country, and this view was supported by the figures of arrests for drunkenness given in the Licensing and the Criminal Statistics. Convictions for drunkenness per 10,000 of population fell from about fifty in 1913 to about twenty in the years immediately after the First World War, and to a little over ten in the late 'thirties.[49] If alcohol is losing ground in this way it may be inferred that its criminological importance is also diminishing. In support of this view Mannheim quotes the decline in persons dealt with for assault, from an annual average of 55,033 for the years 1900-9 to 18,537 in 1938.[50]

However, convictions for drunkenness have risen slightly since 1950 to just over 15 per 10,000.[51] It remains to be seen whether this increase will prove to be temporary and the long-term falling trend will reassert itself.

## Gambling

The extent of gambling, much less its consequences, are almost impossible to estimate. Street gambling is against the law, but is widespread throughout the country. Any estimate of its amount must be the wildest guess. In itself the disrespect for the law thus engendered is a serious thing; and street bookmaking adds greatly to the number of those who gain their livelihood by illegal means, and who thus may be drawn imperceptibly into more serious crime. (On the other hand, the law does at present favour the richer gamblers, who by means of a bookmaker's account or a visit to the racecourse can indulge their weakness without falling foul of the law.) There is undoubtedly also much incidental crime. Some people commit offences in order to get themselves out of financial difficulties resulting from gambling losses, and racecourses are notorious centres of fraud, robbery, and even violence.

It is indeed a bewildering pattern of forces within which we live our lives, and it changes, like a kaleidoscope, with lightning speed. It is, moreover, a large-scale society. Most of us reside in monster urban communities, and we live mass-production lives. And in spite of the number of people with whom we rub shoulders, we live lonely lives, for the warm, direct personal relationships of earlier times have given way entirely, except in the remotest rural communities, to shallow and fleeting personal contacts, at work, in our clubs, or in the streets of the city. How much influence a profound dissatisfaction with such a way of life has upon the amount of crime, it would be impossible to say, but it may not be too fanciful to blame upon it also the growth of mass analgesics, which may include certain kinds of literature or film, but of which alcohol and gambling are the outstanding examples.

In another sense also the level of crime reflects fundamental characteristics of our community life. There is much evidence to show that differences in the moral climate of local communities is connected with differences in their delinquency rates. It may be either a wholesome influence, or a powerful worker of mischief marshalling the public opinion of the neighbourhood behind anti-social trends. The research into this subject will be reviewed in the chapter which follows.

## NOTES TO CHAPTER V

1. These include L. Manouvrier, P. Lafargue, F. Turati, N. Colajanni, and even to some extent the great Enrico Ferri.
2. Bonger, W. A., *Criminality and Economic Conditions*, 1916, p. 322.
3. *Ibid.*, p. 365.
4. The criminology of war is discussed below, pp. 101-6.
5. *Op. cit.*, p. 381 ff.
6. See, for example, Malinowski, B., *Crime and Custom in Savage Society*, 1947.
7. Burt, Cyril, *The Young Delinquent*, 1925, pp. 66 ff. and Table IV, p. 64.
8. "New Survey of London Life and Labour", Vol. IX, 1935.
9. Bagot, J. H., *Juvenile Delinquency*, 1941, pp. 60-2.
10. Shaw, C. R., and McKay, H. D., *Juvenile Delinquency and Urban Areas*, 1942, especially pp. 437-9.
11. See, for example, Healy, W., and Bronner, A. F., *New Light on Delinquency*, 1936.
12. Sutherland, E. H., *White Collar Crime*, 1949. "Is 'White Collar Crime' Crime?", *Am. Sociol. Review*, **10**, 1945, pp. 132-9.
13. Wattenberg, W. W., and Balistrieri, J., "Automobile Theft", *Am. J. of Sociology*, **57**, 1951, pp. 575 ff.
14. What B. S. Rowntree called his "human needs" standard—see his *Human Needs of Labour*, 1937.
15. Mannheim, H., *Social Aspects of Crime in England between the Wars*, 1940, p. 151.
16. See Hurwitz, S., *Criminology*, 1952, p. 319.
17. *Op. cit.*, Chapter 5.
18. Mannheim was writing before the war, when the Dock Labour Board and regular engagements for dockers would have seemed inconceivable.
19. *Op. cit.*, p. 151.
20. East, J. Norwood, *The Adolescent Criminal*, pp. 154 ff.
21. Ranging from 45·5 per cent. at 16-17 to 50·8 per cent. at 18-20, as compared with an absolute maximum of 20 per cent. for the general adolescent population—including students!

22. Van Kleeck, M., "Work and Law Observance in the History of Men in Sing Sing Prison", *American Nat. Commission on Law Observance and Enforcement, Vol. I,* 1931.

23. Clemmer, D., *The Prison Community,* 1940, p. 52.

24. *Op. cit.,* p. 126.

25. Carr-Saunders, A. M., Mannheim, H., and Rhodes, E. C., *Young Offenders,* 1942, pp. 101-4.

26. Ferguson, T., *The Young Delinquent in his Social Setting,* Oxford, pp. 125-6.

27. Cited in Sutherland, E. H., *Principles of Criminology,* 1947, p. 194.

28. Dunn, C. V., "The Church and Crime in the United States", *Annals of the American Academy of Political and Social Science,* 1926, pp. 200 ff.

29. Aschaffenburg, G., *Das Verbrechen und seine Bekämpfung,* 1933, pp. 57 ff.

30. Bonger, *op. cit.,* pp. 207-9.

31. Trenaman, J., *Out of Step,* 1952.

32. Kvaraceus, W. C., *Juvenile Delinquency and the School,* 1945, pp. 101-3.

33. *Report of the Departmental Committee on Children and the Cinema, Cmd.* 7945, 1950.

34. Cited Hurwitz, *op. cit.,* pp. 239-40.

35. *Principles of Criminology,* p. 186.

36. Harris, F., *Presentation of Crime in Newspapers,* Mineapolis, 1932.

37. Gray, B., "Social Effects of the Film", *Sociol. Review,* **43**, 7, 1950, P.S.

38. Blumer, H., and Hauser, P. M., *Movies, Delinquency and Crime,* 1933.

39. *Op. cit.,* pp. 143 ff.

40. Stott, D. H., *Delinquency and Human Nature,* 1950, pp. 363-4.

41. *Ibid.,* p. 364.

42. For details of the various aspects of this investigation, see Gray, B., *op. cit.;* Wall, W. D., and Simson, W. A., *Brit. J. Educ. Psychol.,* **19**, 1949, pp. 53 ff.; **20**, pp. 153 ff.; Wall, W. D., and Smith, E. M., *Brit. J. Educ. Psychol.,* **19**, 1949, p. 121; Dodman, N. D., "The Adolescent and the Cinema", *Education,* Nov. 1948.

43. Barnes, H. E., and Teeters, N. K., *New Horizons in Criminology,* 1945, p. 236.

44. *Op. cit.* There are many references throughout the work.

45. Cited in Hurwitz, *op. cit.,* p. 292.

46. East, J. Norwood, *op. cit.,* p. 56.

47. Burt, *op. cit.,* Table IV, p. 65.

48. East, *op. cit.,* p. 56.

49. Licensing Statistics, quoted Mannheim, *op. cit.,* p. 165.

50. *Ibid.,* pp. 177-8.

51. *Offences of Drunkenness,* 1953 (Home Office, 1954), p. 3.

# CHAPTER VI

## FAMILY AND COMMUNITY

For over a century, the wide disparity in the crime rates of different localities has given rise to speculation. As long ago as 1839, Sir R. W. Rawson[1] observed that crime was concentrated mainly in the larger towns, being less in the smaller mining villages, and least of all in sparsely populated hilly areas such as Wales and the north. There has been a continuous tradition of such studies right up to Burt's careful analysis of the distribution of juvenile delinquency in London.[2] Behind them all lies the implication that crime arises out of the life of the community, a view which is obviously at variance with individualist theories of either the constitutional or the psychological type.

### Chicago Ecological School

A new fillip was given to this theme by the work of the Chicago school, led by Professors R. E. Park and E. W. Burgess, who applied to human social affairs the key biological concept of "ecology". Ecological studies are concerned with the tendency of an organism to adapt itself to its environment. Just as the numbers and local distribution of animal or plant life are governed by the natural environment, so, it is argued, the social ecologist can explain human activities in terms of the social environment.[3] This idea has been fruitful, not only in the researches which it directly inspired, but also in its wider influence upon a whole generation of sociologists, who have come to look upon the ecological approach as of fundamental importance for both research and theory. Well-known criminologists of this school include F. M. Thrasher and C. R. Shaw.

Thrasher's reputation is largely based upon his classical study of gang life among the adolescents of Chicago.[4] The basic tool of the social ecologist is the "social map", showing the geographical distribution of the phenomena under investigation, and especially its relative frequency in different kinds of natural area, such as business districts or residential areas. Thrasher constructed such a map to show the areas in which gangs operated.

He concluded that these were what he called "interstitial areas". Between the more settled localities: the spreading industrial and commercial districts in the centre of the city, and the residential districts retreating all the time further and further towards the outskirts, were left temporarily disorganised gaps.   These areas, adjoining the central business districts on the north, south, and west, were areas of change and dislocation.   One social pattern, that of the residential district, was dissolving, while the pattern which was replacing it, that of the industrial neighbourhood, had not yet matured.   As in the far west during the pioneering period of American history, an organised and settled community hardly existed, and so the institutions, morals, and restraints of the community were weakened and ineffective at a time when the stresses and strains of social life were being vastly increased.   Anti-social attitudes and anti-social gangs were the result.

### Delinquency Areas

Two years later, in 1929, appeared C. R. Shaw's *Delinquency Areas*, and finally, after more widespread and extensive researches, a book which Professor Burgess called a "magnum opus in Criminology"—*Juvenile Delinquency and Urban Areas*, by C. R. Shaw and H. D. McKay.[5]   The home addresses of many thousands of delinquent boys, for various periods from 1900 onwards, were marked on a map of Chicago.   The "spot map" thus obtained could then be compared with maps showing the location of industry, and other characteristics of different parts of the city.

By this means, delinquents were shown to be living predominantly in the central districts, cheek by jowl with the factories, and in very bad housing conditions.   Population in these areas was diminishing, and those who did have to live there, often did so only transiently, en route to something better.   The racial and national constitution was very mixed, with a large proportion of new immigrants.

Here was a picture of social decay which resulted not only in high rates of juvenile delinquency, but also in an impressive accumulation of other social problems.   For these "blighted" areas, as Shaw and McKay called them, showed also the highest figures for tuberculosis, truancy, adult crime, mental illness, and even infant mortality. When a series of concentric circles was drawn on the maps, marking out successive two-mile zones from the centre of the city, rates for each of these community problems were found to diminish steadily and consistently from the centre outwards.   These observations were also borne out by parallel studies in other American cities.

There is one other possible explanation of all this besides the obvious ecological one, namely the human tendency indicated by the old saying "birds of a feather flock together". Could it be that these deteriorating areas attract undesirable or inferior types? Against this view Sutherland points out that the delinquency picture has remained much the same over a period of more than thirty years, although meanwhile the population and its racial composition has almost completely changed.[6] This is hardly conclusive. More to the point are such observations as those of Pauline V. Young, in Los Angeles, where she found that the proportion of Moloccan children who became delinquent increased from 5 per cent. when they first settled there to 46 per cent. five years later, and 83 per cent. at the end of fifteen years.[7]

It would be very rash, however, to assume that there was no process of selection at work. Shaw and McKay themselves implicitly admit the importance of this factor when they stress the temporary nature of the population of the "delinquency area". Those who can move do so, and no doubt those who do not have to, do not settle in such an uncongenial area at all.

In the areas of high delinquency studied by Shaw and his collaborators there are many clearly pathological environmental factors at work, but Shaw and McKay lay most emphasis upon the poverty of their inhabitants. Delinquency, it is argued, has arisen in these areas because of the appetite for a higher standard of life, which the American culture encourages here as elsewhere. This is not merely a desire for a higher level of material satisfaction, but in part for prestige and status in the community, for this is conceded only to those who can show evidence of having achieved material success. Such ambitions are out of the question for the average resident of these impoverished areas so long as he remains law-abiding, but he has before him many well-publicised examples of those who have made money by illegal means. At the same time, the ordinary social controls are weakened by the constant movement of the population and by the babel of voices, the confusion of standards and morals, which results from its mixed national and racial composition. The impact of public opinion on the individual, also, is more impersonal and remote than in smaller, rural communities.

Out of this situation emerges a tradition of delinquency, a delinquent set of socially accepted values. Consequently, the delinquent is not necessarily an abnormal person, maladjusted either within himself or in relation to his social setting. He is, in fact, well adapted to his own environment. "Within the limits of his social world and in terms of its norms and expectations, he may be a highly organised and well-adjusted person."[8]  As, of course, in accordance with the ecological theory of the causes of crime, it is expected that he would be.

## British Local Studies

British criminologists have been slow to follow up the lead given them by Shaw.  There have been, it is true, various valuable studies of delinquency in particular cities, such as London,[9] Liverpool,[10] Bradford,[11] Cambridge,[12] Coventry,[13] Birmingham,[14] and Glasgow;[15] and Mannheim, following another tack, has explored local differences in the relationships between crime and such factors as unemployment and alcohol.[16]  The last two, in particular, are valuable in showing the essential local nature of the equation from which much crime springs, a conclusion which fits in well with the ideas of the ecological school.  But it was not till after the war that real attention began to be devoted to the problem of the public opinion of the neighbourhood as a factor.

In part this lag must have been due to the interest in the psycho-pathology of delinquency inspired by the rapid development of clinical psychology and psycho-analysis.  Most of the research sponsored by such bodies as the Institute for the Scientific Study of Delinquency and the Tavistock Clinic was of this sort.  Also extensive ecological studies require funds, and an interest in criminology in academic circles which has been sadly lacking until recent years.

However, an intensive study of delinquency areas in a small Nottinghamshire town was begun in 1952, under the direction of Professor W. J. H. Sprott, and has recently been completed.[17]  A delinquency "spot map" was first constructed, and then the customs and attitudes of residents in two "black" streets ("black" in the sense of having a high concentration of juvenile offenders) were compared with those of the inhabitants of two "white" streets. The methods of participant observation were used: the observers took jobs in the neighbourhood and joined local social organisations. It was hoped that such a strategy would help them to gain the confidence of the people they were studying, and also to understand local problems better.

The conclusions reached confirm and amplify some of the views of the American investigators.  While the social codes of the "black" streets include much that is desirable, in the way of easy, social relationships, mutual help, and local loyalties, they differ from the "white" streets in other respects which contribute to the greater prevalence of delinquency in the former. Notably these differences include a laxer attitude towards honesty and legality, *laisser-faire* attitudes towards their children, the decisive rejection of remoter in favour of more immediate satisfactions in life, sex laxity, much gambling, and the approval of physical force as the proper way of settling disputes.

Two other more limited investigations call for mention. One is an impressionistic study of a central slum area in Liverpool by J. B. Mays.[18] The members of a university settlement youth club in the area were interviewed by a social worker whom they already knew through their membership of the club. Of the eighty boys interviewed, thirty-four were found to have been convicted at least once, and another twenty admitted committing offences, but had never appeared in court. Thirteen more were borderline cases. Mays estimated that at least 78 per cent. of the group interviewed had been delinquent at some time or another, and compared this with the official delinquency rate for the city as a whole of 1·8 per cent. Not only is the local concentration in Liverpool thus revealed, but also the inadequacy of official statistics, based on convictions. In such areas delinquency is the norm not the exception.

### Delinquency in New Estates

The view, however, that delinquency is necessarily a phenomenon of central slum areas has been challenged by evidence from Leicester. Both Mannheim in Cambridge, and Bagot in Liverpool, had shown that new council housing estates figure prominently in the juvenile delinquency picture. This clue was followed up by the Leicester study in which the addresses of young offenders at different stages in the recent development of the city were plotted on a map. It was found that as slum clearance schemes transferred the inhabitants of the slums to the new estates on the outskirts of the city, delinquency moved out with them. The central areas are now of no greater importance in this respect than the great new housing estates.[19]

The significance of this is the primacy which it gives to established social attitudes over the material conditions of a blighted area. The association between poor housing conditions and crime has often been remarked,[20] but there is obviously no direct causal connection. And housing improvement is not necessarily accompanied by any immediate reduction in crime rates. In the very long run, of course, one might expect that the more wholesome, physical environment will have its effect.

## Conclusions

The results of these various studies may be summarised in the following four propositions:—

(*a*) Juvenile delinquency is often concentrated in certain areas of a city, usually an old slum or a new housing estate.

(*b*) These delinquency areas differ from other areas in their norms and social attitudes, and in a way which seems causally connected with the high delinquency rate.

(*c*) The norms, and the delinquency, persist even in fact of improvements in the material environment.

(*d*) In such areas, delinquency is general and the non-delinquent is exceptional. Official delinquency figures almost certainly under-estimate the amount of delinquency which is actually occurring in these localities.

A great stumbling-block in all studies of this kind, which aim at any sort of statistical measurement, is the inadequacy of the available data. Very rarely, for example, is it possible to make any really accurate estimate of the number of people of different ages who live in the various districts or wards of a city. Without some such idea of the differences in age-structure between different areas, it is quite unsafe (for example) to compare the incidence of juvenile delinquency in one area with that in another. One area may have a larger juvenile delinquency figure than another, but have so much larger a child population that delinquency "per 1,000 at risk" is really very much smaller than in the other area.

Comparisons of total crime figures are usually more practicable, for total population figures for different wards can be obtained through Somerset House. In the Leicester investigation fairly accurate juvenile delinquency comparisons were made possible by the fortunate accident that the City School Attendance Department carry out a regular census of the school population in different districts.

## Other Areal Comparisons

Besides these studies of urban neighbourhoods, the ecological movement has given birth to a number of interesting comparisons between rural and urban areas. Rural crime has been found on the whole to be much less in total than urban crime. This difference is particularly marked where offences against property are concerned, but for offences against the person (much less numerous in total, though they are) the tables are often turned.[21]

There is, of course, more property to take or to damage in the city, but there are other fundamental differences between the two kinds of community also. Vold refers to the social pattern of conformity and stability in the country. This is obviously in striking contrast to the complexity and stimulation, the "bright lights" and temptations of the city. Community pressures in the village are nearer and more personal also, and must therefore be more effective means of controlling behaviour.

Attempts at international comparison have been vitiated by differences in the law, and in the police and judicial systems, between different countries. The same name often does not refer to the same offence, and the extent of criminality in a particular country may be affected decisively by the fact that certain actions allowable elsewhere are there forbidden. Differences in the procedure and even the efficiency of the police have also always to be taken account of. U.N.E.S.C.O. has recognised the importance of international studies, and is engaged at present in working out a classification of crimes which would make international comparability easier, but this will not solve the whole problem. A qualitative re-interpretation of the differences in the light of the social and legal forces at work in the various countries will still be necessary if the bare figures are to mean anything.

## Wider Implications

There is a principle of wider application to be derived from the work of the ecologists. Within the general culture, there may be other sub-cultures, besides delinquency areas, with codes of behaviour and scales of values which are at variance with those of the wider society. Sutherland considers that much "white-collar crime", in the shape of business practices, takes place because the business community in general accepts such behaviour as legitimate, and even praiseworthy. On the basis of his experience as a judge in the Netherlands, N. Muller[22] suggests that many petty offences, such as the stealing of gas and electricity, rifling of meters, and thefts by workers from their place of employment, are due to a widespread tendency among the classes concerned to treat such behaviour as not really criminal.

Mannheim goes much further and boldly asserts that there is really no such thing as an honest person, in any absolute sense. We are, all of us, honest in some situations and dishonest in others, according to the moral climate of the groups to which we belong.[23] Certainly, few can claim that they came through the fire of the war-time rationing regulations without ever breaking the law, and, under the less stringent conditions of the present time, many opportunities of dishonest gain are still taken by large numbers of people who would be shocked beyond measure at any suggestion that they were criminals.    And their own estimate of their acts would undoubtedly be supported by those of their fellow citizens who share their social background.

Even within the bounds of the neighbourhood group there are such sub-cultures.  Shaw and McKay discovered that in their delinquency areas, besides the forces making for delinquency, there were many influences of a more wholesome character, such as the family or the Church, and that these were very powerful in the community as a whole, though not of course in the individual paths trodden by the delinquents.[24]   In the end we reach a position very similar to that of Sutherland, whose "principle of differential association" states that a person becomes delinquent because, in the course of his personal social experience, he encounters cultural pressures towards criminality which are more numerous or more powerful than those ranged against it.[25]

## The Gang

A sub-cultural pattern which is of special interest to the criminologist is the gang.  It plays its part in the aetiology of adult crime as well as that of juvenile delinquency, but the juvenile gang is more accessible to study, and perhaps more illuminating.  All of the empirical studies of gang-life point to the pressure to conform, which these juvenile communities exert upon their members; a pressure which may, if the gang is a delinquent one, sweep with it into criminal behaviour many an otherwise law-abiding youngster.[26]

These facts have sometimes led to wholesale denunciations of gangs as such, but in the light of what is known about the psychological and social development of children, this is a mistake.  Children appear to go through a stage in the pre-adolescent or early adolescent periods when ganging together with others of their own age and sex is normal.  It may even be that loyalty to the gang and its *mores* is a necessary stage on the road to wider community loyalties.  Gang-membership would then be proof that the child is essentially a socially minded and law-abiding person—even though his loyalty to his own little community, if this is a delinquent gang, will bring him into conflict with the laws of the great society.

There is a serious problem here, but it is not one which can be solved by threatening the existence of the gang.  We should be more profitably engaged in finding out why gangs become delinquent in character, and how this can be remedied. Anti-social leadership may provide part of the answer, though we are then faced with the further question of how such a leader is able to carry the gang with him, against all the influences which the wider community can bring to bear. The interpersonal dynamics of the group may be involved here, but it is doubtful if these alignments—loyalties, rivalries, relationships of dependence and domination, and so on—are a sufficient explanation, without reference to the environment within which the gang operates. The ecological principle is as valid in the study of the behaviour of sub-cultural groups such as the gang as in that of individuals.

Thus the tone of a gang may be predominantly delinquent because the social forces impinging upon its individual members are delinquency-producing; or because the tone of the neighbourhood is too tolerant of crime, or even, in extreme cases, actively criminal.[27] More indirectly, the forms of collective activity normal to groups of youngsters may have become impossible in our congested, closely regulated and complex urban communities. Burt gives many examples of this, and it comes out very clearly in the recent Central Harlem Street Clubs Project in New York. Miss E. M. Henshaw found that "enjoyment of adventure" was a cause of delinquency in 50 per cent. of her Bradford cases.[28]

Homer Lane quoted American experience that in two cities with good systems of public playgrounds, the city which arranged for close supervision of the children playing in them, suffered a much higher incidence of juvenile delinquency than the other which had fewer supervisors, and whose playgrounds were, therefore, filled with children playing spontaneously, expressing themselves, and finding adventure and outlets for their energy.[29]

It has long been accepted by social workers in the juvenile delinquency services that too few playgrounds and sports fields in a crowded urban centre may be a major cause of delinquency. A child must have room to move and to breathe. Homer Lane has reminded us that the kind of playground is an equally important consideration, for the child must also have room sometimes to kick and to shout. In a city area in which it is an offence to walk on the grass in the park, or to climb a tree, these conditions are not being met. It is a short step then, to treating the railway siding or the warehouse as a playground, and finding opportunities for adventure and group achievement in doing forbidden things, and perhaps being chased by a policeman.

The existence of the gang then becomes, in its turn, an indispensable condition for the commission of these delinquent acts, for the individual offender needs the support which the group can give him in order to be able to defy the rest of the community.[30]

## The Family

Then at the very core of our community life, the most intimate group of them all, lies the family. Its criminological importance can hardly be overestimated. Many points have already been discussed: for example, familial inheritance, whether of specific abnormalities of physique, intellect or temperament, or of actual criminal tendencies.

All the main psychological theories also lean heavily upon the family, and this is hardly surprising, for after all the family does provide the individual with his total psychological environment during the formative early years, and an ever present and formidable influence throughout most of his life. While recognising the importance of the former, of preserving the mother-child relationship, of love and security in infancy, of sensible early training and the acquisition of wholesome moral standards from one's family background, the importance of the latter should also be fully acknowledged. In particular, during the school years and in adolescence, proper guidance and supervision, and a consistent and enlightened attitude towards character training, can do much to protect the child in his years of inexperience, and to help him to build up the superstructure of his personality on sound lines and find his feet in the world.

The dangers which threaten children without this background are well exemplified by what happened to many children during the war, when their fathers had been called up, and their mothers had gone to work in the factories. Running loose, with no supervision and little guidance, it was only too easy for them to get into trouble. Even in adult married life, an individual may be made or destroyed by the quality of the family life he and his wife have created between them.

## The "Broken Home"

One form of family pathology to which criminologists have devoted much attention is the so-called "broken home". It has been found that delinquency is often associated with the absence of one or both of the parents from the home, through death, desertion, or divorce. It was one element in the factor of "defective family relationships" which Burt found to occur twice as frequently in his delinquent as compared with his control cases.[31] In a national survey, carried out just before the war, broken homes were found to be present in 25·6 per cent. of the delinquents, as compared with 13·0 per cent. of the non-delinquents, in the London area, and 31·5 per cent. as against 18·6 per cent. in a number of selected provincial towns.[32] Numerous other enquiries give similar results.[33] In America, Healy and Bronner,[34] and the Gluecks,[35] are among the many who concur. The case would seem to be proven beyond reasonable doubt.

Yet Ferguson reports figures from Glasgow which lend little support to it: "In this study families from which a parent was absent, were found to produce slightly more than their share of delinquency, but this was true only at post-school ages, not during school days. If both parents were absent, the rate was higher but still only above average at post-school ages."[36]

Still more heretical, Shaw and McKay, after obtaining a general ratio of broken homes for delinquents as compared with non-delinquents of only 1·18 : 1, went on in a study of a particular area on the "Near West Side" of Chicago, to find 25·8 per cent. of broken homes among delinquents as compared with 26·4 per cent. among the controls.[37] Hughes, in a follow-up study of 687 Coventry probationers, obtained follow-up results for delinquents with broken homes which were quite as good as those for delinquents whose homes were not broken.[38]

If the concept of the "broken home" is itself analysed, further reasons for dissatisfaction with it are found. The broken home may imply many crimogenic situations: defective relationships or discipline, conflicts of loyalty, poverty through absence of the breadwinner, and so on: but it is these rather than the broken home *per se* which should be expected to correlate highly with criminality. And they may occur also in a home which is not broken. An unbroken home may be so poisoned by conflict, for example, that the child would be less likely to become delinquent if the parents do separate.

In short, the broken home is not a unitary concept at all, and this probably accounts for the occasional exception to what otherwise has seemed a general rule. In the study of the actual process of causation, and also in the working-out of measures of prevention and treatment (if these aim at being at all specific), the broken home is a blind alley.

Similar objections apply to the frequently noted association between large families and delinquencies. It is almost certainly not the large family in itself which causes children to "go off the rails", but the poverty and overcrowding, the stress, or the lack of supervision, which it may in certain circumstances bring in its train.

## Family and Community

In the main the two great instruments of social control, the family and the neighbourhood, work in amity and concord. This must be so, for parents also have to fit into and make their peace with the community within which they live. Sprott sees the family as the main agency through which the norms of the community are inculcated in each successive generation. "There is no thing called 'culture' which constitutes an additional force."[39]

Where a clash does take place, however, the child is presented with an acute and painful conflict of loyalties. This may be seen in the United States, where immigrants from, say, Western Europe, will often carefully preserve the ways of their original homeland, while their American-born children are faced with the task of finding their feet in a country with a very different way of life. An understandable hunger for social acceptance impels many of these children into gangs.[40] This, and the inevitable confusion about standards in the half-world in which they live, has been postulated to account for the higher rates of juvenile delinquency found among them, as compared with the children of established American families.[41]

This is one manifestation of the factor of "culture conflict", to which Thorsten Sellin has devoted so much attention.[42] Many other phenomena already mentioned, may be brought within this frame of reference, for example, the mixed national and racial composition of Shaw's "delinquency areas", the social disorganisation brought about by war, or in an "interstitial area" or a new housing estate. Even conflicting ideas and values within the family may be included in its scope. Another indigenous American problem, that of negro crime, is also illuminated by it.

We must beware of too crude an application of this concept. Culture conflict is usually only one element in the social situation out of which crime arises, which may also include other factors discussed in this and the preceding chapter. It must not be used to "paper over" the cracks in our understanding of complex social processes. This is what sometimes seems to be happening.

## NOTES TO CHAPTER VI

1. *J. Statistical Soc. of London*, **2**, 1839, pp. 338 ff.

2. Burt, Cyril, *Young Delinquent*, 1944, pp. 70 ff.

3. Basic ecological texts include Park, R. E., and Burgess, E. W., *The City*, 1925; and Burgess, E. W. (ed.), *The Urban Community*, 1926.

4. Thrasher, F. M., *The Gang*, 1937.

5. Shaw, C. R., and McKay, H. D., *Juvenile Delinquency and Urban Areas*, 1942, p. 436.

6. Sutherland, E. H., *Principles of Criminology*, 1947, pp. 141-2.

7. Young, P. V., *The Pilgrims of Russian-Town*, 1932. The Moloccans, a religious community from Russia, settled in Los Angeles in the middle of the nineteenth century.

8. Shaw and McKay, *op. cit.*, p. 436.

9. Carr Saunders, A. M., Mannheim, H., and Rhodes, E. C., *Young Offenders*, 1942. Also certain provincial towns.

10. Bagot, J. H., *Juvenile Delinquency*, 1941. *Youthful Lawbreakers* (Liverpool Council of Social Service), 1948.

11. Henshaw, E. M., *Report on Juvenile Delinquency* (Bradford Education Committee), 1942.

12. Mannheim, H., *Juvenile Delinquency in an English Middle-town*, 1948.

13. Hughes, E. W., *Brit. J. of Ed. Psychology*, **13**: 3, 1943, pp. 113 ff.

14. Chinn, W. L., *Brit. J. of Ed. Psychology*, **8**: 1, 1938, pp. 78 ff.

15. Ferguson, T., *The Young Delinquent in his Social Setting*, 1952.

16. Mannheim, H., *Social Aspects of Crime in England Between the Wars*, 1940, Chapters 5 and 6.

17. Sprott, W. J. H., *et al.*, *The Social Background of Delinquency*, 1954. (Limited circulation by Nottingham University.)

18. Mays, J. B., *Growing Up in the City*, 1954, especially Chapter IV.

19. *Leicester Delinquency Studies*, 1955 (Leicester University College).

20. Clark, J. J., *The Housing Problem*, 1920, pp. 218-20. Mackintosh, J. M., *Housing and Family Life*, 1952, p. 111. Also Winslow, C. E. A., quoted Mackintosh, *op. cit.*, pp. 43-4.

21. Vold, G. B., "Crime in City and Country Areas", *Annals of the American Academy of Political and Social Science*, Sept. 1941, pp. 38-45.

22. Muller, N., *Brit. J. of Delinquency*, **1**: 2, 1950, p. 85.

23. Mannheim, H., Comment on the preceding, *ibid.*, p. 97.

24. *Op. cit.*, Chapter VII and p. 440.

25. Sutherland, E. H., *op. cit.*, pp. 6-8.

26. See, for instance, Mays, *op. cit.*; and Thrasher, *op. cit.* Also Crawford, P. L., Malamud, D. I., and Dumpson, J. R., *Working with Teen-age Gangs*, 1950. Shaw and McKay found that 81·8 per cent. of the boys before the Juvenile Court of Cook County in 1928 committed their offences as members of gangs (*op. cit.*, p. 167). Bagot gives the proportion for Liverpool as 50 per cent., and Mannheim in Cambridge as rather less than 50 per cent. The pre-war national figures reported in *Young Offenders* was 71·6 per cent. for London and 74 per cent. for the group of provincial towns studied.

27. See Benney, M., *Low Company*, for a vivid picture of such an environment.

28. *Op. cit.*, p. 26.

29. Lane, Homer T., *Talks to Parents and Teachers*, 1942, pp. 97-8.

30. Redl, F., "Psychology of Gang Formation", in *Psycho-analytic Study of the Child*, **1**, 1945, p. 369.

31. *Op. cit.*, p. 53.

32. *Young Offenders*, *op. cit.*, p. 62.

33. Banister, H., and Ravden, M., *Brit. J. of Psychology* (General Section), **34**, 1944, and **35**, 1945; Mannheim, H., *Juvenile Delinquency in an English Middletown*, pp. 20-1; Trenaman, J., *Out of Step*, 1952, p. 174; Bagot, *op. cit.*, pp. 80-4, etc.

34. Healy, W., and Bronner, A. F., *Delinquents and Criminals*, 1926, p. 122.

35. Glueck, S. and E., *One Thousand Juvenile Delinquents*, 1934, p. 76.

36. *Op. cit.*, pp. 22-3.

37. Shaw, C. R., and McKay, H. D., *Report on Social Factors in Juvenile Delinquency*, National Commission on Law Observance and Enforcement, Report No. 13, 1932.

38. *Loc. cit.*, Table V, p. 119.

39. Sprott, W. J. H., *Social Psychology*, 1952, p. 162.

40. Of 880 gangs in Chicago for which Thrasher obtained information about race and nationality, only 45 were wholly American, while 396 were dominantly or solidly of some other single national group (*op. cit.*, p. 191).

41. See Barnes, H. E., and Teeters, N. K., *New Horizons in Criminology*, 1945, pp. 125-31.

42. Sellin, T., *Culture Conflict and Crime* (Social Science Research Council Bulletin No. 41, 1938).

# CHAPTER VII

## SEEING THE PROBLEM WHOLE

It is evident from earlier chapters that none of the various theories put forward to account for crime really provide more than a partial explanation. There are always exceptions, always some to whom the theory in question does not apply. Some criminals are temperamentally abnormal, many are not; some are intellectually dull but others are highly intelligent; many of the children in a "delinquency area" get into trouble, but others do not. Obviously the causes of crime are complex, and often probably are also multiple. After all our painstaking researches, the task of unravelling them remains to perplex us.

### Actuarial Approaches

In retreat against these difficulties, some writers have proposed abandoning the concept of cause. Instead, Reckless suggests that we adapt, from the field of insurance, the notion of "actuarial risk".[1] From what we have discovered about the frequency with which certain kinds of person become criminal, or certain kinds of circumstances lead to crime, it should be possible to calculate the probability that other people (whose circumstances, etc., are known to us) will be reported as criminals in their turn. This probability, of course, would hold only "on the average", and therefore must be applied to aggregates and not to individuals; but since crime, as a social problem, is a mass-phenomenon, and measures adopted against it, such as legislation and the social services, will tend to be mass-measures, this is no real drawback.

The principle involved is exactly the same as that used by the insurance company in fixing a life premium by comparing the insured person's health history with what is known about the connection between certain kinds of history and early demise. Insurance companies also make up on the average for what they lose in individual cases.

The strength of this approach is in the planning of practical remedial measures. S. and E. Glueck have shown that the early recognition of the persistent delinquent can be achieved with much more reliability with the aid of prediction tables built up by actuarial methods, than by intensive clinical investigations of the children in question.[2]    Similarly, the choice of offenders for particular forms of treatment, such as probation or Borstal, has been found to be more fruitful, *on the whole*, if made with a prediction table rather than by means of the unaided clinical judgment, even though the latter may be based on a very intimate knowledge of the individuals in question.[3]

This is a saddening situation for those who believe that the individual offender matters, but it is not necessarily permanent, so long as causal research is not jettisoned.    Improvements in our methods of clinical diagnosis depend ultimately on improvements in our understanding of the causal process.    To adopt Reckless's point of view would be to perpetuate the superiority of the more impersonal (and still very imperfect) statistical approaches.

Nor is Reckless really consistent in his rejection of the idea of cause.    No actuarial theorist can be, for his tables are built up from research into a limited number of factors, which presumably are selected because of their possible causal significance from the large number which might have been chosen.

## Action Research

Another possible solution to the problems inherent in studies of causation might be sought through the "action approach": *i.e.* carrying out experiments in prevention and treatment, and thus building up a body of knowledge about the effectiveness of different remedial methods instead of about causes.    It is possible to point to substantial advances in our control over nature in other fields of science as a result of the adoption of empirical methods such as this.    For example, we made use of electricity long before we knew much about its nature.    A more recent example may be taken from psychiatry.    Convulsion methods of treatment have proved dramatically successful in treating certain forms of insanity, but they were originally tried for other types of case, in which they proved quite ineffective.    They were eventually administered almost speculatively to the types of case in which they have since proved so valuable, and even now there is room for debate about their *modus operandi*.    There is no gainsaying these arguments, nor the further point that with its emphasis upon reform, criminology should not neglect such an opportunity of short-cutting the tangle of causal factors, and striking straight at the remedies.    There is all this and more to be said for "action research" in criminology.[4]

On the other hand, unless "action research" is to be a kind of blind groping in the dark, involving a prodigal waste of enthusiasm, money and public goodwill, it must be based upon some under-standing of causes. And as the consequences of the remedial measures are observed, they should enable further hypotheses to be formulated about the causal process itself. If, for instance, a measure of social amelioration such as slum clearance, is followed by a diminution in crime, then this is definite evidence in favour of the view that slums are breeding grounds of crime. In their turn, refinements in our causal knowledge can be fed back into the remedial process, making it possible for the measures applied to be more precise and specific, and to give us even more exact light upon causes. What we should have would be successive approximations to the real causes, each series of experiments in prevention or treat-ment taking us a little nearer the truth. So aetiological research must continue, as the necessary complement and systematiser of what action research has to teach us.

## Causal Studies

As might have been expected, there is thus no way of escape from the complexities of human nature. We must expect to face those complexities, if we hope to understand and to change human behaviour. So we must face the fact that crime is not a single entity. The causes of petty larceny, robbery with violence, and murder are likely to be very different. There is a world of difference also between the high-spirited infringements which almost all boys commit and the carefully planned robberies which some juveniles carry through. If we persist in studying such a miscellaneous hotch-potch of behaviour patterns as this on the plea that they are all "crimes", we must expect our results to be blurred in outline and very uncertain. This does raise immediately the question of "units". Are the aetiological entities the same as the legal ones? If so, it could obviously be only by chance. It has been shown that legal definitions of the same offences differ even in different parts of the United States.[5]

## The Unit of Study

Certain American writers plead for the use of sociological units of study—"behaviour systems". A behaviour system is a group manifestation, involving individuals who identify themselves with one another and share a similar way of life. It emerges, as a recognisable unit, by a characteristic causal process. Sutherland's concept of the "professional thief" is one such behaviour system. "Professional thieves make a regular business of theft." They have traditions and traditional techniques. They have high status throughout the underworld, but associate mainly with each other. "Consequently professional theft is a behaviour system and a sociological entity."[6]   Such a basis of classification would seem to be indispensable for the study of crime as a social process, but, as will be apparent by now, there are other aspects. For example, although "affectionless characters" may be found in many branches of crime, constituting quite different sociological units, it is only when they are grouped together that the significance of their personality abnormalities becomes apparent.

## Interdependence of Factors

But even this gives only a hint of the jungle through which we have to find our way. Even if we deal with particular kinds of crime, and hit upon units which are real aetiological entities, we cannot expect to find any universal relationship between the offences and particular causal factors. For causal factors rarely appear to operate singly, but in groups or constellations, in which, as in constellations of stars, each member affects the operation of each other. Whether a factor is causal or not seems to depend upon how, and with what other factors, it happens to be combined.

Consider those factors, personal to the individual, which are believed to have causal significance. The affectionless or psychopathic personality is again ready to our hand. This particular character formation may be a sufficient cause in itself, but the cases in which it is present are only a small proportion of the total of recorded crime. Psychological maladjustment short of psychopathy does not necessarily lead to crime, for it may end instead in neurosis or insanity, or in non-criminal forms of social maladjustment such as marital unhappiness or alcoholism. Another link is required if the chain is to lead straight through to the particular outcome of criminality, and Healy and Bronner suggest that this is to be found in the main in the individual's social experience.[7]

The studies of the role of mental dullness indicate similarly, what in any case common sense should have told us, that the person who is intellectually handicapped is not therefore inevitably destined to become delinquent. The evidence suggests that he is more likely to do so if he is of unstable temperament, or if, because of his great suggestibility, he falls into bad company. The human personality must, in other words, be considered as a whole: a particular asset may more than compensate for a particular defect. The amount of support and supervision which relatives and friends are able to afford also enters prominently into the equation.

Finally, one must not overlook the complexity of the environment to which he has to make his adjustment. Of the delinquents referred to the Bristol Child Guidance Clinic in 1939-40, only 7·4 per cent. were found to be in that highest grade of mental subnormality which seems to play such an important part in the origin of delinquency. In the following year, as the war got under way and gave rise to increasing social and familial disorganisation, the percentage increased to 31 per cent.[8] The number of subnormals could hardly have changed so strikingly in the interim, but the problem of social adjustment certainly had. As in the case of emotional disturbance, it is not a personal handicap as such which is important, but the individual's ability, handicapped as he is, to cope with a particular environment.

## The Idea of Predisposition

One conceptual framework which might appear to be helpful is the classification of factors as either predisposing or precipitating. Basic personal factors (such as emotional disturbance, or an abnormal constitution) are said to predispose an individual to delinquencies which environmental stresses, temptations, etc., merely operate to precipitate, or bring out. This view has been espoused by many writers. It is fundamental to the work of Healy and Bronner, and of Bowlby. Friedlander refers to the importance of "latent delinquency",[9] and Carr Saunders, Mannheim, and Rhodes compare susceptibility to crime with susceptibility to disease.[11] Stott goes furthest of all, and seems to hold that a single environmental experience is alone enough to precipitate these lurking anti-social tendencies.[11]

None of these authorities would deny that the social environment may be the prime mover in the less serious forms of misbehaviour, but the origin of what Bowlby has called the "stage army of crime", the persistent offenders who return time and time again to crime, in spite of repeated doses of training and punishment, is to be sought in a criminal predisposition, which is (according to the theory adopted) either innate or built into the very structure of the personality by early psychological conditioning. As for the very large number of cases in which there was no sign of personal abnormality, they would be accounted for by the fact that they are perhaps not really criminals, but mischievous or high-spirited persons, or individuals reacting temporarily to stress, who would either return to normal themselves very soon, or upon the application of very minor and simple treatment measures.[12]

If this is true then much of the anti-social behaviour which finds its way into the criminal statistics is not really crime at all.    This is not a very realistic view.    For whatever name we give to such behaviour it remains a major social problem, both quantitatively and qualitatively.    This approach does seem to underestimate the significance of social factors.

At the same time, the distinction between the casual and the persistent criminal is of considerable importance.    Any large increase in the "stage army" must be a matter for the gravest misgivings.    The danger in fact is too real for us to be contented with facile and one-sided generalisations.

Of the various forms of predisposition which have been postulated only that of the affectionless psychopath seems to the writer to lead necessarily to crime.    And though it must be conceded that if this condition is present then the individual in question is very likely to be a chronic offender, it is by no means certain that all life-long offenders are of this type.    The term "habitual criminal" is often used, and suggests that more superficial social processes may sometimes be at work.

"Life story" studies of the kind presented by C. R. Shaw show how this can happen.    In the *Natural History of a Delinquent Career*,[13] Sidney tells how he began to steal at the age of seven, at the suggestion of another, much older boy, and explains that at that age, it was no more than a game to him.    He was an adventurous child, and stealing was a dangerous and thrilling business.    Gradually he was drawn more and more into contact with the criminal world, until he began to identify himself with it and its *mores*.    His circle of friends, his attitudes, habits, and established expectations, indeed his whole way of life, were shaped by and dovetailed themselves with his criminality.    A lifelong process of social growth had succeeded in creating, on a foundation which might just as well have led to a worthy and even a successful career (for he had drive and intelligence), an habitual criminal of the most intractable sort.

Such a character structure might in its turn be described as a form of predisposition, but if so, the term begins to lose its meaning, for it has been built up by the gradual accumulation and assimilation of what would usually have been described as precipitating factors. In such circumstances, the term "precipitating factor" also loses its significance, for, to the professional or habitual criminal, it need hardly exist at all. The impossibility of distinguishing between predisposing and precipitating factors holds right through; even the affectionless criminal is so because of early environmental experiences. Nor is the dichotomy justified as a means of distinguishing the more and the less incorrigible, for the habitual offender as well as the psychopath may be very difficult to reform. There is no ground, for example, for assuming with Stott[14] that only the psychologically abnormal offender needs institutional treatment, and that the socially determined delinquent can be reformed by the shock of being caught, or possibly by a spell of probation. The only virtue of this form of classification is in indicating which offenders are likely to need psychiatric treatment, and which are likely to respond to treatment at the level of social training.

**Dependence of Social Factors**

In their turn, social factors call for minute and careful examination. Just as the unity of the personality precludes us from seizing upon a single trait apart from all the others, and attributing criminal behaviour to its influence, so the social environment must be seen as an organic whole, rather than as a collection of separate stresses and temptations. A good home may protect a child from the baleful influence of a crime-ridden neighbourhood. Mannheim has shown that the influence of unemployment or alcoholism varies tremendously from one community to another.[15] Even the ecologists who speak of the influence of the community as if it were a single factor, the solution of an equation perhaps, but expressed nevertheless through the single agency of the moral tone of the neighbourhood, are forced, in passing, to acknowledge that the skein is a little more entangled than that, and that there are in fact various warring codes within the same community.[16]

Nor is an exclusively sociological explanation any more justified than those discussed above which overstress personal predisposition. Some sociologists, nevertheless, write as if almost all crime could be attributed to social as against personal factors.[17] Perhaps the psychologists and the constitutional theorists do attach too little importance to sociological elements in the causal pattern, but the pendulum can swing too far in the opposite direction. Personal factors are, almost certainly, always important. The traits in question may often be merely individual differences within the limits of normality, but they are none the less effective for that.

This is shown to some extent by the fact that a pathogenic social setting causes delinquency in some cases but not in others.

Delinquency, fortunately for the stability of society, is never as wide-spread as the social forces to which it is attributed. This is supported both by enquiries into the effects of particular social factors and by the ecological study of delinquency areas. An environmental stress is not an objective thing; it differs according to the person who experiences it. In the language of Kurt Lewin, it has a different "valency" for different individuals.[18]

Thus a congested urban environment is likely to be much more frustrating and delinquency-provoking to the more active and adventurous type of child than to his more timid fellow. On the other hand, the less assertive and more easily led type of person is exposed to a rather different set of hazards. He is particularly prone to fall into bad company, and to get into trouble as a member of a gang. This may be because he is "that sort of person" or because he is at the stage of development, around the age of ten, when group membership is always of great importance to the individual. It may also be his reaction to his social situation, like Thrasher's first-generation immigrants, whose need for assimilation and acceptance drives them into gang-membership. Whichever it is, the unique contribution of each individual towards his situation must be appreciated. The social environment exercises a tremendous influence over our behaviour, but it does this through its effect upon the motives and attitudes of individuals, and as part of a meaningful pattern of social stimulus and individual response.

It is the failure of Sutherland to acknowledge the individual contribution which makes his theory of the "professional criminal" so unsatisfying.[19] According to Sutherland, the professional criminal (of whom the professional thief is one kind) takes up his profession for exactly the same reason as the members of any other occupational group: in order to make a large income. He organises his predatory activities efficiently, like a business, and calculates his profits after having charged against them the cost of occasionally bribing the police or the courts. Crime is a business like any other, and requires no further explanation.

This is patently untrue, even in the United States, where in some places, at least, the danger of punishment may be diminished by bribery,[20] for it rests upon an assumption that the law has no moral hold on the individual. If only the financial prospect is sufficiently bright an individual is as likely to "go into crime" as into, say, law or accountancy. When the argument is stated baldly like that its inadequacy becomes apparent. The general impellent is there, but the essentially individual, selective element is lacking. It is likely that Sutherland has relied too much upon the statements made by professional criminals about their motives and experiences.

## Value of the Case Method

If the synoptic or comprehensive view of crime is taken to be vindicated, research interest must shift from the separate contributing factors to the mode in which these combine with each other. Statistics can help us very little, for the techniques which are of most use in the study of complex processes (analysis of variance and factor analysis) can deal only with factors which, though they may be related, remain separate entities. The causes of crime, on the other hand, combine to form new factors—for example, that of "total personality", as distinct from separate personality traits. In the absence of more objective methods, we are forced back upon an attempt to apply our experience and practical judgment in actual individual cases, to this task of evaluating possible causes, and determining their place in the causal complex. The future, in other words, seems to rest for the time being with the case-study. If general laws for the combination of factors do exist, they can only be discovered by empirical grass-roots research of this sort.

## NOTES TO CHAPTER VII

1. Reckless, W. C., "The Implications of Prediction in Sociology", *Am. Sociol. Review*, **6**: 4, Aug. 1954. Also his, *The Crime Problem*, 1950.

2. Thompson, R. E., "A Validation of the Glueck Social Prediction Scale for Proneness to Delinquency", *Brit. J. of Delinquency*, **3**: 4, 1953, pp. 289 ff.

3. For a further discussion of prediction methods, see pp. 161-4.

4. A convincing case for this kind of research is made by various contributors to: *Why Delinquency?—The Case for Operational Research*, 1949. (The Proceedings of a Conference held at the Royal Institution, London.)

5. Cressey, D. R., "Criminological Research and the Definition of Crimes", *Am. J. of Sociol.*, **56**, 1951, pp. 546 ff.

6. Sutherland, E. H., *Principles of Criminology*, 1947, p. 222.

7. Healy, W., and Bronner, A. F., *New Light on Delinquency and its Treatment*, 1936, p. 68.

8. Bodman, F., and Dunsdon, M. I., "Juvenile Delinquency in Wartime", *Lancet*, 8 Nov. 1941.

9. Friedlander, K., *Psycho-analytical Approach to Juvenile Delinquency*, 1947.

10. Carr Saunders, A. M., Mannheim, H., and Rhodes, E. C., *Young Offenders*, 1942, pp. 151-6.

11. Stott, D. H., *Delinquency and Human Nature*, 1950.

12. See, for example, Mays, J. B., *Growing-up in the City*, 1954, pp. 4-8; and Stott, *op. cit.*, pp. 364-5.

13. Shaw, C. R., *Natural History of a Delinquent Career*, 1951.

14. *Op. cit.*, p. 365.

15. Mannheim, H., *Social Aspects of Crime in England between the Wars*, 1940, pp. 169 ff.

16. Shaw, C. R., and McKay, H. D., *Juvenile Delinquency and Urban Areas*, 1942, Chapter VII.

17. The writings of Sutherland often seem to imply as much.

18. Lewin, K., "Environmental Forces in Child Behaviour—in *Handbook of Child Psychology*, 1939, pp. 94-127.

19. Sutherland, *op. cit.*, pp. 213-14 and pp. 222 ff.

20. Kefauver, E., *Crime in America*, 1951.

# CHAPTER VIII

## THE PHENOMENON OF CRIME

In addition to asking, "What are the causes of crime?" we might ask the further question, "What forms does it take?" This is the study of crime as a social phenomenon. It includes such subjects as trends in crime, its distribution between classes, localities, age groups, and the sexes, and seasonal fluctuations in its incidence.

Some of these topics, *e.g.* the class and local distribution of crime, have already been examined for their bearing upon the problem of causation. Those to be dealt with in the present chapter also have their causal implications. But they are important also simply as phenomena, descriptions of one aspect of our social life.

### General Trends

Adolph Quetelet, who first called our attention, over a hundred years ago, to the opportunities for criminological study presented by criminal statistics, argued that crime tended to remain at a fairly constant level. It was, he said, "un budget qu'on paye avec une regularité effroyante". The human qualities which led to crime were very numerous and quite independent of each other. There could, therefore, be no causal trends in the actual course of crime; no single cause was strong enough to achieve this. Chance was the only determinant, and over large numbers a chance distribution tends to remain constant.

Such reasoning led Quetelet to postulate the existence of a "constant criminal propensity" in large groups, though of course not in individuals. Many of the criticisms of his work have been based upon a failure to understand that he was referring to "une homme moyen", a statistical concept, and not to particular individuals. His work provides no support for Lombrosian speculations about the incorrigibility of criminals.[1]

It is of some interest to see how far the course of crime in this country bears out his theory. The figures of "crimes known to the police", since the 'seventies of last century, will be used for this purpose.

Up to the 'thirties, the figures fluctuate about a mean point which might well represent Quetelet's "penchant au crime". Between 1930 and 1939 there was a very considerable increase, but it is

## TABLE V

INDICTABLE OFFENCES KNOWN TO THE POLICE
ANNUAL AVERAGES PER 100,000 OF POPULATION*

| Period | Annual Averages (per 100,000) | Period | Annual Averages (per 100,000) |
|---|---|---|---|
| 1878-82 | 373·87 | 1915-19 | 251·00 |
| 1883-7 | 328·85 | 1920-4 | 279·99 |
| 1888-92 | 293·25 | 1925-9 | 324·87 |
| 1893-7 | 276·64 | 1930-9 | 639·06 |
| 1900-4 | 255·67 | 1940-4 | 972·18 |
| 1905-9 | 285·72 | 1945-9 | 1278·36 |
| 1910-14 | 269·56 | | |

\* NOTE.—After 1949 the basis of this rate was changed. It is now calculated upon the population of eight years old and over. Comparable figures on the new basis are only available as far back as 1930.

arguable that where this was not due to changes in the methods of police recording (*e.g.* the abolition of the Suspected Stolen Book in London in 1932), it was attributable to the Children and Young Persons Act, 1933, which provided a more humane approach towards the juvenile offender, and so encouraged people to bring children before the courts. The increase would then be found largely in the under-sixteen age groups. If the number "found guilty" are used instead of the police figures, in order to eliminate the results of changes in recording methods, and if the figures are then broken down into age groups, this expectation is found to be realised.

## TABLE VI

MALES FOUND GUILTY OF INDICTABLE OFFENCES
NUMBERS PER 100,000 OF POPULATION IN EACH AGE GROUP

| Year | All Ages | Age 10 but Under 14 Years | Age 14 but Under 16 Years | 16 Years and Over |
|---|---|---|---|---|
| 1931 | 326 | 540 | 740 | 157 |
| 1932 | 354 | 592 | 767 | 170 |
| 1933 | 337 | 615 | 807 | 159 |
| 1934 | 351 | 788 | 855 | 151 |
| 1935 | 370 | 983 | 1,006 | 147 |
| 1936 | 383 | 1,051 | 1,053 | 151 |
| 1937 | 404 | 1,222 | 1,125 | 158 |
| 1938 | 407 | 1,183 | 1,143 | 162 |

There is a remarkable degree of stability in the figures for the over-sixteen group during this period, in spite of adverse environmental circumstances, including the economic depression of the 'thirties. Quetelet would seem to be handsomely vindicated.

With the outbreak of the Second World War, however, the torrent overflowed its banks. During the war, crime among all age groups rose to a record height, and has remained high ever since. It is conceivable that the peak has now been reached, and that in the decline which is to follow, the old mean will be re-established. But if the range of variation which is possible can be so great—if the maximum can be as much as five times as great as the minimum, as is the case here—there may be a common element in crime, but it can have very little practical importance.

There are also theoretical reasons why Quetelet's view should be treated with reserve. One might describe the "propensity for crime", as Quetelet himself seems to do, purely as a result of causes within the human personality. Or like van Bemmelen (a modern apologist for Quetelet) one might include the social element.[2] In either case, the validity of the argument depends upon the belief that causes are numerous, weak, and independent. The result of much modern criminological research is directly opposed to such an assumption.

The psychopathologists have shown that the "propensity" within the personality may be affected enormously by changes in the methods of child-training used in a community.[3] The sociologists, for their part, can point to various "mass impellents"—the moral tone of a community, for instance[4]—which can have a very definite effect upon the amount of crime. The course of criminality during the recent war tells decisively against the view that social factors must tend to cancel each other out.

## Crime in War-time

Not that the criminological situation in war-time is a simple one to analyse. Various administrative changes in time of war make it very difficult even to obtain an effective measure of the amount of crime which has taken place. Millions of adult men are conscripted into the armed forces, and are thus prevented from committing civilian offences. Many certainly become army offenders, but there is no way of finding out how many.[5] There is usually also some disorganisation of the civil administration: there is usually, for example, a reduction in the size of the police force, and therefore in its efficiency. Many more crimes must remain unrecorded than before the war.

Other changes work in the opposite direction. Large numbers of regulations are passed, creating new crimes and new kinds of criminals. Thus ration book offences begin to take their place side by side with larceny, and breaking and entering.

Changes in the attitude of the police may also be very important. Studies of juvenile delinquency in Liverpool show that in both world wars an apparent increase in juveniles prosecuted was counterbalanced to some extent by a decrease in the numbers cautioned by the police. A similar shift was discerned in the line of demarcation between indictable and non-indictable offences, the former increasing at the cost of the latter, apparently because of a general tightening up by the police. Any study based (as most are) upon indictable offences may, therefore, possibly tend to exaggerate actual variations in the amount of crime.[6]

It was recording difficulties such as these which led Sutherland to speak of many of the alleged effects of war on crime as "statistical artefacts".[7]

At the same time, the causal process itself seems to be extremely complex. Family life is affected adversely, and parental supervision is relaxed. Prisons are closed for lack of staff, and prisoners have to be discharged earlier. In this country our whole social life was disrupted by the war: with evacuation, schools closed, bombing, and the incursion of large numbers of foreign troops belonging to our allies, and of refugees from countries over-run by the Nazis. On the credit side, the national emergency causes a great wave of patriotism to sweep the country, which in Britain in the last war was found even to have its effect upon the behaviour of men in prison.[8]

Among other favourable developments, one might have included the reduction of unemployment and higher wages which usually result from conscription and the expansion of war industries, but where the balance of advantage lies here is problematical. Long working hours and the employment of women in war factories may well have injurious effects upon the family life of the nation which no improvement in material circumstances could make up for.

There is, therefore, every reason for caution in interpreting crime trends in war-time. Generalisations applied to all wars or all countries seem likely to be particularly hazardous, for the causal equation is probably different in every case. We have here a very good example of the value of the ecological viewpoint.

Striking differences in the course of crime as between one European country and another during the recent war become explicable in the light of local circumstances.[9] For example, the increase in "crimes known to the police" in Denmark between

1939 and 1943 (when the Danish police were dissolved by the Nazis) was 100 per cent., many times as great as that in other countries. In Britain the increase was under 25 per cent. Danish authorities blame this rise mainly upon the military occupation, and upon the special form which occupation took in Denmark.[10]

In Finland, an unparalleled rise in the crime rate occurred after the armistice, during the years 1944-5. The average rate of increase was 70 per cent., while crimes against property increased by 116 per cent.[11] British figures during the same period rose only slightly, and actually fell during the more comparable period of the first post-war year.

TABLE VII

NUMBERS OF ADULTS (17 YEARS AND OVER) AND JUVENILES (AGED 8 BUT UNDER 17), PER 100,000 OF THEIR AGE GROUPS, FOUND GUILTY OF INDICTABLE OFFENCES

| Year | Juveniles | Adults |
|------|-----------|--------|
| 1938 | 494 | 163 |
| 1939 | 558 | 149 |
| 1940 | 776 | 149 |
| 1941 | 821 | 200 |
| 1942 | 739 | 213 |
| 1943 | 752 | 205 |
| 1944 | 794 | 203 |
| 1945 | 857 | 222 |
| 1946 | 730 | 215 |
| 1947 | 702 | 243 |
| 1948 | 881 | 257 |
| 1949 | 808 | 222 |
| 1950 | 843 | 222 |
| 1951 | 923 | 259 |
| 1952 | 859 | 260 |
| 1953 | 724 | 233 |

Professor Vold argues that the war had relatively little effect upon crime trends in the United States, such changes as took place often revealing themselves as parts of long-term trends. The war, he felt, had little effect because it made only a superficial impact upon the structure of American civilisation.[12] Such a statement could only have come from a country as remote from the actual field of conflict as the United States.

The danger of sweeping generalisations is illustrated also by the different course which criminality took in this country in the two world wars. During the war of 1914-18, the number of adults tried for indictable offences decreased, though with a greatly reduced civilian male population, these figures probably disguise a fairly stable crime position. The trend of juvenile offences was much less favourable: the number of young offenders increased by one-third.[13]

In the recent conflict, there were no such equivocal features.

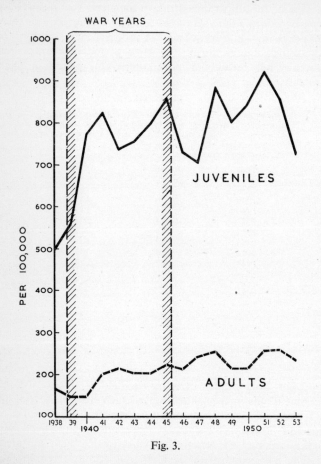

Fig. 3.

The proportion per 100,000 found guilty, for all age groups, rose from 393 for men and 51 for women in 1938 to 554 and 86 respectively in 1945. The distribution of crime as between adults and juveniles is shown in Table VII and Fig. 3. This shows that although the level of juvenile delinquency was nearly two-thirds higher in 1945 than in 1938, adult crime also was about three-eighths higher.

It is sometimes alleged that the violence inseparable from war, and the social approval given to it, are bound to lead to an increase in violent forms of crime. In neither war was this borne out by the statistics of the actual war period. Between 1938 and 1945, the number of persons found guilty of crimes of violence against the person remained steady at about 2 per cent., and sex offenders at around 3 per cent. of the total. Much the greatest increase, in terms of absolute numbers, was therefore in crimes against property, which already constituted the lion's share of the total. Mannheim reported similar conclusions from an examination of the statistics for the earlier war.[14] This is also the experience of other countries.[15]

The explanation may be, as Mannheim suggests,[16] that the human appetite for violence is limited, and that war provides a surfeit of it. Another possibility, not incompatible with the first, is that the increase which might have been expected, did not occur because so many men were away on active service. Either would be consistent with the definite swing towards violent crime in the years *since the war*, the latter being seen as a kind of delayed effect. By 1953, the percentage found guilty of crimes of violence had doubled and the proportion of sex offenders had increased from 3 per cent. to 4 per cent.

The following table, based upon the more complete figures contained in the police returns of "crimes known", gives a better picture of the changes:—

TABLE VIII

INDICTABLE OFFENCES KNOWN TO THE POLICE

|  | Annual Average 1930-9 | Percentage of Total | 1953 | Percentage of Total |
|---|---|---|---|---|
| Violence .. .. | 2,370 | 1·0 | 7,083 | 1·5 |
| Sex .. .. .. | 3,722 | 1·6 | 15,842 | 3·3 |
| Receiving, Fraud, and False Pretences .. | 18,606 | 8·1 | 35,549 | 7·5 |
| Burglary, House-breaking, etc. .. | 39,243 | 17·0 | 88,607 | 18·7 |
| Larceny .. .. | 160,535 | 69·5 | 308,578 | 65·2 |
| Robbery and Extortion .. .. | 325 | 0·1 | 1,088 | 0·23 |
| Malicious Injury to Property .. .. | 475 | 0·2 | 5,309 | 1·1 |
| Others .. .. | 5,749 | 2·5 | 10,933 | 2·3 |

It is seen that the actual number of crimes of violence known to the police increased threefold, and sex crimes more than fourfold. It is probably significant that the greatest increase among crimes against property were in those containing an element of violence: robbery and extortion, and malicious injury to property. Although total numbers in these classes of offences remained small, the former reached a level more than three times greater in 1953 than during the pre-war period, while malicious injury to property was more than twelve times as great.

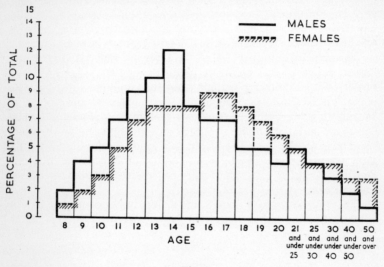

Fig. 4.

**Crime and Age**

Most of our crime is committed by juveniles. This is quite clear from Fig. 3. Various studies in recent years have shown that the peak age for crime in this country fluctuates around thirteen years.[17]

To speak solely of peak ages, however, may be misleading. The peak age for males in 1953 was fourteen, with 2,115 persons found guilty per 100,000, but 88 per cent. of the offenders in that year were of ages other than fourteen. The actual distribution of indictable male criminality among the various age groups in 1953 is shown in Fig. 4. It can be seen that the distribution is skewed towards the ages below fourteen, rather than those above. The age distribution for female offenders is also given in Fig. 4.

The real significance of the peak age is that it indicates a kind of climacteric in the criminal life cycle. Until the peak age is reached, new offenders are being recruited, but beyond that age the grip of crime gradually relaxes. It seems that at present the climacteric for males occurs at about the age of puberty. For girls it is a little later, about seventeen, though there has been a tendency since the war for the gap between the sexes to be narrowed by a general fall in the ages of female offenders.[18]

Some authorities have put the age of maximum criminality higher than this. Goring found it in the age group 15 to 20,[19] but there is some evidence that the age has been falling steadily since the middle of the last century, when it was estimated to be as high as 20 to 25, or 20 to 30.[20] In America, the ages of offenders seem to be higher than in this country. Sutherland estimates that delinquency in the United States "increases from the age of about six to about nineteen, where it remains nearly constant until the age of twenty-seven, after which it declines sharply with increasing age".[21]

One lesson which can be drawn from all this variability, is that age itself, in the sense of "a stage of organic evolution and involution",[22] is not the only factor to be considered. Thus it would be over-simplifying the problem to attempt to account for the location of the peak age in this country in terms of the puberty crisis. A particular age represents a different social status, and confronts the individual with different social problems, in different societies.

This is true even of basic physiological stresses such as those connected with the attainment of sexual maturity. For it may be assumed that the latter will bring with it greater conflict in a culture such as ours, where public opinion and economic forces combine to delay marriage, than in Eastern countries where marriage and full sexual gratification are possible shortly after puberty.

In the words of von Hentig: "The fact that you are a baby, a centenarian, or an adult of twenty-five, determines what your sociological habitat is, and whether you play a prominent part or are merely an extra in the drama of human interrelations. Age itself is not the causative factor, but rather the forces that render age an essential physiological and sociological problem".[23]

If children's offences are excluded, the amount of crime at different ages remains fairly constant until the age of thirty, when a steady decline sets in, criminality becoming very little indeed in old age. The percentage of the total found in the age group sixty and over is less than 1 per cent. Ever since Goring,[24] it has been recognised that most adult crime occurs in early manhood.

American figures have already been quoted. In Denmark, the first real decline, according to 1947 figures, commences after the age of twenty-four. A similar pattern is found in Sweden and in Belgium.[25]

The regularity with which the same broad pattern repeats itself suggests that here at least some factor of a permanent character is involved. Sellin implies this in saying that the curve of crime "is no different from any other activity curve depending on the vitality of man".[26] If this were all, however, it would be difficult to account for a decline at or just before the age of thirty, for a man is then in his physical prime. The explanation is probably to be found in the fact that most people have usually settled down in life by this time. They are established in their jobs. They have married and perhaps acquired children, and these new responsibilities and satisfactions have become stabilising forces in their lives They have found a niche for themselves in society: they have friends, and a reputation to preserve. The curve of vital energy, like so many other constitutional factors, plays a part, but only that of a limiting factor. Within the wide limits which it sets, there is much room for socially determined variability.

We should, therefore, look with considerable scepticism upon a theory such as that of the Gluecks, which purports to show that the criminal passes through a process of maturation, and that, unless he is mentally abnormal, he tends to reform at the end of a fixed period of time (about seven years) from his first delinquency.[27]

This conclusion was based upon a series of follow-up studies of offenders over a period of fifteen years. The methods used in establishing it are open to criticism: for example, the mentally abnormal are admitted to be exceptions to the theory, and mental abnormality has been defined very widely indeed. More serious is the effect of the theory in focusing our attention upon meaningless average trends, rather than upon the dynamic interrelationships out of which crime emerges. If the Gluecks' arithmetic is vindicated, and a period of about seven years is found to be the "allotted span" for criminal behaviour, this can only be asserted so long as social conditions do not change drastically. Yet it is to a change in these circumstances, in the shape of new methods of treating and preventing crime, that we look for some alleviation of the problem. They should take place, and may well do so. The task of the criminologist is to attempt to assess what results such changes are likely to have, not to abandon them in favour of mere statistical uniformities.

Apart from the general trends, there is a marked tendency for certain types of crime to be commonest among certain age groups. Aschaffenburg found the incidence of grand larceny among men aged eighteen to twenty-one to be 150 times as great as among the over-seventies. Sex crimes, on the other hand, were four times as common among the older group.[28] Taking an average age of 33·7 as the dividing line, Vernon Fox, in a study of a large number of American cases, found that the emphasis shifted in the older group from such crimes as kidnapping, burglary, and robbery, to forgery, fraud, embezzlement, and sex crimes.[29]

English Criminal Statistics show the following distribution:—

TABLE IX

TYPES OF CRIME COMMITTED AT DIFFERENT AGES
PERCENTAGE IN EACH AGE GROUP IN 1953

|  | 8 but Under 14 | 14 but Under 17 | 17 but Under 21 | 21 but Under 30 | 30 and Over |
|---|---|---|---|---|---|
| Breaking and Entering .. | 31 | 22 | 15 | 21 | 11 |
| Larceny .. .. .. | 20 | 14 | 10 | 21 | 35 |
| Robbery .. .. .. | 19 | 15 | 21 | 34 | 11 |
| Receiving .. .. .. | 12 | 10 | 7 | 22 | 49 |
| Violence .. .. .. | 3 | 5 | 14 | 38 | 40 |
| Sex .. .. .. | 7 | 13 | 11 | 20 | 49 |
| Fraud and False Pretences | 2 | 2 | 5 | 24 | 67 |

This table confirms the conclusion of the other investigators. In middle and old age there is a definite shift from the more overt forms of property crime, such as robbery, and breaking and entering, to sex crimes, and violence, and more subtle types of property offence such as receiving, fraud, and false pretences. With regard to the latter observation, von Hentig makes an illuminating comparison between the criminality of old men and the crimes committed by women. Both, he sees, as either instigators of crime in others, or as committers of crime in which craftiness has an important place.[30]

It is becoming more and more apparent that persistent adult offenders are in the main those who began their criminality in childhood. This is the conclusion to be drawn from Goring's data, already quoted.[31] In a more recent analysis by Mannheim of the records of nearly 1,300 offenders having at least four convictions, 59 per cent. were convicted for the first time before the age of twenty-two, and 13·6 per cent. of the male cases before the age of fourteen.[32]

This fact brings home to us very forcibly the importance of treating juvenile delinquency seriously. Much of it may be youthful high spirits, and is soon given up. But in some cases it may be evidence of serious psychological disturbance, or the beginnings of associations and habits which will lead to a life of crime. If we want to solve the problem of the adult recidivist, we cannot afford to neglect these early manifestations of criminality. Indeed, we ought perhaps to spread our net even wider, for the Gluecks have shown that truancy, running away from home, and lying (in that order), are also connected significantly with later criminality.[33] The difficult child (even though at first a non-offender in the formal legal sense) is also a potential recidivist.

## Female Criminality

Criminal statistics the whole world over show a much smaller amount of criminality among women than among men. In this country, for example, since the war, female criminality has varied at between one-seventh and one-eighth of the male total.

Some writers have suggested that this difference is more apparent than real, being the result of the greater leniency with which women offenders are treated. Women are less likely to be charged, and more likely to be acquitted when they are charged.[34] There is some evidence that partiality of this sort does exist. The acquittal rate for females tends to be a little higher than that for males. In 1953, for all courts, it was 6·8 per cent. for females, as against 4·4 per cent. for male offenders.[35] There is also some evidence for the view that women are less often brought to book for their crimes; criminal abortion and prostitution both have a notoriously low detection rate.[36] It would be unreasonable, however, to attribute more than a small part of the enormous difference in criminality between the sexes to these factors. Other more powerful influences seem to be at work.

It is tempting to find these in biological differences. Some criminologists have been content with this kind of explanation. Women, it is reasoned, are weaker, and less daring and aggressive than men. Their biological role is essentially passive, while that of the male is active. Men, therefore, attack their environment more vigorously than women. The dependence of women upon their menfolk is a further natural consequence of these essential differences between the sexes, and in its turn would account for the frequently noted fact that women often instigate crimes committed by men instead of carrying them out themselves.[37] For much the same reason, the man of the house is responsible for the economic security of his family, and is, therefore, especially exposed to risk at times of economic stringency.

There is, however, an obvious social component in these situations. For one thing, the degree of female dependence varies in different communities, and at different times. Women are far less dependent than they were in the Victorian period. Moreover, the claims of the family upon a man are themselves socially conditioned, and the part played by general economic conditions must not be overlooked.

There is ample statistical evidence to show that society does play its part in determining the male-female crime ratio. Hacker has shown that this ratio varies widely in different countries. The female share of the total amount of crime is greatest in those countries where women are most emancipated. It reaches vanishing point in those countries of the East and Middle East, where their social experience is rigorously circumscribed.[38]

If these deductions are suspect because of the difficulty of making valid international statistical comparisons,[39] there is the careful analysis of Polish statistics by Radzinowicz.[40] This shows that even within the boundaries of a single country, the crime ratio between the sexes varies considerably in different districts, or according to age, religion, or marital status. Thus in the more primitive rural areas, the ratio was as small as 12·8 per cent. but rose to 23·5 per cent. in the urban "voivodship" of Warsaw. The female proportion is generally lower in the rural than in the urban areas: 16·6 per cent. in the former as compared with 23·5 per cent. in the latter. The female proportion also increases with age: from 17·8 per cent. to 38·6 per cent. The influence of marriage is quite marked, married women having a much lower ratio than the rest.

The biological factor may play its part then, but it is by no means the only one. We have to take account also of the current view as to the social role of women. Girls are trained from their earliest years to be "modest" and "nice", while a boy is expected to be rougher and tougher. Possibly because of the danger of pregnancy, growing girls are protected and supervised more than boys. And when they are grown up, even in Western countries where women are now relatively emancipated, they live a more cloistered life than their menfolk. It is, for example, still considered hardly right among many groups for women to go alone to certain kinds of mixed gatherings (to public houses, for example, or dances). Again, if one member of a family has to stay at home to keep house, or to look after an ageing relative, it is always one of its female members.

Equally interesting is the difference in the types of crime committed by men and women. Certain types of crime are obviously going to be a male monopoly. These include rape, and most violent crimes against property, such as housebreaking[41] and robbery. Similarly there are others which women commit much more frequently than men. They include many offences against the person: cruelty to children, attempts at murder, and suicide. Among female property crimes, shoplifting stands supreme, while others include forgery and fraud.

Perhaps more significant than any of the other female crimes, however, are those connected with prostitution. Some criminologists argue that prostitution is the female equivalent for crimes against property—as a way of providing an income other than by honest work—and that no satisfactory sex-ratio for crime can be calculated which excludes it.[42] But even if the number of convictions for prostitution are included, it is almost certain that this would be a gross underestimate of the amount of prostitution which is actually taking place, for it has a very low conviction rate. There were, for example, only 9,640 convictions for this offence in 1953. Brothel-keeping is also a preponderantly female offence; twice as many women as men were convicted for it in 1953.

## Seasonal Fluctuations

Seasonal variations in crime also call for discussion. Why should crime be more prevalent in particular months, or on particular days of the week?

That it is so is fairly generally agreed. Take for instance, the question of the monthly distribution. Writers in various countries have shown that while crimes against property reach their maximum in the winter, crimes against the person are at their greatest during the summer months.[43]

Various attempts have been made to explain these facts in terms of human physiology. Ferri spoke of a reduced output of energy in warm weather, leading to a surplus which could be released in acts of violence.[44] The observed correlation, however, is with season rather than weather. More plausible are the speculations about a connection between the increase in sexual crimes which starts in spring, and the occurrence of a natural biological tide at this season of the year. It is a time of intensified sexual activity among all forms of life: the season of creation and procreation.

The sex urge in human beings seems also to achieve its climax then.[45]

It has been denied that there is any periodicity in human sexual behaviour,[46] but this is hardly in accordance with common observation. Burt found a close correlation between the monthly figures for conceptions and those for adult sexual crimes, and an even closer one with what he called "the more natural sex offences of the young".[47]

For other types of offence it may be that human physiology plays only a very subordinate part, if any part at all. Climatic conditions may be important, but for their social rather than their biological significance. The dark nights of winter in the northern hemisphere are very convenient aids to the thief or the burglar. Winter is also a time when nature is niggardly. Then, if at all, there will be high prices and material privation. The economic provocation is likely to be at its strongest during the darkest months of the year.

The light and (at least relatively) warm months of the summer, on the other hand, facilitate social intercourse. It is easier to meet people—and to fall out with them. The location of the main annual holiday during the summer tends to the same end.

It is necessary to beware of over-simplifying; there are exceptions to the general trends. Murder seems to have no fixed peak, in contradistinction to the other crimes of violence which mount during the summer months. Local influences must also be given due weight. Thus Verkko shows that in Finland, during the period 1934-8, thefts reached their maximum during the summer at the same time as crimes of violence.[48] A well-known study of homicides in Seattle, identified the peak as occurring during the winter, and attributed it to a specifically local cause, the seasonal influx of migratory workers during the autumn.[49]

The daily peaks for crimes against the person are, as one would expect, at the week-ends. Sunday is usually the day when most offences of this kind are committed, closely followed by Saturday.[50] This is readily explicable as a result of the week-end holiday, together with the customary Friday pay-day and its effect in making for more week-end drunkenness. Other crimes seem to be fairly evenly spread over the whole week.

Various studies have been carried out in this country of the daily fluctuations in juvenile offences. These show that juvenile offences of all sorts reach a clear peak on Saturday and Sunday, with a minor peak in mid-week.[51] There is again the obvious association with holiday periods. Surprisingly enough, in view of this fact, there is no evidence that juvenile offences do follow the school holidays at all closely. In a study of juvenile delinquency in Leicester it was found that there was very little difference between delinquency rates during term and in the holidays.[52] Bagot contended that the peak occurred not during the holidays, but shortly afterwards.[53]

## NOTES TO CHAPTER VIII

1. Quetelet, A., *Sur l'Homme, ou Essai de Physique Sociale*, 1836. For a summary of his views, see van Bemmelen, J. M., "The Constancy of Crime", *Brit. J. of Delinquency*, **2**: 3, 1952, pp. 208 ff.

2. van Bemmelen, J. M., *loc. cit.*

3. See Chapter IV.

4. See Chapter VII.

5. For studies of many aspects of crime in the armed services, see Spencer, J. C., *Crime and the Services*, 1953; and Trenaman, J., *Out of Step*, 1952. These books effectively refute the hoary myth that war-time conditions and service life can cure the chronic delinquent. On this point see especially Spencer, Chapter VII.

6. Bagot, J. H., *Juvenile Delinquency*, 1941, pp. 20-1.
*Youthful Lawbreakers* (Liverpool Council of Social Service), 1948, p. 15 and Table I.

7. Sutherland, E. H., *Principles of Criminology*, 1947, p. 195.

8. Report by the British panel, in Sellin, T. (ed.), *Effects of War on Criminality*, Bull. International Penal and Penitentiary Commission, 1951.

9. Sellin, T. (ed.), *op. cit.*

10. *Ibid.*, pp. 559-60.

11. Hurwitz, S., *Criminology*, 1952, pp. 301-2.

12. In Sellin, T. (ed.), *op. cit.*, p. 785.

13. Mannheim, H., *War and Crime*, 1941, p. 94.

14. *Ibid.*, pp. 91-4.

15. See Sellin, T. (ed.), *op. cit.*

16. *Op. cit.*, p. 127.

17. Carr Saunders, A. M., Mannheim, H., and Rhodes, E. C., *Young Offenders*, 1942, especially the appendix by Mannheim, pp. 160 ff. Also the annual volumes of Criminal Statistics.

18. The female age group fourteen and under seventeen has now replaced the group seventeen and under twenty-one as the most important, in spite of the supremacy of age seventeen.

19. Goring, C., *The English Convict*, p. 201.

20. Carr Saunders, Mannheim, and Rhodes, *op. cit.*, p. 160.

21. *Op. cit.*, p. 96.

22. von Hentig, H., *Crime: Causes and Conditions*, 1947, p. 129.

23. *Ibid.*

24. *Op. cit.*, pp. 122 ff.

25. Hurwitz, *op. cit.*, p. 262.

26. Quoted, *ibid.*, p. 263.

27. This theory has been developed in a number of criminological follow-up studies. For a summary account of the work, see Glueck, S. and E. T., *After-conduct of Discharged Offenders*, 1945, Chapter VII.

28. Aschaffenburg, G., *Crime and its Repression*, 1913, p. 154.

29. Fox, V., *Journal of Criminal Law and Criminology*, **37**, 1946, p. 141 ff.

30. *Op. cit.*, p. 152.

31. See above.

32. Mannheim, H., *Social Aspects of Crime in England Between the Wars*, 1940, pp. 358-9.

33. Glueck, S. and E. T., *One Thousand Juvenile Delinquents*, 1939, p. 95.

34. Grunhut, M., *Penal Reform*, 1948, pp. 411-12.   Mannheim, H., *op. cit.*, pp. 341 ff.

35. At the end of last century the proportions were given as one-quarter and one-sixth respectively.   (Morrison, W. D., *Juvenile Offenders*, 1896, p. 46.)

36. Mannheim, H., *op. cit.*, questions this, but see also Pollak, O., *Criminality of Women*, 1950.

37. Mannheim, *op. cit.*, pp. 344-5.

38. Hacker, E., *Kriminalstatistische und Kriminalaetiologische*, 1941.

39. See Chapter II.

40. Radzinowicz, L., in *Sociol. Review*, **29**, 1937, pp. 76-102.

41. Between 1938 and 1953, breaking and entering by females has doubled, from 1·8 per cent. of the total to 3·5 per cent.

42. Radzinowicz, *loc. cit.*, pp. 99-100.

43. See especially Aschaffenburg, *op. cit.*, pp. 16-30.

44. Cited Hurwitz, *op. cit.*, pp. 246 and 249.

45. Ellis, Havelock, *Studies in the Psychology of Sex*, 1920, pp. 122 ff.

46. White, R. Clyde, in *Am. J. of Sociol.*, **32**, 1937, pp. 800-95.

47. Burt, Cyril, *Young Delinquent*, 1925, pp. 173-4.

48. Quoted Hurwitz, *op. cit.*, p. 248.

49. Schmid, C. F., in *Social Forces*, **4**, 1926, pp. 745-6.

50. For an account of various European studies on this question, see Hurwitz, *op. cit.*, pp. 251-2.

51. Bagot, J. H., *op. cit.*, pp. 39-40.   Burt, *op. cit.*, p. 159.

52. *Leicester Delinquency Studies*, 1953.

53. Bagot, J. H., *op. cit.*, p. 39.

# CHAPTER IX

## THE NATURE OF PUNISHMENT

One of the disadvantages of continuing to use such words as "punishment" and "penal", in that part of criminology which is concerned with treatment, is that the real complexity of public attitudes towards the criminal tends to be obscured. The purely punitive element still has to be reckoned with, but it is by no means all. It is possible to trace the operation of at least six motives, some of which are punitive, and some not, viz. (a) expiation, (b) restitution, (c) retribution, (d) deterrence, (e) reformation, (f) prevention.

These different motives are never clearly separated in our minds; in practical situations they are entangled with and masquerade as one another. We move without realising it from one to the other apparently at the behest of our emotional needs. Any sort of rational approach to treatment is going to depend upon a careful preliminary analysis of the nature of punishment, and a wider diffusion of insight on these matters throughout the community.

The criminologist, for his part, has to do his work within the existing context of social attitudes. He needs a clear idea of how these attitudes are compounded if he is to understand the part they play, and to allow for them in proposing remedial measures.

### Expiation

The essence of the expiatory view is that in suffering his punishment, the offender has purged his guilt, has "paid for" his crime, and that his account with society is therefore clear. This is the attitude, for example, which lies behind the commonly expressed reluctance to hold a man's record against him after his discharge from prison. To pursue him further would be vindictive. This lenient attitude is rarely undiluted: only too often an ex-prisoner does remain a "gaol-bird" for a long time after he has served his sentence, but mixed with and mitigating this attitude is a general sense of fairness which makes for a more compassionate approach.

On his side, the offender himself often seems in a vague sort of way to welcome a penalty of some sort, and to feel that it really does lighten the burden of guilt upon him.

Expiation, in fact, seems to be a fundamental need of our moral nature. It is, therefore, only to be expected that it will find an

116

important place in our religious doctrines and practices. Most of the great religions of the world testify to its importance,[1] though the means which they prescribe for its achievement may vary widely from one religion to another. In Christianity the idea is a central one, the Cross being a symbol of the supreme act of expiation by Jesus Christ. The expiatory significance of such practices as Penance and Confession is also obvious.

To the criminological reformer, expiatory trends are double-edged. On the one hand, they temper social attitudes towards the criminal, making it possible to propose measures of penal reform with some chance of acceptance. On the other hand, they may give rise, as Wills has argued,[2] to the belief that as the slate is now wiped clean by punishment, further delinquencies can be embarked upon. Or, alternatively, wrong-doing may be justified on the ground that the offender is, after all, prepared to "face the music" afterwards.

## Restitution

With restitution, the rights of the victim come into the picture. On this view, the criminal should make good the damage or the loss he has inflicted upon his victim. This is perhaps the most primitive of all the elements of punishment, for it brings out in a naked form the personal interests involved, which the public administration of justice has tended to overlay. As comparative social anthropology shows,[3] compensation or revenge was originally exacted by the victim himself or his kin, but as punishment became more and more a public matter, so did the offence take on more the character of an offence against the community, eventually a "breach of the king's peace". The possibility of restitution is rarely considered by British courts of criminal jurisdiction nowadays.[4]

But this does not mean that the *idea* of restitution has no influence upon the pattern of punishment. There is little doubt that the absence of anything in the nature of real restitution disposes people more favourably towards severe punishments. The victim, as he cannot be recompensed, is to be revenged. Like Shylock he is entitled to his pound of flesh.

It would be more constructive to attempt to infuse into our system of criminal justice more opportunities for real reparation. As Mannheim shows, some possibilities already exist within the framework of the present law, but the courts make too little use of them.[5] More opportunities of the same kind, however, are also needed. There is no danger that the interests of the state in the maintenance of public order would suffer as a result.

**Retribution**

The motive of retribution is often confused with expiation, with which it certainly has much in common.  Like expiation, retribution is concerned with restoring the moral balance, disturbed by the criminal's behaviour.  However, it has no concern with the moral purgation of the criminal himself.  The difference might be indicated by stating that while expiation is both the right and the duty of the offender, a retributive punishment is his desert.  Retribution is punishment in its purest form.  No other motive is involved than that of inflicting pain or loss on the offender as his just meed. The purgation of the offender and the reduction of crime are equally irrelevant to it.

Most of the argument about the validity of punishment has therefore centred around the question of retribution.  The belief in its importance is universal.  Not only is the general public usually adamant in demanding the retributive punishment of the offender, but the doctrine has a well-established place in British jurisprudence.  Among our great legal authorities, both Stephen,[6] and Kenny,[7] insist upon the importance of retaining it.  Lord Justice Fry wrote that "the object of punishment is to adjust the suffering to the sin".[8]  Among contemporary jurists, Goodheart argues, "Retribution in punishment is an expression of the community's disapproval of crime, and if this retribution is not given recognition then the disapproval may also disappear.  A community which is too ready to forgive the wrong-doer may end by condoning crime".[9]

How strong a hold this principle has upon us is shown by the fact that even our religious teachers, the leaders of a Church which teaches forgiveness as the cardinal virtue, lend it their support—even as generous and gentle a cleric as William Temple.[10]

The case for retribution is, nevertheless, a very dubious one. How, for example, can we, in the words of Edward Fry, hope to "adjust the suffering to the sin"?  For this means first assessing the moral culpability of the offender;  and this is quite a different thing from the seriousness of his crimes, for to assess it involves taking account of the temptations to which he has been subjected, as well as the many conditions which have helped to make him what he is.  Indeed, such an analysis may lead us to the conclusion that he should, perhaps, not be held responsible at all.

In the second place, how can we really administer a penal system so that the amount of pain suffered is graduated in relation to any criterion, whether of guilt or otherwise? Suffering is essentially subjective. Any two offenders may differ widely in sensitivity, and in the sorts of punishment to which they are sensitive. As a result, social opprobrium, for example, or imprisonment, may be much more painful to one than the other. Yet if sin and suffering are not proportional, it follows from the principle of retribution itself that a punishment is unjust.

A third and more fundamental objection is that advanced by philosophers from Socrates to Hobhouse: that the infliction of evil upon anyone can never in itself be good.[11]

Any more detailed discussion of such ethical issues would be out of place in a book of this sort.* The important point for present purposes is that there is a deeply ingrained belief in our culture in the importance of "just punishment" for wrongdoing. This general chorus of approval for the idea of retribution has inevitably had its effect upon our correctional institutions, where in spite of the lip-service paid to the theory that they exist solely for the retraining of the offender, actual practice is still dominated by punitive, essentially retributive motives.[12] Public opinion can be relied upon to resist any steps towards the amelioration of the condition of prisoners, if it involves the abandonment of this principle. It finds expression also in the social censure and even ostracism to which conviction exposes the offender, even when no formal punishment has been imposed.

Exceptionally, however, and rather unexpectedly, the community's view of what constitutes just retribution sometimes ranges it on the other side of the fence. Thus the reluctance of our judges to impose two sentences for one crime, has saved many habitual offenders from the long preventive sentences envisaged by the Prevention of Crimes Act 1908. Again, the ordinary man's sense of justice may sometimes be outraged by the proposal that a youth, whose offence might otherwise have earned him a comparatively short prison sentence, should be sent to Borstal for three years, although the longer period of training is necessary for his rehabilitation. No doubt the similar provisions for corrective training and preventive detention under the Criminal Justice Act 1948 are open to criticism on the same grounds.

In either case, whether it operates on the side of severity or lenity, the retributive motive is a conservative force. It focuses attention upon the offence rather than the offender, and so is

* A valuable general discussion of the ethics of punishment will be found in Ewing, A. C., *The Morality of Punishment*, 1929.

doggedly opposed to any scientific approach, aimed at the individual delinquent, and intended to deter him from further delinquencies or to reform him.

Yet it would be unduly pessimistic to assume that this must always be so. There was a time when even animals or inanimate objects were punished. In ancient Athens, an axe which had injured a citizen could be tried, and if found guilty be ceremoniously exiled by being hurled over the city boundary. In England, according to the law of Deodand which was extant well into the nineteenth century, a cart which ran over a man could be confiscated and sold for charity. If an ox killed a man, the Hebrews stoned it to death, and its flesh could then not be eaten.[13] We now recognise that even some human offenders may not be fully responsible for their criminal acts, if for example they are juveniles, or can legally be held to be insane. Even in the case of the normal adult, extenuating circumstances may sometimes be admitted by the court; and the doctrine of the guilty mind (*mens rea*) is no longer the indispensable precondition for conviction that it once was.[14]

The chief obstacle to further progress is going to be, not the moral question, for as the psycho-analysts have shown this is very largely a rationalisation, but our need for a scapegoat, on to whom we can erupt the hostile feelings pent within us all. We feel justified in hating and punishing the wrongdoer, and so, by attacking him, can find an aggressive outlet about which we need not feel guilty.[15]

### Deterrence

With deterrence, the real aim of the criminologist, that of reducing crime, at last comes into view. Although ethical considerations can never be avoided in any social science which proposes practical measures, they loom less large here than in the discussions of expiation, reparation, and retribution. The aim in deterrent punishment is to instil in the individual a regard for the law because of his fear of the punishment which will follow if he transgresses. The first ethical question is, therefore, whether legally correct behaviour maintained for such reasons is worth having.

To pose the question in such a way, seems to the present writer to be very naive. The element of fear does already enter to a very considerable extent into the social training of all of us. As Archbishop Temple saw very clearly, this in no way derogates from the value of the sentiments we afterwards build on these foundations.[16] They may begin as rationalisations for our real motives of fear, but they develop into sincerely held moral principles, to which, when they are matured, we cling in the face of the most appalling temptations and difficulties.

Apart from this problem, there is only that of the sort of deterrent punishments which are permissible. How severely are we justified in punishing our criminals merely to reduce the amount of criminality? The Nazis showed us just how far a government could go in torturing the rebellious human spirit into grudging obedience. How far we should go is obviously going to be determined by our sense of compassion and decency. And that means that punishments in this country are going to be very rigorously restricted.

At this point, however, we move at last into the field of empirical enquiry. The fact that we do feel thus, imposes a practical limitation upon the utility of very severe punishments. Where common feeling adjudges the criminal law to be too severe, the latter tends not to be enforced, and so to defeat its own ends. The outstanding example of this was the ubiquitous death penalty at the beginning of the nineteenth century. Magistrates began to acquit obviously guilty persons because they were not prepared to impose the death penalty for petty offences.[17]

But the belief in the value of even moderate deterrent punishments also calls for critical examination. Behind it is an assumption that we are rational beings, who make a careful calculation of possible gains and losses before deciding upon our actions. In the Benthamite phrase, it is assumed that we always act in accordance with our own "enlightened self-interest".

This view has long been abandoned in certain other social sciences. In economics, for example, although this supposition is still made, it is now recognised that it is an abstraction, and that any conclusions drawn must be qualified if they are to be applicable to real life. We now know much more about the complexity of human motives. The new psychology of the unconscious has taught us that our real motives may be essentially irrational, *i.e.* infantile, unrealistic, or even self-destructive.[18]

Thus the affectionless psychopath[19] is an individual for whom the prudent calculation of gains and losses required by the deterrent theory would be quite impossible. Many observers have noted that criminals of this type, who constitute a substantial proportion of our persistent offenders, are quite incapable of learning even from the experience of punishment, much less from the threat of it. Criminals "from an unconscious sense of guilt"[20] must be even less amenable to deterrent methods. They seek and welcome punishment, and its existence is a constant provocation to them to commit further offences and bring it on themselves.

But quite apart from abnormal cases of this sort, the result of punishment is not always what might have been hoped. We all know of the schoolboy whom a hiding turned into the hero of the school. Many young offenders certainly gain much prestige with their fellows from having served a term in an approved school; if they manage to achieve the lofty heights of a Borstal or a prison sentence, they can boast that they really are "big-timers". We have it on Mark Benney's authority that a prison sentence is the passport to respect even in the underworld.[21]

What also of the sense of resentment which is often felt about a punishment which the recipient considers to have been unjust? Many criminals seem to have a smouldering sense of injustice, which has helped to perpetuate their anti-social tendencies. More detailed case-studies are needed before we can hope to decide how valuable deterrent methods can be in cases like these.

Where the appropriate motives are there to be capitalised, however, the usefulness of deterrent punishments is going to depend upon how thoroughly the law is enforced. If there is a good chance of avoiding detection, the fear of punishment loses much of its persuasive force. The efficiency of the police and of the courts is therefore of the first importance. In this country the efficiency and integrity of the courts may be taken for granted, but this is not so everywhere. In the United States, for example, charges of corruption have been made against the courts from time to time; and, in less democratic and more backward countries, bribery of the judiciary may be even more widespread.

In all countries, however, the weak link in the enforcement of the law seems to be at the level of detection. This is not a question of graft. In spite of the occasional scandal, there is no evidence that widespread corruption exists in the British police service (such as, for example, has often been laid to the charge of local American forces). It is more a question of the inability of any police force, however efficient, to bring to book more than a small proportion of those who break the law. In a more autocratic country, with more police, possessing more arbitrary powers of enquiry and arrest, and in which the individual's daily life is in any case more closely supervised by the state, detection may perhaps be more complete. But this would be bought dearly, at the cost of certain fundamental values which we shall not voluntarily relinquish.

As a result, only a small proportion of the total amount of crime committed actually ends in a conviction. All authorities are agreed that many crimes are committed which never come to the notice of the police, and some which do are, for various reasons, never recorded.[22] It is, therefore, a striking fact that even of this truncated total, fewer than a half are actually cleared up each year. In 1953, of 472,989 indictable crimes known to the police, only 222,100 were cleared up.[23] There is plenty of room here for the development of such attitudes as, "It's the other fellow who'll be caught", or "It's worth the risk".

A unique opportunity for making an evaluation of the deterrent approach to crime was presented by Danish experience during the war. In 1944, the German occupying forces deported the Danish police, and for some time the country had only a local guard force invested with police authority. There followed an immense rise in the number of robberies, thefts, frauds, etc., but no comparable increase in murder or sexual crimes.[24] While this experience does show that crime is reduced very considerably by the prospect of detection and presumably punishment, it suggests that deterrent methods are of less value in reducing the incidence of those crimes in which strong passions or deep psychological problems are involved. Moreover, it underlines the point which has already been made about the importance of incomplete enforcement.

This Danish experience is clearly relevant to the debate about the value of capital punishment, contradicting the view, still widely held in this country, that the death penalty is an important deterrent to those who might commit murders or other violent crimes. If the death penalty did not exist, goes the argument, more criminals would carry weapons, crimes of violence and attacks upon the police would soar, and even murders would be much more common. The evidence submitted to the Royal Commission on Capital Punishment by the various European countries which have abolished the death penalty also fails to bear out these fears.[25] Although in these countries, there seems usually to have been a wave of violence immediately after capital punishment was given up, this soon subsided, and no unfavourable long-term effects can be discerned. The case for capital punishment, at any rate, it seems cannot be based upon arguments about deterrence. If the death penalty is to be justified at all, it can only be on frankly retributive grounds.

With these qualifications, the value of deterrent punishment would seem to be established. This is borne out also by the deeper psychological studies of the psycho-analysts. Flugel explains that deterrent punishments are the ally of the law-abiding individual in his struggle to keep his own anti-social wishes under control. "The criminal, by his flouting of law and moral rule, constitutes a temptation to the *id* [*i.e.* to our own unconscious and primitive wishes]; it is as though we said to ourselves, 'if he does it, why should not we?' This stirring of criminal impulses within ourselves calls for an answering effort on the part of the super-ego, which can best achieve its object by showing that 'crime doesn't pay'. This, in turn, can be done most conveniently and completely by a demonstration on the person of the criminal. By punishing him we are not only showing him that he can't 'get away with it' but holding him up as a terrifying example to our own tempted and rebellious selves."[26]

The limitations of deterrent punishments must still be borne in mind. There is much crime, especially of the more serious sort, on which it has little effect, and many criminals, particularly of the more persistent type, on whom it will make little impression. Above all, we need at some point in the process of treatment to move beyond it. We do not wish to have in our midst a growing and explosive group of dissidents, kept in reluctant subjection by the constant threat of punishment. We need to set in motion some radical change within each criminal, which will make the social tensions inseparable from deterrent punishment a little less necessary. Thus deterrence should lead naturally to the consideration of ways of achieving reformation.

## Reformation

This concept has gradually begun to change its meaning over the past hundred and fifty years. To John Howard and many of those who followed him, reformation was at bottom a spiritual process. They did not preach at the prisoners: they laid more stress on example and changes for the better in the prison regime—but all to the end, as Mary Carpenter put it, of "touching the inner spirit".[27]

In other words, the criminal was to be treated as a free moral agent, and to be led to abandon his evil ways by the aid of religion and moral exhortation. Even as John Howard wrote, an Act was being passed (in 1773) which made it easier for the justices to appoint salaried chaplains in the county jails, and Howard noted with pleasure that most of them had acted upon it.[28] Great preachers like John and Charles Wesley prayed with and ministered to the prisoners.[29]

It would be misleading to suggest that this kind of attitude is no longer important. The chaplain is still believed to fulfil an important reformative purpose in British prisons and Borstals, and there is strong official pressure on prisoners to attend religious services.[30] The persistence of retributive motives in punishment also testify to the persistence of the belief in a free moral will. But this "moralistic" attitude has been forced to retreat in the face of the growing body of knowledge about the causes of crime. Scientific criminology, set securely on the right path by Lombroso, has become the advocate of scientific methods of reformation. Attention is being directed increasingly towards education, and the improvement of adverse environmental circumstances. Developments in psychology have led to a new appreciation of the therapeutic importance of personal relationships—with, for example, the probation officer or the Borstal housemaster. Psychological treatment proper is already acknowledged to be necessary, though only in the more obviously abnormal cases.

This does not mean that there is no room for punishment as a reformative measure. That issue still has to be decided. Some of the drawbacks of punishment from the point of view of reformation are being realised, and its positive value is obviously less than had once been thought. Nevertheless, it probably has its value, on condition that it is used very discriminately indeed.

On the whole, however, for many criminologists "reformation" is rapidly becoming synonymous with "cure". The criminal is no longer a "bad man" but a "sick man". Some see great dangers in a development such as this. It is argued that if the criminal is encouraged to believe that the fault lies in his circumstances rather than in himself, even such will to improve as he may have will be sapped. Even wider consequences may follow. If such a determinist philosophy is widely accepted, the moral fibre of the whole community may be damaged.[31] Even criminologists are not immune from these doubts, for Dr Mannheim finds it necessary to say: "But on principle to divorce the idea of punishment by the state from moral considerations has, in the long run, proved a fatal error. Only on a moral basis is it possible to argue with the law-breaker".[32]

These arguments have about them all the appeal of the familiar and the well established. At the same time there is no reason why they should prevent the criminologist from continuing with his researches on a completely empirical basis. If moral restraints are important, they will be vindicated.

## Prevention

Traditionally the word "prevention" has been associated with the deterrent function of punishment. "General prevention" was the deterrent effect which the punishment of the criminal "as an example", had upon the rest of the population. "Individual prevention" was its effect upon the criminal himself, either as a deterrent, or if he was imprisoned, also as a physical restraint for the duration of his sentence.

As in "preventive medicine", however, the idea of prevention in criminology is now more appropriately applied to the remedying of the basic conditions in our society out of which criminal potentialities spring. This is prevention in a more fundamental sense than the mere repression of criminal tendencies. Here the notion of punishment has probably least scope of all. At this point also the teriritory of criminology ends, for here its frontiers meet those of the neighbouring provinces of genetics, psychology, and general social reform.

### NOTES TO CHAPTER IX

1. Westermarck, E., *Origin and Development of the Moral Ideas*, 1908, pp. 356 ff.
2. Wills, W. D., *Hawkspur Experiment*, 1941, pp. 89-90.
3. Hobhouse, L. T., *Morals in Evolution*, 1929, Chapter III. Hobhouse, L. T., Wheeler, G. C., and Ginsberg, M., *Material Culture and Social Institutions of the Simpler Peoples*, 1930, pp. 53 ff.
4. Mannheim, H., *Dilemma of Penal Reform*, 1939, pp. 224-5.
5. *Ibid.*
6. Stephen wrote: "It is highly desirable that criminals should be hated, that the punishment inflicted upon them should be so contrived as to give expression to that hatred and to justify it". Quoted, Page, L., *Crime and the Community*, 1937, p. 71.
7. Kenny, C. S., *Outlines of Criminal Law*, 1902, pp. 33 ff.
8. Quoted, *ibid.*, p. 34.
9. Goodheart, A. L., *English Law and the Moral Law*, 1953, p. 93.
10. Temple, W., *Ethics of Penal Action: First Clarke Hall Lectures*, 1934.
11. See, for instance, Hobhouse, L. T., *Elements of Social Justice*.
12. See below, p. 217.
13. Seagle, W., *History of Law*, 1946, p. 126.
14. Jackson, R. M., in Radzinowicz, L., and Turner, J. W. C. (eds.), *Modern Approach to Criminal Law*, 1945, pp. 262 ff.
15. Flugel, J. C., *Man, Morals and Society*, 1945, p. 169.
16. *Op. cit.*, pp. 26-7.
17. Trevelyan, G. M., *English Social History*, 1945, pp. 348 ff.
18. This view is not confined to psycho-analysts, but is a commonplace of modern psychological thought.
19. Above, pp. 51 ff.
20. Above, p. 45.
21. Benney, M., *Low Company*, 1936, p. 291.
22. See pp. 16 ff.
23. *Criminal Statistics*, 1953, *Cmd.* 9199. Howe has estimated that 35-40 per cent. are cleared up. (*J. Royal Stat. Soc.*, **114**: 2, 1951, p. 160.)

24. Hurwitz, S., *Criminology*, 1952, p. 303.

25. *Royal Commission on Capital Punishment, Minutes of Evidence*, 1949, pp. 797 ff.

26. *Op. cit.*, p. 169.

27. Carpenter, Mary, *Reformatory Schools for the Children of the Dangerous and Perishing Classes*, 1851.

28. Hinde, R. S. E., *The British Penal System*, 1951, p. 17.

29. Simon, J. S., *John Wesley and the Religious Societies*, 1921.

30. See Fox, L., *British Prison and Borstal Systems*, 1952, Chapter XII.

31. Goodheart, *op. cit.*

32. *Op. cit.*, p. 21.

# CHAPTER X

## ORIGINS OF OUR PENAL SYSTEM

The criminologist cannot help but be a critic of the penal system so long as we continue to refine our understanding of the problems of treatment. He is, therefore, very prone to fall victim to that occupational disease of the reformer: the tendency to lose one's sense of proportion, and to see nothing good at all in the object of criticism. It would be well to be immunised against this in advance, and the best way of achieving this is perhaps to study the history of the present system, whereupon the very real progress which has been made will become apparent.

There has, of course, been some form of imprisonment from time immemorial. We read in the Old Testament of Joseph being imprisoned in Egypt, two thousand years before Christ.[1] But prison was always used in the ancient world as a means of safe custody pending trial or punishment, not as a form of punishment in itself. There were frequent exceptions to this general rule, but its status as an accepted principle was confirmed when Justinian enacted it as Roman Law in the fifth century A.D.

This was the prevailing attitude towards imprisonment throughout the Middle Ages; not until the nineteenth century, with the emergence of the penitentiary movement, was it used as a penal instrument in itself. Meanwhile actual punishments ranged from forms of public humiliation, such as the stocks and the pillory, to flogging, banishment, and death. According to Blackstone, death was the penalty for more than one hundred and sixty offences in 1769.[2]

### Early Prisons

Not that the prisons of any country in Europe were at this time really suitable for use as a means of treatment. In eighteenth-century England, the county gaols were situated in all sorts of unlikely buildings: "Anything might serve, from the cellar of an inn to the gatehouse of an abbey".[3] They were the nominal responsibility of the justices, but these worthy men disposed of their interests to private contractors, who ran them as profit-making enterprises, making their profits out of the fees they were able to charge the prisoners. A man would have to pay a fee on admission, and another on discharge. He could be charged for the putting-on of irons—and for taking them off again. Food, sometimes all food, and sometimes all except a bare minimum, had to be paid for. And the man who could not pay, soon found that his hunger, his chains, and his misery were greatly increased.

Naturally, like any astute business man, the jailer saved on his overheads whenever he could. There was no separation according to sex or age. Ventilation was often non-existent, and dirt and stench abounded. Disease was rampant; typhus was known as "gaol fever", and killed a quarter of the prisoners every year.[4]

Such conditions must, in themselves, have been demoralising enough, but the jailer, in his avarice, added further refinements in the shape of the brothel and the tap. Riotous and degrading scenes were common. John Howard wrote, "If it were the wish and aim of magistrates to effect the destruction present and future of young delinquents, they could not devise a more effectual method, than to confine them so long in our prisons".[5] Here was no potential agency of reform, but a social evil of the first magnitude.

## The Bridewells

For a time it had seemed likely that the Houses of Correction, or Bridewells, developed during the latter part of the sixteenth century, would provide the reformative institution which was needed. They were not originally intended for criminals, but for ne'er-do-wells and vagrants, who were to be made to work for a living, and trained in good working habits. The first Bridewell (hence the name) was the Palace of Bridewell, given to the City of London in 1552 by Edward VI as a place of correction for the "thriftless poor".

Others followed throughout the country, and indeed throughout Europe.[6] So well did they compare with the prisons of the time that Lord Coke, a great judge, wrote: "Few or none were committed to the common gaol . . . but they came out worse than they went in. But few are committed to the House of Correction . . . but they come out better".[7] The Bridewells were not farmed out, but were administered by the justices. The discipline seems to have been strict, but wholesome and constructive. Recalcitrants were punished, but there were also well-organised industrial departments, and for boys, training in skilled trades. Nearly two hundred years before the progressive stage system in prison[8] was even thought of, the inmates of the Houses of Correction were offered the prospect of more attractive work as a reward for hard work and good behaviour. The incentive of wages was added later.

Gradually, however, they became corrupted. Funds for their maintenance became inadequate. The justices and the public lost interest. Work programmes became less effective, and eventually ceased. The distinction between gaol and House of Correction became blurred. Thus an Act of 1630 provided that the House of Correction should adjoin the common gaol, in order that it might be utilised to provide work for the prisoners, and in 1730 the justices were empowered to commit both vagrants and criminals to either at their discretion. To all intents and purposes, the Bridewell as a distinct kind of institution, had disappeared.

## The Reformers

A Dark Age then supervened, and lasted for another forty years. Not until 1767 did ideas of reform stir once more, with the translation of Beccaria's famous *Essay on Crime and Punishment.* This adumbrated a principle of punishment which was so advanced that we await its full realisation even now. The only justification for punishment, said Beccaria, is the protection of society by the prevention of crime. He left no room at all for the motive of retribution.

JOHN HOWARD. Among those to whom Beccaria's ideas came as a clarion call was John Howard, soon to be High Sheriff of Bedfordshire. He saw very clearly the evils implicit in the farming-out system, and pleaded for its abandonment in his own county. But the Justices of Bedfordshire demanded a precedent before they would agree to any change. It was to provide them with this, that Howard embarked upon those visits to prisons throughout the country, which he described in *The State of the Prisons.*[9]

Howard found no precedents for reform during his travels, but much to cause him agony of the soul, and he therefore set out to alleviate these evils by all the means in his power. He argued for the segregation of women, young offenders, and debtors from hardened criminals, and for separate cells for sleeping. He urged that all prisoners should be employed in useful labour. Taps should be abolished, and gaolers should be carefully chosen for their honesty and humanity, and should receive an adequate salary. Proper medical treatment, and better standards of cleanliness, light, ventilation, and sanitation should be enforced.[10]

With the aid of Alexander Popham, the member for Taunton, two reforming Acts were actually passed in 1774, and individual followers of Howard, such as Sir George Onesiphorus Paul of Gloucestershire, persuaded their brother magistrates to institute reforms. But a few years later, Howard himself observed that the Popham Acts had been strictly obeyed in only fifteen out of 130 prisons. When he caught the plague and died in 1790, while studying the incidence of this disease in Eastern Europe,[11] most English prisons were still largely untouched by the hand of reform.

Howard's influence upon the minds of others, however, was tremendous. He had lit a torch which his followers carried throughout the world. Penal reforms since have owed everything to his inspiration, and not a little to his ideas.

BENTHAM AND THE PANOPTICON. Prominent among the reformers who followed him were Jeremy Bentham, the great radical philosopher, and Elizabeth Fry. Bentham's many-sided genius gave birth to his plan for a "panopticon", a prison so designed that the director could keep the prisoners under constant surveillance, and direct everything they did in accordance with the best penal principles. This was to be achieved by seating him in a central observation chamber encircled by tiers of windowed and lighted cells.[12] The government were at first attracted by the scheme, but later abandoned it. When the first penitentiary at Millbank did appear in 1821, it bore no resemblance to what Bentham, appropriately applying a mechanical metaphor, had called his "mill for grinding rogues honest and idle men industrious".

As for the spirit which should inform a prison, Bentham, in spite of his utilitarian philosophy, proved less of a purist than Beccaria. Although he agreed with the latter that punishment should be imposed only for reformation or deterrence, he believed that the victim should be allowed, if only as a by-product, to enjoy the satisfaction of feeling revenged.[13] The reconciliation of these two principles provides a pretty problem in logic and ethics.

At a more practical level, the great Utilitarian pleaded for careful classification and for work which would lead the prisoner to "love labour instead of being taught to loathe it",[14] but ranged himself at the same time beside those who wished to preserve the discredited system of private contractors. In few of his proposals for social reform did Bentham's doctrinal belief in "enlightened self-interest" lead him further from a realistic appraisal of the situation than here. Like Howard, few of his plans reached fruition in his lifetime, but his influence entered strongly into the ferment of ideas out of which practical reforms did emerge in due course. And many of those reforms bore the clear stamp of that rational and utilitarian approach to social questions which we owe to him.

ELIZABETH FRY. Elizabeth Fry was a very different kind of person. She was no theorist, but a compassionate woman with the courage and determination to tackle apparently insoluble problems, and the ability to capture the hearts of those whom she sought to help.[15]

The state of Newgate Prison had long been causing disquiet to philanthropically minded people. As long ago as 1702, a deputation from the newly formed Society for the Promoting of Christian Knowledge, led by a Dr Bray, had visited it and other London prisons, and shocked by what they had seen, had published exhaustive proposals for improvement.[16] These had little effect. Reforms were introduced in the middle of the century by a pious keeper named Abel Dagge; but by 1813 its condition was again such that Stephen Grellet, a travelling Quaker preacher, who visited the prison then, could still describe it as an "abode of woe and misery". It was at Grellet's suggestion that the delicately nurtured Quaker lady, Elizabeth Fry, began her work among the women prisoners there.

She set up a Ladies' Prison Committee among her Quaker friends, and with its help provided the women prisoners with comfort and understanding, the decent clothing so necessary for their self-respect, and the opportunity of work. A prison school was organised for the children. Sincere religious feeling pervaded all the proceedings, and seems often to have been communicated to the prisoners themselves. As a result, the women's side at Newgate was transformed. A place which had previously been called "Hell above Ground" had become peaceful, clean, and industrious.

Mrs Fry did not rest content with what had been achieved. She sat up with condemned women during their last hours, offering them what consolation she could. She extended her operations to the Hulks, floating prisons on the Thames, and effected the same miracle there. She had become a person to be reckoned with, and was called as an expert witness before a House of Commons Committee. She helped to set up Ladies' Committees at other prisons, and travelled far and wide on her civilising mission. Such influential persons as Frederick William IV of Prussia admired and were influenced by her.

She did not stand entirely alone. In 1816 the Society for the Reformation of Prison Discipline was founded, under the leadership of Thomas Fowell Buxton and Samuel Hoare. This society was the lineal ancestor of the present Howard League for Penal Reform. Fowell Buxton was himself an outspoken critic of the state of the prisons. "Punishments," he declared, "are inflicted that crime may be prevented, and crime is prevented by the reformation of the criminal."[17]  No present-day criminologist could improve on that as a statement of principle.

Yet these remained the views of reformers, of those exceptional individuals whose religious or humanitarian feelings made them detest the abuses they saw about them, and want to do something about it.  Their views were not typical of their time; most of their contemporaries who gave any thought to the question of the punishment of crime, would probably have found the views of the Rev. Sidney Smith more congenial. "Prisons," he wrote, "are really meant to keep the multitude in order, and to be a terror to evildoers . . . There must be a great deal of solitude; coarse food; a dress of shame; hard, incessant, irksome eternal labour; a planned and regulated and unrelenting exclusion of happiness and comfort."[18] The prison system was about to enter, not an epoch of sympathy and reformative endeavour, but of grim and soul-destroying deterrence.

### Transportation

Meanwhile the expedient of transportation was being tried. Banishment was, of course, a very ancient form of punishment, but with the development of the American colonies, it took a new turn. From the beginning of the seventeenth century, "dissolute persons" (in the words of an Act of James I) were transported direct to America, where they were sold into bondage to the colonists.[19] Transportation became an alternative to other forms of punishment, eventually, as an act of grace, a commutation of the death penalty, and by 1663 there were so many criminals in Virginia that the colonists lived in daily fear of revolt.

The American Declaration of Independence in 1776, therefore, caused an immediate crisis.  What was to be done with the large numbers of offenders who had previously been shipped off to the colonies?  As an immediate measure, prisoners were confined on old ships, the Hulks, in the Thames, where they could be employed in clearing the river channel.  But providentially Captain Cook discovered another New World, and in 1784 transportation to Australia began.

The first Governor of New South Wales, Arthur Phillip, was a humane man, but lack of organisation in London and unbelievable over-crowding and squalor on board the transport ships, made his task an impossible one. Many died en route, and when they reached Australia there was famine, and the most rigid and cruel discipline.

Gradually, however, order and system began to appear, reaching its zenith under Sir George Arthur, Lieutenant-Governor of Van Diemen's Land (now Tasmania) 1824-36. The administration was highly centralised and efficient. Discipline was hard, for while a convict could earn an amelioration of his condition by good behaviour, or perhaps even a remission of part of his sentence, the intractable received punishments which were, in the words of Arthur himself, "as severe as they could be afflicted on a man". According to Grünhut, only about one-quarter of the convicts avoided such punishments.[20] It was small wonder that many committed capital offences in order to secure release from their misery.

At the beginning of their sentences the convicts would be employed directly by the government, in clearing the bush, building roads, or other public works, but later would be assigned to colonists as unpaid servants. This assignment system led to many abuses; a convict's condition would depend almost entirely upon the sort of master he obtained. Later he might even be given an appointment in the police, or be freed. A rudimentary system of what we now call "progressive stages" was thus being applied.

Transportation had often been attacked by the reformers, though oddly enough, in the light of what we know of conditions in the settlements, often on the ground of undue leniency. There is little doubt, however, that the general public favoured it as an easy way of getting rid of their more troublesome fellow-citizens. Therefore, in spite of a scathing denunciation of the system by a Select Committee of the House of Commons in 1838, and a determined attempt to secure its abolition, much of it was retained. The assignment system was abandoned, and convicts were no longer to be sent to New South Wales, but Van Diemen's Land and Norfolk Island continued to receive their quotas of reluctant immigrants.

FAILURE OF TRANSPORTATION. But during the 'forties, the colonies themselves took a hand in the game. They refused to take more convicts, and from that moment the system was doomed. In 1853, penal servitude at home was instituted as an alternative to transportation, and four years later all further transportation was forbidden. Penal servitude remained with us until 1948, by which time it differed hardly at all from ordinary imprisonment, and as a separate form of sentence was a complete anomaly.

In the end transportation proved a failure because too many irreconcilable aims were being sought through it. The assignment system made nonsense of any theory of just and equal retribution. Convict labour was not of the hard-working, self-reliant sort, for which the healthy development of a new colony calls. The rigours of life in the penal settlements were designed to deter potential offenders in Britain, but the remoteness of Australia from the mother country made it difficult even for those in official positions in Britain to know just what was happening there. This kind of treatment, in its turn, was not likely to effect much of a reformation, in the sense of a real change of heart, in those who were subjected to it.

ALEXANDER MACONOCHIE. One outstanding figure and one seminal idea only could be placed to its credit. In 1840 Captain Alexander Maconochie became Superintendent of Norfolk Island. He took over more than a thousand convicts who had been removed there because they had proved troublesome in New South Wales or Van Diemen's Land. Maconochie had the worst problem of all, and yet by sympathetic handling and an appeal to the men's better feelings, by the abandonment of savage punishments and the inculcation of a high moral code in his officers, he succeeded, in the four years during which he ran Norfolk Island, in showing how much good a penal settlement could do if its function was solely and unambiguously that of reformation.

He himself believed that the most powerful of the weapons to his hand was his Marks System. Its aim was to give the prisoner a real motive for reform, by making it possible for him, through his own efforts, to shorten his sentence. As he made progress, he would be awarded marks, until at last he had earned enough to secure his release. In the hands of Maconochie, the important idea of progressive stages, towards which the transportation system had been fumbling, came to life as a potent incentive.

## The Irish System

However, there was no legal authority for the remission of sentences in this way. Not for another fifty years, with the passage of the Prison Act 1898, was remission recognised by the law of this country. In Ireland, however, under Sir Walter Crofton, it was adopted, together with a system of progressive stages by which the prisoner could earn more and more freedom, until at last he was liberated under the supervision of the police.

Crofton must have been well aware of the effect of long prison sentences in developing what has been called, rather uncouthly, "institutionalisation". When a man is released after a long period of incarceration, during which all his contacts with the outside world have been severed, he is at first lost and bewildered. He misses the security of the prison routine, and is unused to assuming any responsibility, for in prison all important decisions are made for him by his captors. Moreover, after all those years away from normal society, he finds it not only trying, but also strange and rather frightening. He is in no condition to stand on his own feet and resist further temptation.[21]

Crofton tackled this problem by inserting into his stage system an intermediate stage, immediately before actual release. The convict would be freed from the ordinary disciplinary system, except for the ultimate penalty of demotion to a lower stage. He would do his work without supervision, and the work itself would approximate to that which he was likely to obtain after his discharge. The aim was to expose him to some of the difficulties and temptations he would meet after discharge, both to accustom him to these conditions and to give the authorities some idea of how far he was ready to go out into the world.

## A New Penal Philosophy

The progressive stage system was not entirely overlooked in this country. It found a place in the system of penal servitude at home, which replaced transportation, but the main interests of penal administrators lay elsewhere. They had finally accepted the idea of a penal and reformative, rather than simply a custodial, prison service, but its main features were to be solitary confinement and deterrence.

The idea of a Penitentiary, a government-administered prison which should set itself a positive reformative aim, had had a long period of incubation. Acts passed in 1779 and 1791 all proved abortive, and not till 1821 was Millbank Prison completed. By this time the Hulks, which had never been intended to be more than a temporary measure, were becoming so over-crowded that action to provide further accommodation was unavoidable.

SEPARATE CONFINEMENT VERSUS THE SILENT SYSTEM. This development gave new point to a long-standing controversy about prison methods. Should prisons be based upon the principle of separate confinement, or ought provision to be made for groups of prisoners to work together?

This issue had been debated even in the time of John Howard. Howard himself, contemplating the over-crowding and promiscuity of the county gaols, was in favour of separate confinement at night, but argued that there should be a common day-room, and provision for work in association. Others, however, led by the eccentric Jonas Hanway (whose many services to his fellow-countrymen included the introduction of the umbrella into this country), were in favour of a more austere regime, involving complete separation day and night.

It was in America, however, that these two approaches were first put to the test. Quaker Pennsylvania, as part of its reform of the notorious Walnut Street Jail in Philadelphia, instituted a regime of solitary confinement in 1790. This was partly the result of a misunderstanding of John Howard, whose ideas the reformers had accepted, but it must also have been a plan which accorded well with the Quaker religious conception of the "inner light". For it was hoped that solitude would enable the prisoner to meditate upon his misdeeds, and to accomplish a real change within himself. One is reminded of the meditation which is enjoined upon the members of religious orders as a means of spiritual improvement.

The isolation of the more serious offenders was complete; for minor offenders it was confined to the first part of the sentence, being then held in reserve as a punishment. Many visitors from Europe brought back glowing accounts of what they saw. Only the more sensitive, like Dickens, who attacked the system in "American Notes", saw the dreadful apathy which lay behind the orderliness and the meek demeanour of the prisoners. To normally gregarious human beings, there could be no deprivation as severe as solitary confinement. And as the prisoners adapted themselves to it by introversion, they became less and less able to cope with normal social life. With the best will in the world, the pious Quakers of Pennsylvania had ended by imposing upon their prisoners an inconceivably cruel punishment. In the attempt to reform their criminals, they succeeded only in dehumanising them.[22]

It was not on these grounds, however, that the Pennsylvania system was rejected in other States of the Union. It suffered from serious practical disadvantages which militated against its general adoption. Building costs for a cellular prison were high. It was also difficult to provide suitable work for prisoners who had to be isolated in their cells all day long, and prison industries were often a valuable source of profit to the authorities.   Many States, therefore, preferred the Auburn system, so-called because it was first developed at Auburn Prison in New York State, after the collapse there of an experiment in solitary confinement.

Under the Auburn plan, prisoners were confined in separate cells at night, but worked in groups during the day.   However, no talking was permitted, and this rule of silence was enforced by severe disciplinary measures, including "such regulations as down-cast eyes, lockstep [close formation] marching, no prisoners ever face-to-face, no talking, and constant activity when out of the cells".[23]

VICTORY OF THE SEPARATE SYSTEM.   These were the two systems which fought for supremacy in Britain during the first half of the nineteenth century, and if the victory eventually went to the Pennsylvania system, it must be put down to the general revulsion against the abuses of the "congregate system" in the county gaols. Sir George Onesiphorus Paul's Gloucester gaol, the House of Correction at Southwell, and various other model institutions had taken the separate form, and in the contrast which they presented to the general disorder elsewhere, they provided a very convincing argument for separate confinement.   Millbank, and later (1852) Pentonville, provided separate cells, and the British version of the "solitary system", the "separate system", began to take shape.

Many of its advocates argued that it was more humane than the Pennsylvania system proper in that it allowed contact between the prisoner, and the chaplain and other officers.   As the Rev. Hinde states, there was probably little practical difference as far as the prisoners were concerned.[24]   Certainly the most rigorous separation from the other prisoners was insisted upon.   While being exercised in the prison yard, the prisoners wore masks, and in chapel each man sat in a stall enclosed on three sides, which effectually shut him off from his fellow-worshippers.

These unnatural conditions of life seem to have led to a great increase in insanity among prisoners.   Mayhew and Binny calculate that for the period 1842-50, the rate of insanity in Pentonville, where the separate system was first fully applied, was ten times as great as during the same period in the country as a whole.[25]

Deterrent motives were very much to the fore.   The views of the Rev. Sidney Smith have already been quoted; the deterrent aspects of separate confinement were emphasised by him and many others.

Programmes of work were also designed to deter rather than to stimulate. Useless and monotonous forms of toil, such as the "crank" and the "treadmill" were advocated. To some extent they were necessitated by separate confinement, which ruled out the prison workshop and many of the more constructive forms of occupation, but the principle of deterrent punishment also lent them support.

CENTRALISATION. The next fifty years showed a steady development towards centralisation and uniformity on the basis of deterrence and the separate system. In 1835 the first Inspectors of Prisons were appointed. From the beginning they were convinced supporters of the new regime. They attacked the "silent system", and pointed out that in Coldbaths Prison, where it had been adopted, there were, in the year 1836, no fewer than 5,138 punishments imposed for the single purpose of enforcing silence. Some local prisons which had prosperous and lucrative workshops attached, resisted the New Order, but it continued to spread, and in 1877, when the local gaols were finally taken over from the justices by the State, it became the rule.

Edmund du Cane was the first Chairman of the Prison Commission, set up to control the new national prison system. He soon showed himself an able administrator. The organisation of all the prisons was tightened up, and the less suitable ones closed. However, the handling of human beings calls for imagination and sympathy as well as efficiency. During the du Cane period, both of these humane qualities went into eclipse.

Detailed regulations on treatment and discipline were drawn up and enforced for the whole country. A rigid progressive stage system was introduced. Isolation and unconstructive hard labour became obligatory. During the du Cane period, lasting for twenty years, our prisons became soulless machines, aiming to place the same stamp upon all the sensitive and infinitely variable human beings committed to their charge.

**The Gladstone Committee**

The blame was not all to be laid at du Cane's door; this was the system which Parliament had itself prescribed in the Acts of 1865 and 1877. His fault lay not in being a highly successful administrator of this policy, but in being nothing else.

By 1895, an ageing du Cane had become more and more despotic, and after press attacks upon him, a Departmental Committee, the

Gladstone Committee, reported in favour of immediate changes.[26] The most significant of its conclusions was that which challenged the uniformity of which du Cane was so proud, and enunciated instead the principle of individualisation of treatment. "We think," stated the Committee, "that the system should be made more elastic, more capable of being adapted to the special cases of individual prisoners; that prison discipline should be more effectually designed to maintain, stimulate or awaken the higher susceptibilities of prisoners, to develop their moral instincts, to train them in orderly and industrious habits, and whenever possible, to turn them out of prison better men and women physically and morally than when they came in." Du Cane's life-work had fallen in ruins about his head.

The old man retired, and was replaced by Ruggles Brise; and the Act of 1898 replaced the New Order by a newer one. This took the first timid steps towards a more elastic system of treatment, by placing much more power in the hands of the Prison Commission to determine the details of policy. Previously all such details involved legislation; now the Secretary of State was empowered to make the necessary regulations. It is a pity that a similar discretion has still not been accorded to the governors of the individual prisons, for it is here, in the "fighting line", that individualisation of treatment must take place. Even to-day, although the system is far less centralised than in du Cane's time, treatment is still hampered and hidebound by regulations and red tape.

As a further step towards individualisation, the courts were to pass sentences of imprisonment to be served in either the first, second, or third Division, in order of increasing severity. This proved of little value, and has now been abandoned. By the same Act, the remission of part of a sentence for good behaviour at last received legislative sanction.

### NOTES TO CHAPTER X

1. *Genesis*, Chapter 39.
2. *Blackstone's Commentaries*, 1769, IV, p. 18.
3. Fox, L., *English Prison and Borstal Systems*, 1952, p. 20.
4. *Ibid.*, p. 21.
5. Howard, John, *State of the Prisons*, 1784, p. 8.
6. See Grunhut, M., *Penal Reform*, 1948, pp. 17 ff., for developments on the Continent.
7. Coke, Sir E., *Institutes of the Laws of England*, II, p. 729.
8. See below, pp. 134 ff., 173, 183.
9. First published in Warrington in 1777. Subsequent editions, incorporating the results of further investigations, appeared in 1780 and 1784.

10. *State of the Prisons, op. cit.*

11. He had published the results of earlier enquiries in this field in: *An Account of the Principal Lazarettos in Europe*, 1789.

12. "Panopticon or the Inspection House", *Works IV*, 1791, pp. 37 ff.

13. *Theory of Legislation*, 1891 (trans. from the French of E. Dumont), pp. 309-10.

14. *Works IV*, p. 144.

15. For an account of her life, see Whitney, Janet, *Elizabeth Fry*, 1937.

16. "An Essay towards ye Reformation of Newgate and the other Prisons in and about London"—reprinted in Hinde, R. S. E., *The British Penal System*, 1951, pp. 21 ff.

17. Buxton, T. F., *Inquiry whether Crime and Misery are prevented or produced by our Present System of Prison Discipline*, 1818.

18. Smith, Sydney, *Works*, 1845, I, p. 459.

19. Nominally it was their labour which was sold, but no real distinction is involved.

20. *Op. cit.*, p. 77.

21. Dendrickson, G., and Thomas, F., in *The Truth about Dartmoor*, 1954, pp. 200-1, give us an inkling of how this looks from the point of view of the discharged prisoner.

22. Barnes, H. E., *The Evolution of Penology in Pennsylvania*, 1927, contains the most complete account of developments in this State from the colonial period to the end of the nineteenth century.

23. McKelvey, Blake, *American Prisons*, 1936, p. 8.

24. *Op. cit.*, p. 112.

25. Mayhew, H., and Binny, J., *Criminal Prisons of London*, 1862, p. 104.

26. *Report of the Departmental Committee on Prisons*, 1895.

# CHAPTER XI

## THE PATTERN EMERGES

The Report of the Gladstone Committee was a milestone in English penal history. It defined the aims of a progressive penal system, and although the realisation of these aims proceeded only slowly, it was a gain to have had them so clearly acknowledged.

### New Kinds of Institution

The outcome was to be seen in two main trends during the early years of the new century. One was concerned with the better classification of offenders, and the establishment of specialised form of treatment for the different classes. The other was a definite movement away from the prison solution altogether. Both approaches are represented in the English penal system as we see it to-day.

BORSTAL. Ruggles Brise, du Cane's successor as Chairman of the Prison Commission, himself experimented with special training institutions for adolescent prisoners, modelled on the Elmira Reformatory in New York State.[1] After initial experiments at Bedford Prison, the first of these new institutions was set up in 1902 in the village of Borstal, near Rochester in Kent. The village eventually gave its name to the system. The extension of the Borstal system was provided for in the Prevention of Crimes Act 1908,[2] which also instituted Preventive Detention for persistent criminals. There are now (at the end of 1953) twenty Borstal institutions of various kinds, and the system is world-famous.[3]

PREVENTIVE DETENTION. The aim of preventive detention was the protection of the public. The habitual criminal did not appear to be amenable to treatment, and must, therefore, be shut up in prison, where he could do no further harm, for a prolonged period. This was to be achieved by providing that, if a person who was sentenced to penal servitude had had three previous convictions since reaching the age of sixteen, the court could impose, in addition to the sentence of penal servitude, a further sentence of between five and ten years preventive detention.[4] In acknowledgment of the fact that the latter was preventive not punitive, the convict was to receive extra privileges and comforts when he had completed the first (penal servitude) half of his sentence.

Comparatively little use was made of this provision by the courts. In 1913-14, the average daily population in preventive detention was only 171, and by 1947 it had fallen to 31. It was not in accordance with the tradition of just retribution, which dominates judicial thinking in this country, to impose two penalties for one crime, and on the whole the courts were not prepared to do it.

### Trends away from Imprisonment

Many, however, believed prison in any form to be incompatible with a reformative approach. In his evidence before the Gladstone Committee, Sir Godfrey Lushington said, "I regard as unfavourable to reformation the status of a prisoner throughout his whole career; the crushing of self-respect, the starving of all moral instinct he may possess, the absence of all opportunity to do or receive a kindness, the continual association with none but criminals . . . the forced labour and the denial of liberty. I believe the true mode of reforming a man is exactly in the opposite direction of all these. But, of course, this is a mere idea; it is quite impracticable in a prison. In fact, the unfavourable features I have mentioned are inseparable from prison life".

Such a conclusion must have been inescapable to anyone who could look at the prisons of the time with a detached eye. They were predominantly punitive and deterrent in character. Many will go even further, and say, with Lushington, that they can never hope to be anything else. They are no longer harsh and cruel, as during the du Cane era, but they do seem, from their very nature, to be ill-adapted for reformative work.

DEVELOPMENT OF PROBATION. Those who have felt like this, have directed their efforts towards keeping offenders out of prison, and their greatest achievement in this direction has undoubtedly been the development of probation.

From the 1870s, in a devoted effort to break the vicious circle of sentence, contamination, and sentence, agents of the Church of England Temperance Society had been working in the police courts. They had no official standing, but the Summary Jurisdiction Act of 1879 and the Probation of First Offenders Act 1887 had permitted magistrates to suspend sentence in suitable cases, and so enabled the Society's reclamatory work to take place on an informal basis.

The work prospered and expanded. By 1907 it was well established, and, by means of the Probation of Offenders Act of that year, it was for the first time put on a proper basis.   Probation, like so many of our social services, had had first to serve its apprenticeship as a privately sponsored experiment.   It had proved its worth, and was now to be acknowledged as a service which the State itself ought to maintain.   Under the terms of the Act, courts were authorised to appoint their own probation officers, and the nature of probation was carefully defined.   The courts were empowered also to order that an offender should be under the supervision of a probation officer, something which had previously depended upon more informal arrangements—though lip-service continued to be paid to the idea that the probationer accepted probation of his own free will by the proviso that he must give his consent before an order could be made.

The Act of 1908 had one major defect: it did no more than advise the appointment of probation officers; no court was bound to appoint one until 1925.[5]   Fourteen years after the Act, nearly a quarter of our police courts still had no probation officer.[6]   Nevertheless, probation has gained ground steadily, especially in the treatment of juveniles.   By the end of 1953, there were 1,182 full-time probation officers in England and Wales, and 45,741 probation orders in force.[7]

OTHER DEVELOPMENTS.   Other statutes passed during this period which tended towards this same end, of keeping people out of the corrupting atmosphere of prison, included the Mental Deficiency Act 1913.   This recognised the futility of sending the mental defective to prison, and provided for supervision or institutional placement instead.   The Criminal Justice Act 1914 allowed time for the payment of fines, and the Money Payments Act 1935 required magistrates to enquire into the means of an offender who had failed to pay a fine, before committing him to prison in default.   These two Acts together must have saved many thousands of petty offenders from prison sentences.

### Keeping Children Out of Prison

By the great "Children's Charter", the Children's Act 1908, the first statutory limitations were also placed upon the power of the courts to imprison juveniles.   "Children", *i.e.* under the age of fourteen, were not to be committed to prison under any circumstances, and "young persons", those aged fourteen and under sixteen, only if they were "unruly or depraved".   Now, under the terms of the Criminal Justice Act 1948, there are restrictions on imprisonment up to the age of twenty-one.

REFORMATORY SCHOOL MOVEMENT. Much, however, had already been done by this time to keep children out of prison. As early as 1788, the Philanthropic Society had set up a family-type institution, to look after the children of convicts, as well as juvenile offenders. In 1817 came the Farm Colony at Stretton-on-Dunsmore, with the aim of rescuing children from prison and redeeming them.

The State lagged sadly behind. Until 1838, children committed to prison were sent to the common gaol to mix with confirmed criminals, prostitutes, and the rest. Parkhurst was set aside as a special prison for juveniles in that year, but it was no more than a prison. Such callousness was in sharp contrast to the indignation which many of our legislators were expressing at this time on behalf of Negro slaves, thousands of miles away. Even young children, it seems, had to be sacrificed on the twin altars of deterrence and retribution.

Private philanthropists such as Mary Carpenter of Bristol and Barwick Lloyd Baker in Gloucestershire showed the way, however, and as more and more voluntary institutions were opened, Parliament was forced to take cognisance of them. In 1857, the Reformatory Schools Act was passed to regulate them, and they were assigned a special Inspector of Prisons. Industrial schools, for pre-delinquents under the age of fourteen, were dealt with four years later. Voluntary philanthropy has kept its lead in this field; local authorities were not empowered to provide correctional schools until 1872, and even to-day about three-quarters are still in the hands of voluntary bodies.

Du Cane states that there were still a hundred children under the age of sixteen in prison in 1894, and until the 'nineties it was still necessary for all children committed to a reformatory, first to serve a few days in prison, but by this time there were many hundreds of children living under the milder and more benevolent rules of the residential school. By the turn of the century, probation had also "arrived", and is now used even more widely than the approved schools.[8]

JUVENILE COURTS. Potentially the most revolutionary step in the recognition of the special needs of the young offenders was the creation of juvenile courts by the Children's Act 1908. Our juvenile courts were based on developments in the United States (where the first juvenile court in the world, at Boston Mass., had been founded in 1899), but unlike their American counterparts, they retained their character as criminal courts, and with it the normal legal procedure of a court of criminal jurisdiction.

However, they were to be held in a different place from the adult court, and their hearings were to be private. Every care was to be taken to see that children appearing before the court did not come into contact with adult offenders. The juvenile court has been improved since, especially by the Children and Young Persons Act 1933, which provided for panels of magistrates with special experience of children, and restricted membership of juvenile courts to those who could qualify for inclusion on these panels.[9]

The aim of juvenile courts was to encourage new and less punitive attitudes towards juvenile offenders. For although they have had from the beginning many welfare functions in connection with the care of neglected and deprived children, it is clear that even in dealing with delinquents, the juvenile courts were intended from the beginning to be mainly concerned with their welfare. This has become explicit in the 1933 Act which requires that juvenile courts "shall have regard for the welfare of the child or young person, and shall in a proper case take steps for removing him from undesirable surroundings and for seeing that proper provision shall be made for his education and training".

It is anomalous to place such a duty upon a criminal court, and in attempting to carry it out, they can, as might have been expected, claim only partial success. Remaining courts of criminal jurisdiction, they do, as such, quite often show their teeth. Until children have been removed entirely from the purview of the criminal courts, a punitive element is bound to remain. Nor are the rules of evidence in such a court as well adapted as the more informal methods used by the Americans for exploring delicate and complicated social and family situations. But this issue will be discussed further in the next chapter.

### Contribution of Alexander Paterson

In spite of the Gladstone Committee, the Act of 1898, and the efforts of Ruggles Brise, and although the separate system had gradually been relaxed, to be finally abandoned under the pressure of productive needs during the war of 1914-18, British prisons were subjected to a further devastating attack in 1922 by a group of educated and intelligent men who had experienced imprisonment during the war as conscientious objectors. They described the regime under which they had served their sentences as one which was more likely to predispose prisoners to crime than to reform them, and likened it to the much despised du Cane regime.[10]

It was true that Ruggles Brise himself often openly espoused a retributive philosophy,[11] and boasted about the uniformity he maintained in the prisons. He was, it seems, too committed to the ideas of the older system to be wholehearted in his efforts on behalf of the new. Others were needed to nurse it through its long infancy, notably Alexander Paterson. Paterson was appointed a Prison Commissioner (he was never Chairman) in 1922, and immediately brought imagination and new vitality into the work of the Commission. He tried to define and restrict the retributive element in a prison sentence. "It must, however," he wrote, "be clear from the outset to all concerned that it is the sentence of imprisonment and not the treatment accorded in prison, that constitutes the punishment. Men come to prison as a punishment, not *for* punishment."[12]

He could, therefore, place the emphasis in prison on positive training, an aim to which our prison system is now thoroughly wedded. Training is a less high-flown concept than reformation or deterrence; it aims at fitting a man for a law-abiding life by practical measures such as education, work, controlled association with other prisoners, and the exercise of responsibility.[13]

Wakefield Prison was the first proving-ground for Paterson's concept of training, but the Wakefield system, as it was called, is now operated in seven regional training prisons, and has inspired the new sentence of corrective training in the Criminal Justice Act 1948. It breathed new life also into the Borstals. They became less prison-like, and in the 'thirties began, with Lowham Grange and North Sea Camp, the new tradition of open pioneering institutions.

## Criminal Justice Act 1948

A new Criminal Justice Bill was under discussion just before the war with Hitler, but the national emergency caused it to be pigeon-holed. In 1948, the substance of it was at last enacted,[14] and this Act, together with the Prison Act 1952 and relevant sections of the Children's Act 1933, forms the basis of our present system.

The 1948 Act has provided two new sentences for persistent offenders: corrective training, and preventive detention. The former is for persons of twenty-one or over, convicted of an offence punishable by at least two years' imprisonment, who have had two similar sentences since they were seventeen. The court must first consider any report submitted by the Prison Commission on their suitability for training, and may then pass a sentence of from two to four years corrective training.[15]

The new sentence of preventive detention replaces that contained in the Prevention of Crime Act 1908.   Unlike the earlier, and largely abortive system, preventive detention is not now to form part of a dual system in which it follows a prior sentence of imprisonment: there will now be only a single sentence, of between five and fourteen years preventive detention.   It may be passed upon any person aged not less than thirty, who is convicted of an offence punishable by imprisonment for at least two years, and who has had at least three similar convictions since the age of seventeen, and if the court is also satisfied that such a sentence is "expedient for the protection of the public".[16]   The preventive as against the corrective nature of this sentence is obvious from the wording of the final phrase.

The Act also abolished "hard labour", and penal servitude, terms which had been losing their meaning ever since the Gladstone Committee laid it down that all prisoners should be required to work as a means to their rehabilitation.   Work is now, as Bentham urged it should be, an aid to training, not an additional punishment imposed only upon the worst cases.   The attempt at classification by the court, which the 1894 Act attempted through its three divisions of imprisonment, has also been abandoned.

In a more fundamental sense the ascendancy of the courts has been challenged by the tentative steps which the Act has taken towards relatively indeterminate sentences.   The Rules made under the Act provide that the length of a sentence of preventive detention shall depend to some extent upon the detainee's progress, as assessed by the prison authorities, who alone are likely to know when he is fit for discharge.   Also the Act itself provides that sentences to Borstal shall no longer specify the period to be served, but be simply to "Borstal training", and the trainee may then be released, at the discretion of the authorities, at any time between a minimum of nine months and a maximum of two years after committal.[17]

Further restrictions have also been imposed on the power of the court to send juveniles to prison.   The minimum age for committal by a court of summary jurisdiction is seventeen, and for superior courts, fifteen: this compares with a general minimum previously of fourteen.   Even then a court must not imprison offenders under the age of twenty-one unless no other appropriate treatment is available, and the court must state its reasons in writing in each case in which it does so.[18]

Two new methods of treatment for juveniles have been introduced.   Detention centres are intended to provide a short period
of training, up to six months, for young people who might otherwise
have been sent to prison.[19]   Attendance centres provides a course of
non-residential training, up to a total of twelve hours, which
offenders are required to undertake in their spare time, *i.e.* in the
evenings and at week-ends.[20]

The variety in forms of treatment is gradually increasing, and
that is a very good thing.   We still know too little about crime and
its correction to lay down hard and fast rules.   Even more variety
would be welcome.   It would help a good deal, for instance, to
release the creative talents of the social workers in our correctional
services, by relaxing central control a little.   To diversity in type of
provision we should then add diversity in personal approach, and
the latter is the real key to the individualisation of treatment.

The dispensation now established is, in fact, neither perfect nor
final.   We have travelled a long way since the days of John Howard,
but the horizon is always receding.


### NOTES TO CHAPTER XI

1. This institution, however, founded in 1876, was for young adults as
well as adolescents, receiving males between the ages of sixteen and thirty.
A brief account of its origin and the methods used there will be found in Barnes,
H. E., and Teeters, N. K., *New Horizons in Criminology*, 1945, Chapter XXIV.

2. Prevention of Crime Act 1908, Part I.

3. The subsequent history of the Borstal system is outlined in Chapter XV.

4. Prevention of Crime Act 1908, Part II.

5. Criminal Justice Act 1925.

6. *Report of the Departmental Committee on the Training, Appointment
and Payment of Probation Officers*, 1922.   *Cmd*. 1601.

7. *Howard Journal*, **9**: 2, 1955, p. 156.

8. See also Chapter XVII.

9. The law with regard to juvenile courts is contained in the Children and
Young Persons Act 1933, Sections 45-9, and the Second Schedule.   On the
whole subject see: Elkin, W. A., *English Juvenile Courts*, 1938; and Watson,
J. A. F., *The Child and the Magistrate*, 1950.

10. Hobhouse, S., and Brockway, A., Fenner (eds.), *English Prisons Today*,
1922.

11. Leslie, Shane, *Sir Evelyn Ruggles Brise*, 1938, especially p. 163.

12. *Paterson on Prisons* (ed. S. K. Ruck), 1951, p. 23.

13. Paterson's concept of training is discussed in Fox, Sir L., *English
Prison and Borstal Systems*, 1952, pp. 66 ff.

14. Criminal Justice Act 1948.

15. Sec. 21 (1).

16. Sec. 21 (2).

17. Sec. 20 and the Second Schedule.

18. Sec. 17.

19. Sec. 18.

20. Sec. 19.

# CHAPTER XII

## PROBLEMS OF ADJUDICATION AND DIAGNOSIS

Although most progressive thinkers have now abandoned the retributive approach to crime, and it is on the wane even in our prisons, it is still the dominant idea at the stage of adjudication. The apportionment of blame and the imposition of punishment remain the chief aim of our criminal courts. Exceptions have been made for special classes, notably the very young and the insane, but proposals for the more general adoption of a therapeutic instead of a punitive approach have been fiercely resisted in this country, in spite of successful experiments with Treatment Tribunals in the United States. It is proposed in this chapter to discuss first the narrower issues of the legal position of children and the insane, and then the wider topic of how far our courts of law, as at present constituted, are capable of satisfying the need for careful diagnosis and the planning of treatment.

### The Age of Criminal Responsibility

The limited responsibility of children is already acknowledged in all countries. In Britain, no child under the age of eight years can be guilty of an offence.[1] From eight years to fourteen, there is a presumption that he could not know he was doing wrong, unless the prosecution can rebut this by "clear and strong evidence of design, concealment or exceptional ferocity".[2] These conditions are not likely to be very difficult to satisfy, and in practice, knowledge of wrong is usually taken for granted in cases involving children of these ages.[3] From the age of fourteen onwards, a child is held fully responsible—except that he is immune from the death penalty until he is eighteen[4]; and his liability to imprisonment is limited under the age of twenty-one.[5] With few exceptions, then, the child of eight and over must accept full legal responsibility for his actions.

This position is not very favourable to children, as compared with the corresponding laws in many other countries. In very few countries on the continent of Europe is the age of responsibility lower than thirteen.[6] In France and Poland it is thirteen. In Austria, Germany, Norway, and Czechoslovakia it is fourteen. In Denmark and Sweden it is fifteen, and the Swedish police would like it raised to sixteen.

For years, reformers have been urging that we should raise the age in this country at least to fourteen[7]; Dr Grunhut asserts categorically that school children ought not to be brought before a court of criminal jurisdiction.[8] This does not mean that nothing would be done about school children who got into trouble, but that instead of being dealt with by a criminal court, they would become the responsibility of some kind of social welfare agency. Behind these proposals one can hear distinct echoes of the main debate, the need for treatment rather than punishment being more readily conceded in the case of children.

It is difficult to find an objective criterion by which to justify any particular minimum age of criminal responsibility. For one thing, maturity is not merely a matter of chronological age. It seems to be connected also with climate, and with the amount of social experience which children can gain in different cultural settings. Possibly for climatic reasons, Italians are said to develop more quickly than the British[9]; and the working-class youth of eighteen in this country, who has already been at work for three years, is usually more sophisticated and worldly-wide than his middle-class opposite number, who is still confined within the monastic walls of his boarding school.

The level of intellectual ability is also relevant. Individuals differ very widely in intelligence, and therefore in the power to understand their experience and make use of it. One child of fourteen may have a mental age of only twelve, while another may have as much intelligence as the average person of sixteen. Here is a difference of four years in intellectual age, yet both must be treated by the law in exactly the same way.

Grunhut gives an interesting lead, in suggesting that until school-leaving age (that would be fifteen at present), the young offender should be treated as an educational problem.[10] This solution has at least the advantage of intelligibility. The very fact that we keep our children at school until such an age implies that they are still developing. The idea should also commend itself to those who oppose any major inroads on the conception of full criminal responsibility. For if it provides a good case for limiting the responsibility of children, it is an equally cogent argument against the extension of similar concessions to older offenders, who are no longer under tutelage. To others this will tell against it, as perpetuating, and indeed confirming the retributive principle.

The case for raising the age at least to fourteen or fifteen seems to be overwhelming, but there is almost as good a case for limiting legal responsibility until children have worked through the many stresses connected with adolescence and starting work. The Norwegians exclude most young offenders under the age of eighteen from the jurisdiction of the criminal courts, and treat them as "welfare" cases.[11] But short of this, there are many opportunities under the existing British law for treating young adults under twenty-one in a special and constructive way. The main need is for courts which will make use of these opportunities, and that probably means special courts. Mannheim suggests for this purpose, a special division of the adult court.[12]

## Insanity and the Courts

The legal formula governing the criminal responsibility of insane persons was first laid down over a hundred years ago, and has been the subject of heated controversy ever since. In 1842, Daniel McNaghten shot a man whom he mistook for Sir Robert Peel. It appeared that he acted under the delusion that Peel was persecuting him. He was held to be "not guilty, on the grounds of insanity".[13] The battle was immediately joined, and following a debate in the House of Lords, the judges worked out a set of general principles to guide the courts in future cases of this sort.

The McNaghten Rules, as these are called, state that the plea of insanity can only be sustained if the defence can show that the prisoner was labouring under such a defect of reason, from disease of the mind, that he (a) did not know the nature and quality of the act he was doing, or (b) did not know that it was wrong. A third rule states that where neither of these apply, and the prisoner is suffering from delusions, he is in the same position with regard to responsibility as he would be if the delusions were true. This last provision has given rise to many legal puzzles, and is rarely invoked nowadays.[14]

Although these Rules are not in themselves law (for judges have no power to make law by general declarations of this sort), they govern the administration of the law relating to insane offenders throughout the Commonwealth, and in many states of the U.S.A.[15] It should be noted that they do not pretend to define insanity as such, but only the grounds on which legal responsibility may be waived by reason of insanity.

Where an offender is found "guilty but insane",[16] he is committed to a mental hospital, usually Broadmoor, during Her Majesty's pleasure. Such an alternative is generally felt to be severer than most sentences of imprisonment, and the plea of insanity is therefore entered by the defence only in murder cases, where it might save the offender from a capital sentence.

The wording of the McNaghten Rules was fairly obviously determined by the fact that the case on which they were based was one involving delusions. The insanity of a deluded person takes the form of false beliefs. Where delusions are not involved, the knowledge factor, on which the Rules lay so much emphasis, may not be the really important thing. It may be a case, for example, of an insane impulse, which the individual is quite unable to control. The much greater importance of emotional disturbances of this sort in insanity, as against disturbances of "reason", has been increasingly recognised as psychiatry has uncovered the irrational impulses of the unconscious during the early years of the present century. Very few cases of insanity, clearly pathological though they may be, do in fact satisfy the very restricted McNaghten criteria.

The psychiatrists never ceased to attack the Rules. As early as 1864 Maudsley indicated them.[17] In 1884 the Medical Officers of Hospitals and Asylums for the Insane exposed their inadequacies.[18] Before official committee after official committee, medical opinion has been uniformly hostile. The Atkin Committee on Insanity and Crime (1924) actually recommended changes in the law, and an amending Bill was introduced into the Lords by Lord Darling, but was rejected. An impressive display of unanimity on the part of the medical profession before the recent Royal Commission on Capital Punishment, has been equally ineffective.[19] The Rules remain just as they were drafted all those years ago, in spite of the revolution which has taken place meanwhile in our understanding of the nature of mental illness.

There have been signs in recent years of a more generous interpretation of the Rules by the courts, so as to admit the "irresistible impulse". Various witnesses before the Royal Commission on Capital Punishment attested to this. Dr J. Ivison Russell explained the matter in this way: "The person who acts on an irresistible impulse is really doing a non-volitional act; he is not knowing the nature and quality of his act in such a way as to form a rational judgment on that act, and that is a case of not knowing the act".[20] Between 1901 and 1922, of 1,445 persons tried for murder, 485 or 34 per cent. were found guilty but insane. W. T. S. Stallybrass concludes, "No one can suppose that the 485 satisfied the tests imposed by the Rules in McNaghten's case".[21]

Yet there is no real solution in such a shift. The words do not really bear the extended meaning which is being attached to them, but are being juggled with to make them fit. Therefore, while some judges, in their directions to the jury, interpret them in this lenient sense, other judges continue to interpret them very strictly.[22] And there will always be a tendency to restrict their meaning when cases arise, of brutal murder, for example, in which strong feelings of horror and indignation are aroused.

There is, in theory, a "safety-net" for any insane murderer who may have slipped through the many gaps in the Rules. If the Home Secretary has reason to think that a person under sentence of death* is insane, he has a statutory duty to order a special medical examination. This is usually carried out by a panel of three doctors, who may declare their view as to the sanity of the prisoner on the basis of clinical considerations alone, unfettered by such legal limitations as the McNaghten Rules.

Statutory medical enquiries of this sort have been ordered more frequently in recent years. Of 284 murderers convicted and sentenced over the period 1900-9, only thirty-two were made the subject of such an enquiry, while during the period 1940-9, eighty-six in a total of 262 were investigated in this way. About one-half of those referred to the medical panel are either certified insane as a result, or have their sentences commuted to imprisonment.[23]

The number of cases in which the sentence of death imposed by the court was set aside as a result of these medical enquiries (forty-one between 1940 and 1949)[24] does highlight the defects of the McNaghten formula. But this sort of intervention, after sentence, has grave disadvantages of its own. The sentence of death will already have been pronounced, and the prisoner and his relatives will then be forced to endure a period of mental agony and uncertainty while the medical enquiry is carried out. No one should be subjected to such an ordeal.

Nor is the "safety-net" necessarily fool-proof; it may be that insane persons are still hanged. In *Just Murder* by Edward Robinson, thirty-six instances are described in which, in spite of medical evidence that the accused was insane, all were hanged. The occurrence of such cases may be due to the predominance given to the official medical services in the medical panel, making for a conservative view of what constitutes insanity. Or it may be due to the fact that reprieve is a public act by a politician who dare not

---

* In February 1956 the House of Commons voted in favour of the suspension of the death penalty for a trial period of five years. At the time of writing, it is not yet clear to what extent and in what ways their vote will find expression in legislation.

court unpopularity. It might be more than his political future was worth to reprieve a murderer whose atrocious acts had aroused strong public hostility.[25]

The difficulties are not confined to the diagnosably insane. Many criminals, and a substantial proportion of our murderers, appear to be psychopathic personalities, who suffer from none of the established types of mental illness, but who are, nevertheless, not really responsible for their actions.

Sir David Henderson, the distinguished authority on the psychopathic personality, said, "If you think of such characters or personalities as Ruxton, Neville Heath, or John George Haigh, or many others a little less spectacular, you will admit that these are indeed strange beings who are ruled by the most primitive feelings, but yet throughout the greater part of their lives have shown social qualities which, for a time at least, enabled them to be regarded as reasonable companions . . . They are far more dangerously imperfect in their structure than the unfortunate victims of idiocy, imbecility, or feeble-mindedness, and yet they continue to be treated with far less sympathy and understanding. For the most part they are regarded by the public and by the law as sane bad men who are fit to 'thole their assize'. My contention is that this conception is narrow, rigid, uncivilised, and that drastic changes are required".[26]

Their real pathology, being well-hidden behind what Cleckley has called a "mask of sanity",[27] they cannot claim the protection of the McNaghten Rules, nor can they be declared insane by a panel of doctors. Yet experience shows that they cannot and will not be deterred by any sort of punishment. Even to impose a retributive penalty on them, in view of what we know about their mental economy, seems as primitive as to punish a cart, a tree, or an ox.[28]

The main proposal for reform is still, as it has always been, for the recognition of the "irresistible impulse", though nowadays expert medical opinion prefers to speak of the "inability to control" an impulse.[29] Such a definition would include clear cases of psychopathic personality, as well as insanity. Lawyers are doubtful, however, of the possibility of defining irresistible impulse in such a way as to leave the onus of self-control upon the normal offender.[30] Henderson suggests abandoning all attempts at definition in favour of a straightforward question to the jury about the accused's sanity.[31] The Royal Commission on Capital Punishment finally decided in favour of the latter solution. The jury they proposed should be "left to decide on all the evidence whether the accused was at the time of the offence suffering either from a disease of the mind or from mental deficiency to such a degree that he ought not to be held responsible".[32]

This proposal, if carried into effect, would place a very heavy burden upon the "twelve just men and true", and one which they are really unfitted to bear. The diagnosis of insanity and mental deficiency,[33] and of their effect upon behaviour, are highly technical matters. They should be the responsibility of psychiatrists not of lay persons, however conscientious.

Medical advice is tendered to the jury from psychiatric consultants for the defence, and a prison medical officer on the other side.[34] But the combative nature of British judicial procedure places the medical advisers of the two sides in a position where they have to try to rebut each other's arguments, rather than collaborate to produce a better and more balanced diagnosis. Conflicting medical opinions of this sort are of little help to the jury.

A better solution would probably be to refer the question of the accused's mental state to a medical board, similar to that used in the statutory medical enquiry, but with perhaps a stronger independent representation. The question of legal responsibility would still remain for the duly constituted judicial authority (judge or jury) to decide, with the aid of such light as the board can throw upon his personality and problems.

### Treatment Tribunals

Recent opinion in some countries has gone much further than this. It has been alleged that the inadequacy of the present procedure is not confined merely to cases in which the mental state of the offender is in question, for all criminal cases (even those in which psychiatric issues do not arise) involve difficult problems of social and psychological diagnosis. The legal guilt of the accused can be determined by the traditional means, but the prescription of treatment is a very different matter. Here legal issues and legal experience are quite irrelevant. It is a matter which calls instead for the special skills of the experienced social worker.

SCANDINAVIAN CHILD WELFARE COUNCILS. In Norway, delinquent children under the age of fourteen are no longer dealt with by the courts, but by Child Welfare Councils. Those between fourteen and eighteen are dealt with in a similar way if the public prosecutor decides that treatment rather than punishment is required, and in practice this is done in most cases. The Child Welfare Council, after satisfying itself that the child has committed the offence charged to it, may then take one of a number of alternative courses. The child may be reprimanded and warned, or the parents or the school be asked to administer some form of corrective punishment. Where more drastic action is called for, the child may be taken away from his home, and either be boarded-out, or be placed in a residential school. Only the older children or the more serious offenders are likely to be placed in a more specialised reformatory school.[35]

Thus the Child Welfare Council deals with many cases which in this country would fall within the purview of the criminal courts, and with some, aged seventeen to eighteen, who would be too old even for our juvenile court, and would have to appear before the adult court.

We go still further in our legalism in England than even this comparison suggests. Our juvenile courts are not restricted to dealing with delinquents; they deal with many juveniles who have committed no crime, but are "in need of care and protection".[36] In such instances, the judicial element in any decision would be at a minimum. It should be treated as a social-work question—of deciding in the light of a knowledge of the social problems involved, what action would best serve the child's interests.

Experts in this field, however, have often told us that there is no material difference between the child before the court for an offence and the child "in need of care and protection". Both have the same sorts of defective home background, and it seems more or less an accident whether a child has actually committed an offence or not.[37] The vital need in both kinds of case is for the planning of appropriate measures of treatment.

All the criticisms which could be levelled at the courts as a forum for deciding upon the sanity of an offender apply here also. The expert knowledge of the social worker is lacking. Often, it is true, a probation officer may be asked to visit the home and report on the case, but the final decision always rests with the court itself, and courts vary a good deal in the use which they make of their probation officers, and the attention which they pay to their reports.

There are hardly any facilities beyond this: for example, for clinical investigation and prolonged observation.[38] The combative atmosphere and the rules of evidence are a further handicap. They are most inappropriate for delicate social enquiries of the sort required, in which, for example, it will be necessary to find out about personal relationships and confidential family matters. And the respect for precedent in a court of law, safeguard though it may be against arbitrariness, is diametrically opposed to an approach which sees every case as unique and unprecedented.

YOUTH CORRECTION AUTHORITIES IN AMERICA. In the United States, juvenile courts are already chancery courts, acting *in loco parentis*, and not criminal courts as in this country. American pioneers, therefore, felt free to concentrate upon the adolescent age group. A plan produced in 1940 by the American Law Institute proposed that a Youth Correction Authority should be set up in each state. All adolescents (all, that is, over juvenile court-age and under twenty-one), after being found guilty of an offence by a criminal court, should with very few exceptions be committed to the Authority for study and a decision as to the treatment required. This scheme, with modifications, was carried into effect by a number of American states, including California, Wisconsin, and Minnesota.

The California Youth Authority Act did not stop there, but extended the jurisdiction of the Authority to include those of juvenile court-age also. The Authority was also made responsible for most of the correctional institutions for juveniles in the state. The Youth Authority is very powerful, and can immediately discharge the delinquent, or send him away for a long period of training. Alternatively, although the Authority does not directly control the probation service, it may place young people who are in its care on probation. Even more daring, the Californian legislature has set up an Adult Authority with similar powers and responsibilities towards adult offenders.[39]

These revolutionary experiments have been supported in principle by many British writers,[40] and by such a well-known and experienced magistrate as Claud Mullins.[41] It has been urged that such a procedure not only makes for better diagnosis, but also reduces the inconsistency in the penalties prescribed as between one court and another.[42]

Where also, as in the Californian system, the Treatment Tribunal is responsible for the administration of treatment as well as its prescription, this is in itself a great gain. It has long been regretted that the court which commits an offender to some form of correctional treatment rarely has anything more to do with him.[43] The only exception to this is the close relationship which exists between the probation service and the petty sessional court. The magistrates of each court are required to set up a probation-case committee to review cases from time to time with the probation officer. In all other cases, even if the judge or the magistrates retain a sense of responsibility in spite of their remoteness from the actual execution of the treatment they have prescribed, they cannot have any real knowledge of the nature of that form of treatment. This does not make for sound decisions.

The Californian system also leaves more scope for flexibility. The Youth Authority is able to learn by its experience in attempting treatment, and can change a decision quite easily, or change its policy, if experience suggests that this is desirable. To this end it has also developed new kinds of institution and forms of treatment, and has been able to weld the many and varied forms of treatment which exist in the state into a co-ordinated and flexible instrument, capable of being applied in a highly individualised way.

But Treatment Tribunals have their dangers. Highest on the list is that of arbitrary power, unrestrained either by precedent, or by the impartiality which a judge derives from his legal training and his regard for judicial traditions.[44] In California there is no appeal from a decision of the Youth or Adult Authorities. It is also urged that the introduction of such a system would denude the courts of their most interesting and significant functions. The judges would not want to be confined to the mere determination of guilt, and the profession would cease to attract the more able jurists if it was limited in this way.[45] Such considerations have led Mannheim,[46] and others, to urge that the Treatment Tribunal should be advisory only. The court should remain the final arbiter.

The threat which the bureaucrat, even the social welfare officer, can offer to our liberties is a very real one. "Power corrupts, absolute power corrupts absolutely," wrote Acton. This dictum still has much wisdom in it. Yet the Home Office and the Prison Commission already carry out analogous functions to those of a Treatment Tribunal. For instance, although the court may commit an individual to either prison or Borstal, it is left to the Prison Commission to decide whether this shall mean close incarceration, or placement in an open institution. The length of the sentence, through the system of remissions, is also partly determined by the Commission.

The classifying schools set up by the Home Office for juveniles committed to approved schools perform a very similar function to that of the diagnostic clinic run by the California Youth Authority at the Preston School of Industry. The Treatment Tribunal would need to add to its armoury other forms of treatment besides the institutional ones, and unlike the Home Office or the Prison Commission, would move into action before sentence, not afterwards.

THE INDETERMINATE SENTENCE.  The indeterminate sentence is probably an essential part of such a scheme, and this is a most controversial matter.  It entails that the period for which the offender is committed to the care of the Tribunal is not absolutely fixed by the court, but is varied at the discretion of the Tribunal itself.[47]

Some writers distinguish the indeterminate sentence sharply from remission systems such as the British, where a definite sentence is imposed, but can be reduced by recognised amounts at the discretion of the prison authorities.[48]  The difference would seem to be purely formal.  In any case, however, there is already a degree of indeterminacy, in the narrowest sense of the word, in our present system.  It is already accepted in committals to approved schools and Borstals, and in the new sentence of preventive detention under the 1948 Act.[49]  A Borstal sentence, for instance, is for not less than nine months nor more than three years.  How long, within these limits, a Borstal inmate actually serves, is decided by the Prison Commission.

Unless a similar discretion can be given to a Treatment Board in respect of all the cases with which it deals, it will be very much hampered in its task of working out individualised programmes of treatment.  Only those actually carrying out a programme of treatment can know how an offender is responding to it, or how much more treatment he is likely to need.

Californian experience has shown, however, that the morale and peace of mind of the prisoner depends upon his knowing that he will be free on a certain date.[50]  To meet this need, and as an ultimate safeguard against arbitrary imprisonment, a maximum sentence might be fixed by the court, the principle of indeterminacy entering to permit earlier discharge in suitable cases.

INEQUITY OF A TREATMENT APPROACH?  Another criticism is likely to loom large in the mind of the man in the street: what will often seem to him to be the unfairness of a treatment decision as compared with one based on punishment considerations.  Judge F. Perkins, the main American opponent of the original A.L.I. plan, made much of this point.[51]  He invented a number of hypothetical cases in which, because the circumstances of two offenders were different, they would be dealt with very differently, even though the offences which they had committed were the same.  One, for example, might be immediately discharged because there was very little chance that he would offend again, while another might be placed in a reformatory for a period of years.

There is no gainsaying the plausibility of this kind of appeal, but it is the sort of objection which the uninstructed person is likely to make to any approach to crime through treatment rather than punishment. The relatively long sentences involved in commitment to Borstal or corrective training lay them open to a similar kind of attack where the alternative would have been a much shorter sentence of simple imprisonment. But the constructive training at which these special forms of sentence are aiming would be impossible if the sentence were very short. The answer must be found in the skill with which the case for treatment is presented to the public.

On the whole, American experience with these Boards over the past fifteen years has not borne out the fears expressed by Judge Parker and his supporters. As Mannheim says, some changes in this direction seem certain to come. There is more doubt, however, whether as much need be conceded to judicial scruples as Mannheim suggests. Our freedom, and the status of the judges, would seem to be adequately preserved by retaining a judge as a member, perhaps the chairman, of a Treatment Tribunal with direct authority.

## Prediction Tables

A Treatment Board would have the assistance of clinical experts, and would presumably set up its own classifying and allocation centre, similar to those at present maintained by the Prison Commission for the allocation of corrective trainees or Borstal boys, and by the Home Office for classification within the approved school system. The establishment of a classification centre was the first major task undertaken by the California Youth Authority.

Recent statistical work, however, has thrown grave doubts upon the assumption that the intensive study of individual cases in this way is the best basis for treatment decisions. It has been suggested that statistical tables, based on actuarial studies of past experience with the different forms of treatment, provide a sounder guide.

Prediction tables, as these actuarial tables are called, have been constructed to show the extent to which individuals displaying certain superficial features of background or character have in the past become confirmed offenders, or have succeeded or failed after receiving a particular form of treatment, e.g. probation or Borstal. They are "risk tables", based upon past experience with large numbers of cases, in every way similar to those used by insurance companies. Not only are they said to be more reliable than individual methods of diagnosis, but they also require far less time and skill for their application.[52]   For the "risk factors" included in them are chosen because they are relatively easy to determine, as well as for their association with criminality or response to treatment.

Although the first prediction tables were designed by E. W. Burgess,[53] the more refined tables developed in recent years have been associated with the names of the Gluecks. Their "social prediction scale", for the early identification of juvenile delinquents, may be taken as an example. As a result of their researches into the causation of juvenile delinquency reported in "Unravelling Juvenile Delinquency", they isolated five social factors which correlated highly with subsequent criminality in young people, viz. discipline of boy by father, supervision of boy by mother, affection of father for boy, affection of mother for boy, and cohesiveness of the family. These, after being weighted according to the prominence which research gave to them, formed the basis of the table.[54]

R. E. Thompson has compared the effectiveness of the Glueck social prediction scale with that of clinical study by a team of three experts (a psychiatrist and two psychologists) employed on the Cambridge-Somerville Youth Study.[55]   One hundred Youth Study cases in which the outcome over a period of years was already known were sorted according to the Glueck table. No information about the personalities or background of the boys, apart from the facts called for by the table, were made available to the predictor. The clinical team, on the other hand, in their predictions, made in the early stages of the Youth Study, had had the advantage of personal interviews and all the background information which could be collected, as well as consultation with each other. It was, nevertheless, found that while the tables made a correct prediction of subsequent delinquency or non-delinquency in 91 per cent. of the cases, the three clinicians were successful in only 54 per cent., 56 per cent., and 62 per cent. of their predictions respectively.[56]

Mannheim and Wilkins, who constructed a table for the prediction of response to Borstal treatment, similarly found the table to be significantly more reliable than the judgment of Borstal staff members, who had lived with a boy over a long period and knew him intimately.[57]   Other tables have been designed to predict response to probation,[58] for selecting prisoners for release on parole,[59] and for identifying probable adult recidivists.[60]

These devices must be of the utmost importance to those who are faced with treatment decisions, and the Gluecks have suggested that they should be made available to the courts to help them in this task.[61]   However, they can tell us nothing directly about individual cases. Although they do appear to be remarkably successful, it is only in the aggregate, and there will always be a percentage of "hard cases" in which a table is certain to fail if it is applied automatically. For this reason, the Gluecks themselves recommend that prediction tables should be used as an adjunct to, rather than a substitute for, clinical investigations.[62] The Third International Congress on Criminology, held in London in 1955, which came to the same conclusion, suggested further that it might be dangerous to place a prediction table in the hands of judges, who might be tempted to rely on it too exclusively. It should instead be provided as an aid for the professional workers employed by the court to study the case.[63]

Other reservations ought perhaps to be made. Firstly, prediction tables are concerned only with statistical associations, and are as superficial as all statistical correlations must be. We can deduce nothing from them about the nature of the connection between the correlated factor and the observed result, or even whether the connection is causally relevant at all.

If there is a shift of research interest from causal studies to the establishment of such associations because of the practical utility of the latter, the progress of criminological science is going to be greatly handicapped. This is not only because the main incentive for research, the prevention and treatment of crime, will have been transferred from causal to prediction studies, but also because of the attraction which any result expressible in a numerical form tends to have. As the cult of the I.Q. has shown, a quantitative result creates an illusion of scientific precision and certitude by comparison with which the results achieved by more subjective but more realistic studies cut a very poor figure.

Another objection strikes at the actuarial principle itself. Unlike the factors which an insurance company take into account, the social factors which enter into the problem of crime change constantly. Probabilities based upon past experience are, therefore, a rather unsure guide for a somewhat uncertain future.

This affects the long-term validity of tables designed, like those of the Gluecks, to identify juvenile delinquents or adult recidivists, but would be even more important in its consequences, in the case of tables constructed to predict response to different forms of treatment. They would necessarily be based upon treatment as it was when the table was constructed, and would be inapplicable if methods were afterwards improved. They would, in fact, give good results only so long as the process of treatment remained unchanged,

and so would constitute a conservative force, making for the reten-
tion of out-moded techniques.

The results achieved from any form of treatment may be partly
the result of the response of the criminal, but are also a function of
the effectiveness of treatment methods themselves. Prediction
tables neglect this whole side of the question. Clinical methods of
diagnosis and prognosis, on the other hand, are based upon an
examination of the intimate dynamics of treatment, and call in
question both the types of cases allocated to it and the methods
used.

To sum up: prediction tables are likely to be of great value, and
are probably here to stay. At the same time, their limitations must
be remembered, and they must not be used to the exclusion of more
fundamental approaches.

## NOTES TO CHAPTER XII

1. Children and Young Persons Act 1933, Sec. 50.
2. Stallybrass, W. T. S., in Radzinowicz, L., and Turner, J. W. C., *Modern
Approach to Criminal Law*, 1945, p. 413.
3. Williams, G., *Criminal Law: The General Part*, 1953, pp. 652-3.
4. Criminal Justice Act 1948, Sec. 16.
5. *Ibid.*, Sec. 17.
6. Williams, G. (ed.), *Reform of the Law*, p. 156.
7. Mannheim, H., *Dilemma of Penal Reform*, 1939, pp. 190 ff. Grunhut, M.,
in Fry, M., *et al.*, *Lawless Youth*, 1947, p. 31. Williams, G. (ed.), *ibid.*
8. *Op. cit.*
9. Stallybrass, *op. cit.*, p. 414.
10. *Op. cit.*
11. See below, pp. 156-8.
12. *Op. cit.*, p. 199.
13. In 1883 the form of sentence was changed by statute to "guilty but
insane". This illogical wording was a result of pressure from Queen Victoria;
a would-be assassin who shot at her was found "not guilty because insane",
but the implacable Royal lady insisted that he most certainly did shoot at her,
and that any sentence should therefore begin with the word "Guilty . . .".
14. Williams, G., *op. cit.*, pp. 330 ff.
15. However, there are differences of interpretation: in England, knowledge
of the "wrongfulness" of an act means legal wrongfulness, but in U.S.A. and
Australia it means moral wrongfulness. (Hall Williams, J. E., *Brit. J. of
Delinquency*, 5: 1, 1954, pp. 72-3.)
16. See note 13 above.
17. Robertson, C. L., and Maudsley, H., *Insanity and Crime*, 1864.
18. Williams, G. (ed.), *op. cit.*, p. 158.
19. See the *Report* and the *Minutes of Evidence, Royal Commission on
Capital Punishment*, Report: *Cmd.* 8932.
20. *Minutes of Evidence*, Para. 6665.
21. *Op. cit.*, p. 416.
22. *Report*, *op. cit.*, pp. 81-5.
23. *Ibid.*, Table V, p. 125.
24. *Ibid.*

25. It is only fair to add that the Royal Commission on Capital Punishment was convinced that the statutory medical enquiry provided an effective safeguard against the hanging of an insane person (para. 243).

26. Henderson, Sir D. K., *The Psychopathic Personality*, Inaugural Postgraduate Lecture, St Andrew's University, 1951-2.

27. Cleckley, H., *The Mask of Sanity*, 1941.

28. See above, p. 120.

29. See the evidence of the B.M.A., *loc. cit.*, p. 315, and of the Institute of Psycho-analysis, pp. 545 ff.

This form of words places the emphasis upon inadequate ego or character development, shown by Bowlby and others, to be of great importance in the creation of the psychopathic personality. The strength of the impulses which have to be controlled must, nevertheless, enter into the picture.

30. Goodheart, A. L., quoted Stallybrass, *op. cit.*, pp. 417-18.

31. *Minutes of Evidence*, *loc. cit.*, pp. 459 ff.

32. *Report*, *loc. cit.*, Para. 356.

33. As mental deficiency is due to lack of development, not disease of the mind, the McNaghten Rules cannot legitimately be applied to such cases.

34. Not psychiatrically qualified. If a psychiatric consultant wishes to give evidence it can only be as a witness for the defence. This is in itself a matter for concern.

35. *Lawless Youth*, *op. cit.*, pp. 235 ff.

36. Children and Young Persons Act 1933, Secs. 61-3.

37. *Report of the Care of Children Committee*, 1946, Cmd. 6922, Para. 38.

38. There are juvenile observation centres within remand homes in certain areas, but they are very few. Nothing of the sort exists for the study of adult offenders.

39. Barnes, H. E., and Teeters, N. K., *New Horizons in Criminology*, 1954, pp. 810-12.

40. Fry, S. M., *Future Treatment of the Adult Offender*, 1944. Mannheim, H., *op. cit.*, pp. 200 ff. Also *Criminal Justice and Social Reconstruction*, 1946, pp. 223 ff.

41. Mullins, C., *Fifteen Years Hard Labour*, 1949, p. 192.

42. Mannheim, H., *Criminal Justice and Social Reconstruction*, pp. 227 ff.

43. See, for example, Laski, H. J., *Grammar of Politics*, 1938, p. 564.

44. Mannheim, H., *Dilemma*, p. 207. Grunhut, M., *Penal Reform*, 1948, p. 362.

45. Mannheim, H., *op. cit.* Page, Leo, *Sentence of the Court*, 1948, pp. 161-2.

46. *Ibid.*

47. *The Indeterminate Sentence* (United Nations, Dept. of Social Affairs), 1954.

48. Mannheim, H., in *Howard Journal*, **9**: 2, 1955, pp. 169-70.

49. See below, pp. 174, 201, 214.

50. Scudder, Kenyon J., "Progress in Handling the Adult Offender", *Yearbook of the (American) National Parole and Probation Association*, 1947, pp. 13 ff.

51. Perkins, F., *Common-sense and Bad Boys, and other Essays*, 1946.

52. The actual construction of prediction tables is, of course, a very time-consuming business.

53. Burgess, E. W., "Workings of the Indeterminate-sentence Law and Parole Systems in Illinois", in Bruce, A. A., Harno, A. J., Burgess, E. W., and Landesco, J., *Parole and the Indeterminate Sentence*, 1928.

54. Glueck, S. and E., *Unravelling Juvenile Delinquency*, 1950, Chapter XX.

55. Powers, E., and Witmer, H., *An Experiment in the Prevention of Delinquency*, 1951, describes the Cambridge-Somerville Youth Study. See also below, pp. 255-6.

56. Thompson, R. E., "A Validation of the Glueck Social Prediction Scale for Proneness to Delinquency", *Brit. J. of Delinquency*, **3**: 4, 1953, pp. 289 ff.

57. Mannheim, H., and Wilkins, L. T., *Prediction Methods in relation to Borstal Training*, 1955.

58. Monachesi, E. D., *Prediction Factors in Probation*, 1932.

59. Vold, G. B., *Prediction Methods and Parole*, 1931.

60. For a summary of the work of the Gluecks on the prediction of adult recidivism, see their *After Conduct of Discharged Offenders*, 1945, Chapter VI.

61. *Ibid.*, pp. 68 ff.

62. For example, *Unravelling Juvenile Delinquency*, pp. 269-70.

63. See the form of resolution eventually approved by the Congress.

# CHAPTER XIII

## ENGLISH PRISONS

Our prisons are easily recognised. These Bastille-like buildings, with their towers and battlements, their huge walls and great gates could be nothing else. Built, most of them in the nineteenth century, to match a prison philosophy we have now out-grown, they are the chief obstacle to progress in penal methods. So long as they last, real treatment is going to be obstructed at every turn—and they look as if they might last for ever.

### Prison Buildings

When they were built, the keynote of the prison system was separate confinement and the futile "hard labour" of the crank and the treadmill. So they usually consist of galleries of small cells, radiating like the spokes of a wheel from an observation chamber in the centre—and little else. From the centre, all the galleries may be kept under constant surveillance.

Security considerations are naturally important, and the cells are at least strong and safe. In spite, therefore, of the modern belief in the value of controlled association, prisoners tend to be locked up too often and for too long. They are not only shut up in their cells at night, but for large parts of the day also, whenever staff shortages (as at present) make the supervision of large numbers of men in association a difficult proceeding in prisons built like this.

As work and recreation in the company of other prisoners was never intended, prison buildings provide no accommodation for this. Additional structures, inconvenient and not very secure, have therefore had to be built to provide workshops. Often the space available within the prison is so limited as to make this very difficult, or even impossible. For instance, in Leicester prison, a choice had to be made at one point between more huts and leaving some room for exercise. Films and concerts, as often as not, have to be held in the chapel.

The regulations provide that (subject to the governor's discretion) all prisoners, after a short initial period, shall be entitled to eat their meals in association, but in fact, because of lack of accommodation, only a few of those entitled to this privilege are able to enjoy it, and even then must often eat their meals in the well of a cell-block, or in

one of the larger cells converted for the purpose.   Every step away
from a repressive and deadening cellular regime is accompanied by
the greatest difficulties.

These massive brick and iron structures are a constant obstacle
also to fruitful classification within the prison.   It is difficult to
segregate classes of prisoners within a single prison built on the
radiating pattern.   There is little chance, either, of flexibility and
enterprise in treatment methods within such a rigid framework.
And the size of these units, with accommodation for hundreds of
prisoners, is inimical to the establishment of the personal relationships which (as will be argued later) are indispensable for a real
approach to reformation.

Mr Herbert Morrison, when Home Secretary during the war,
publicly expressed the heartfelt wish that all our prisons might be
blown up.   The objections of the Treasury notwithstanding, something of the sort should be a first priority in penal reform.   Our
Victorian architects were only too successful in their attempts to
carry into effect the penological ideas of their time; they have
succeeded in making the adoption of any others almost impossible.
If we want to see real progress in prison methods, we have to face
the expense and upheaval involved in turning bulldozers in to browse
upon our Pentonvilles, Armleys, and Strangeways.

### Over-centralisation

The "dead hand" of the nineteenth century is to be found also
in the administrative system under which our prisons are governed.
When the prisons were nationalised in 1877, it became possible to
close unsuitable buildings, to raise standards all round, and to use
more economically and efficiently the accommodation which was
retained.   These advantages still obtain.   One has only to compare
the British system with the jumble of Federal and state penitentiaries
and county and city jails in America, and to compare our institutions,
in spite of their shortcomings, with the sordid conditions which
exist in some of the American jails, to realise what we have gained
from our centralised system.

At the same time, because a centralised system very easily
becomes bureaucratic, the initiative and enterprise of the prison staffs
has often been stultified by it.   In 1911, Ruggles Brise, then Chairman of the Prison Commission, boasted in New York, "It is now
4.30 in the afternoon, and I know that just now, at every local and
convict prison in England, the same things in general are being done
in the same way".   The Prison Commissioners make great play

nowadays with the freedom which the individual prison governor has to determine his own policy "within the regulations",[1] but in reality, routine, diet, and punishments, the classification system and the overall daily programme are all laid down for him in those regulations.   This is quite apart from the constant administrative pressure from the Commissioners themselves.   Well might an American observer write that "British prisons, with only a few exceptions, are still dominated by uniformity, monotony, and drabness".[2]

This is particularly damaging because of the importance of flexibility in the correctional process.   In our prisons we are trying to reform human beings, not to train animals or tune up machines. Interpersonal influence of the sort which our prison staffs should be exercising is dynamic and a little capricious.   Every prisoner is different, and (what is often forgotten) so is every prison officer, and every prison governor.   There is no "right" method of treatment appropriate to all individuals and circumstances, and no method is going to be right all the time, even for the same prisoner. The ideal is the classical one of the greatest degree of individualisation in treatment that it is possible to achieve.

The nearest that the system approaches to this aim is to provide different types of institution for different classes of prisoner.   The regime in different types of institution within this scheme may indeed be very different, though within each such prison, uniformity of treatment remains the governing principle.

## The Classification System

Even so, a classification system of this sort is the first requirement of a rational treatment programme, for it enables our prisons to avoid the evils of contamination, and to bring together those who are most likely to be helped by the elements which must be common in a particular regime.

The British classification system is at present somewhat complex, various criteria, in actual practice, combining with or cutting across each other.   However, after the separation of debtors and other civil prisoners, the formal criteria used are sex, age, length of sentence, criminal experience, and suitability for a particular type of training.

The criterion of age has resulted in the segregation of young prisoners, i.e. those under the age of twenty-one.   The relevance of length of sentence is also obvious: the approach to a floating prison population must be different from that to a body of prisoners who are likely to be available for training for a longer period.   There is also the question of criminal contagion to be borne in mind, for short-term prisoners are often petty first offenders, at the beginning of their criminal careers. Special accommodation is provided for short-sentence men, and a sentence of at least eighteen months is now fixed as the minimum for placement in a regional training prison.

The consideration given to the prisoner's criminal record has led to the distinction between Stars, or offenders serving a first prison sentence, and Ordinaries. Finally, there is the criterion of suitability for a particular type of training, which has tended to cut across that between Stars and Ordinaries, a group known as "trainable Ordinaries" being grouped with Star prisoners in the regional training prisons.

The Criminal Justice Act 1948 adds its own contribution to the classification system with the conditions it lays down as necessary before sentences of corrective training and preventive detention can be passed. These include not only age, and criminal experience, but also social criteria—that of "suitability" in the case of the former, and "dangerousness" in the case of the latter.[3]

Of these various planks of the classification system, all can be easily and objectively determined except "suitability". One feels that to determine whether a prisoner is suitable for a particular form of training must necessitate a careful study of his background and personality. This task, for all cases of simple imprisonment, is, however, allotted to the Reception Board at the local prison, consisting of the Governor and his senior assistants. The process is necessarily hurried, and psychological advice is rarely available. The court records are provided for the guidance of the Board, but only in a few instances is there a social worker to visit the prisoner's home and try to find out what part has been played by his social and family background. Until recently, at least, none even of the few social workers thus employed had received any training in social work to help them perform their important and highly skilled tasks.

This procedure is in sharp contrast with that adopted in the classification of corrective trainees. The court, before passing a sentence of corrective training, must consider any report received from the Prison Commission on the suitability of the offender for this form of treatment, and the preparation of this report is once again the responsibility of the local prison. But once the sentence has been passed, the trainee is sent to an allocation centre where professional workers (including psychologists and social workers) are available. On the basis of the evaluation of his potentialities at the allocation centre, he may be sent to an open prison, a regional training prison, or a corrective training prison with a strict discipline.

In defending the policy of mixing trainable Ordinaries with Stars, Sir Lionel Fox emphasises the importance of careful selection,[4] but can hardly claim that the present method is careful enough. If the memoirs of one ex-inmate are to be believed, the dangers of contamination are very real.[5] There may, indeed, as Fox says, be "many who must be classed as Stars who are more likely to corrupt the minds of their fellows than many who must be classed as recidivists", but this is no argument against the more careful personal evaluation of the prisoners, but rather the contrary. In fact, together with better clinical facilities for classification, should go an increasing reliance upon the personal evaluation rather than upon the more superficial distinction between Stars and Ordinaries.[6]

## Types of Institution

What institutions exist to meet the correctional needs of the different classes of prisoner? Here the position has improved immensely in recent years. There is a wide range of provision, from open camps, buzzing with industry, to the rigorous and secure corrective detention prisons, or the aimless local prisons, with their polyglot populations.

LOCAL PRISONS. It is the mixed, and on the whole unpromising, nature of their populations which is usually put forward to excuse the drab purposelessness of local prisons. They are not only prisons in their own right, but also local collecting centres, and contain a large proportion of transients, awaiting trial or transfer to another institution. Many others are short-term committals, who are in prison for too short a time for real training. The rest are either civil offenders (*e.g.* debtors), or prisoners who are not considered good enough material for the training prisons or the camps.

The local prison must also at present, unfortunately, pay the price for the improvements in other types of institution. If the more hopeful cases in the training prisons and the camps are to receive the sort of training which they need, the local prison must go short of both staff and constructive occupations, for there is at present an overall shortage of both. As a result, its inmates spend long hours locked in their cells, or working at the soul-destroying tasks of mail-bag making or repairing.

The problem of the local prison, then, must await the solution of wider problems of staffing, the availability of suitable work for prisoners to do, and above all the replacement of present buildings by more suitable ones.   But this is no excuse for delay; it means only that these wider problems have become very urgent ones indeed.

REGIONAL TRAINING PRISONS.   In these institutions the pattern of intensive training worked out at Wakefield in the inter-war years is now applied to populations consisting of those corrective trainees who are classified as suitable for this form of training,[7] together with trainable Ordinaries and Stars in the proportion of not more than two Ordinaries to every three Stars.

As all the inmates of a training prison are there for at least an eighteen-months' sentence, there is time to carry through a pro-gramme of training.   Interesting and varied kinds of work are available: there is little need to resort to the old standby of mail-bag work.   Vocational training, evening classes, and even correspondence courses can be taken.

Staffing ratios are better than in the local prisons, and this has the advantage of enabling prisoners to be out of their cells more often, either for education or recreation, or merely to chat.   It is very doubtful, however, if the staff are either numerous enough or well-enough trained to do much more than maintain order and security.[8]

The degree of custodial security maintained varies.   Some training prisons are completely open, many of their inmates working outside the prison walls.   One, the Verne, at Portsmouth, while maintaining complete peripheral security, allows much freedom within the purlieus of the prison.   Others are closed institutions, but have an open camp attached, to which the better prisoners can be transferred.

OPEN PRISONS.   Open prisons and camps have already been referred to in connection with training prisons, but there are also open institutions of other types, e.g. for civil or for short-sentence prisoners, and for women.[9]   According to the *Report of the Prison Commissioners for* 1954, there were no fewer than twelve open prisons or camps of various kinds at the end of that year.[10]

The earliest of these (in this country) was New Hall Camp, built in the woods near Wakefield, the first practical result of Alexander Paterson's dictum that "you cannot train men for freedom in a con-dition of captivity".[11]   And as an impressive symbol of the revolution thus effected, one of the first buildings was constructed of cast-off cell-doors.

Inmates for these new prisons necessarily have to be selected very carefully. If many run away, leaving a trail of further offences behind them, the public reaction would probably be violent enough to put back the clock for many years. The classification is, nevertheless, a positive one, concentrating upon the probability of prisoners being able to benefit from training under open conditions, rather than automatically excluding those with bad records. Personality considerations are kept well to the fore. Thus in 1950, Leyhill Camp in Gloucestershire contained twenty-one murderers, while one-quarter of its population had been sentenced for violent crimes, and one-fifth for sex offences. Abscondions have been gratifyingly few: in the first four years of Leyhill the numbers were respectively 9, 14, 8, and 5, and up to 1950, only one serious crime had been committed by a prisoner "on the run".[12]

When the bogy of security no longer haunts every activity in the institution, it is possible to concentrate whole-heartedly upon the task of training. Relations with officers are improved when the latter are no longer mere gaolers; and the way is opened up at last for the exercise of real personal influence. The general atmosphere of the institution improves, becoming more like that of a normal free community, and the men respond by becoming more co-operative and hopeful. American experience with open prisons, at Seagoville in Texas, and at Chino in Southern California, has been very similar.

PREVENTIVE DETENTION. By the time the 1948 Act had come into operation, the number of men committed to preventive detention under the Act of 1908 and still in prison were very few. Now in Parkhurst, they still retained certain privileges and extra amenities due to the dual nature of the law under which they had been sentenced.[13] Under the new legislation, there was to be only a single sentence, and, as administered by the Commissioners, it was to be a period of constructive training and not mere segregation. For instance, the principle, under the older act, of giving the preventive detainee extra privileges, in consideration of the purely preventive element in his sentence, has been abandoned in favour of additional stage privileges, which have to be earned.

A progressive stage system lies at the core of the whole scheme. The first stage, of about twelve months, is spent in a local prison. The detainee is then transferred to a central prison, where he becomes eligible for various privileges, superior to those available to the ordinary prisoner.

An indeterminate element enters into the sentence at this point. If the detainee serves the rest of his sentence in the second stage he is entitled to a maximum remission of one-sixth of his sentence, but if he can secure admission to the third stage, the amount of remission possible is increased to one-third. He must not, in any case, be transferred to the third stage until he is within a year of serving two-thirds of his sentence, and will then serve in the third stage for a period of between six and twelve months. The decision as to whether he shall be promoted to the third stage is in the hands of an Advisory Board, who are required to consider, not simply his behaviour in the institution, which may of course be very misleading, but whether they believe he will be fit for discharge after serving his time in the third stage.

The Prison Commissioners seem to be well aware of the danger that long terms of imprisonment like these may make a man so dependent upon institutional support that he will be unable to stand on his own feet when at large. They are, therefore, experimenting with pre-release methods which are very reminiscent of Sir Walter Crofton's famous "intermediate institution". Men in the third stage live in a separate block, with their own common-room, discussion groups on discharge problems, unlocked cells, and relaxed supervision.[14]

A number are then transferred for the last few months of their sentences to a hut in the grounds of Bristol Prison. Each of the hut-dwellers goes out to work in the city, collects his wages himself, and pays for his board from them. He is able to go out of the prison quite freely to attend classes or go to the cinema. An Assistant Governor is in charge of the hostel, and has under his charge there a group which is small enough for him to get to know them all very well.[15]

These are very imaginative and worth-while developments, the value of which may be found not to be confined to preventive detainees.

WOMEN IN PRISON. The number of women in prison is much fewer than the number of men. Thus the daily average population in prisons and Borstals in 1953 was 22,430 for men, but only 1,137 for women.[16] This is partly due to the general discrepancy between the level of recorded criminality for men and women, but not entirely, for the proportion of women in prison is even lower than this general figure, and is falling. It appears, in fact, that women are more leniently treated by the courts than men.[17]

The fact that such small numbers are involved is often cited as if it were a real handicap to progress. Thus Sir Lionel Fox claims that it is impossible to set up a training centre for girls under twenty-one, because there are usually fewer than twenty of them.[18] This complaint seems to arise from the failure of the powers that be to see the virtues inherent in small institutions.

As, in fact, practice in the women's wing of various local prisons shows, a small prisoner-group gives the staff a real chance of establishing personal relationships with inmates, and breaking down the traditional rigidity of the disciplinary framework, if only a little. As a result, the contrast between the small wing for women in many local prisons, and the great echoing galleries on the men's side, is quite striking. There is none of the overtone of mutual hostility which poisons the atmosphere of many of the men's prisons.

Small institutions tend to be more expensive to run, especially in staff, but if the Prison Commission could be persuaded to think more often of smaller groups for male prisoners, much good might result. The preventive detention small-group experiments already described are a step in the right direction.

Birmingham, Manchester, and Holloway women's prisons, with daily average populations in 1953 of 100, 171, and 337 respectively, are in rather a different category from the other establishments, none of which achieve a daily average population of 100.[19] In Holloway especially, difficulties are apt to be much more frequent and acute than those of the large men's prisons, partly perhaps because of the complicated way in which women manage their relationships with each other in our culture. Whatever other reforms may be required, and although Joan Henry may have over-stated her case,[20] it seems that many serious problems do exist. A first priority should be to break-up Holloway into a number of smaller self-contained institutions.

The administrative set-up for women is much the same as for men.[21] Only women, however, have a choice from several styles and patterns of dress. They are also allowed to do their hair as they wish, and to use make-up.

One recent development which should be mentioned is the annexe for neglectful mothers at Birmingham Prison.[22] Women who are sent to prison for child neglect are assigned to Birmingham to receive an eight-weeks' course in child-care and home management. Twelve women are trained at a time, and they live together in a hostel in the prison grounds. The actual courses are planned and provided by the Birmingham Education Committee.

This scheme is a great improvement upon an unconstructive term of imprisonment, but it has defects which may be irremediable. The difficulty of providing training in child-care in the absence of children is one such. Others are the shortness of the course (it is, after all, only eight weeks), and the fact that some women who have finished their training have to go back to prison to complete their sentences. These are an inevitable result of any sentencing procedure: with the limits which must be imposed upon the length of a sentence, and the need to commit when the offence is tried and not when there happens to be room in the training annexe. There are similar establishments run by voluntary organisations outside the prison system,[23] and it is to be hoped that the courts will make more use of their power to place women on probation with the condition that they attend these, instead of imposing a prison sentence.

YOUNG PRISONERS. Prisons being what they are, it is very desirable that young offenders should be kept out of them as much as possible. The Commission have done something by providing for the complete segregation of all young prisoners in young prisoner centres, or on a special landing in local prisons.[24] Their daily routine, however, does not vary much from that of the adult prisoners, and seems to be far less constructive than that in the best Borstals.

The 1948 Act has given an opportunity for a new departure. Besides further restricting the conditions under which young people under twenty-one may be sent to prison, the Act provided for the setting up of detention centres. Two such have been set up: one for junior boys, and one for seniors.

Discipline in the detention centres is designedly strict, and the boys are required to be "alert, well-mannered, punctual, and clean".[25] The training is obviously at a rather superficial level. However, the boys are encouraged to go to the Warden or his staff with their troubles.

It seems to have been believed in some quarters that detention centres would replace, as a "short, sharp shock", the former sentence to twenty-eight days' punitive detention in a remand home, which had been much criticised.[26] It is the sort of sentence which might have been very useful with first offenders, as a cold douche to bring them to their senses. But as Dr Grunhut has shown,[27] the courts are sending to the detention centres rather more serious cases than the remand homes had received. Only nine of the first hundred boys received into the Kidlington detention centre were first offenders, as compared with 22·4 per cent. in senior remand homes during the period 1945-8. Fourteen per cent. had had more than three previous convictions. Forty-four per cent. had previously been on probation, and 26 per cent. in approved schools.[28]

The new sentence seems, therefore, to be developing partly as an alternative to imprisonment in certain serious cases of juvenile recidivism. It may be that this use of it is inconsistent with its use also as a "short, sharp shock" for first offenders. Something other than prison is needed for the confirmed young delinquent, but surely something which penetrates more deeply than the detention centres are doing.

THE MENTALLY ABNORMAL. There is at present no special institution for the treatment of mentally abnormal prisoners. Offenders who are in need of treatment are placed either in Wormwood Scrubs or Wakefield, or Holloway in the case of women, where the services of psychotherapists are available.

Psychological treatment in prison began with a study of its possibilities by East and Hubert during the period 1934-8.[29] They reported favourably upon it, and recommended that a special institution should be created, in which it could be more efficiently organised. The Prison Commission have now secured planning permission for the erection of such an "East-Hubert" institution on a site in Buckinghamshire.[30]

The Home Office Advisory Council on the Treatment of Offenders has also recommended the provision of a special institution, but has urged that it should not be part of the penal system, and should "be removed as far as possible from the prison atmosphere".[31] Even if we do not go to such lengths, a separate therapeutic institution of some sort is required. For although East and Hubert, and the psychotherapists who have followed them,[32] have shown that treatment can be effective in a general prison, it must, in such a setting, be greatly handicapped.

For instance, the atmosphere of a prison is not conducive to the development of the warm and trusting attitude of patient towards therapist which is indispensable for successful psychotherapy. There is also the danger of encouraging malingering or invalidism among prisoners who do not really need psychological help. The attitudes of the prison staff, and of prisoners who are not under treatment, is also likely to be unhelpful. The staff are apt to feel that the prisoner-patients are being spoiled: other prisoners to jeer at them as mental cases.[33]

If the new psychiatric institution provided accommodation for "difficult" or psychopathic prisoners, even if they were not considered good subjects for psychotherapy (as East and Hubert intended it should), the ordinary prison would be relieved of a very heavy burden of responsibility, and milder prison discipline methods might be encouraged. Although the Departmental Committee on Punishments in Prisons, etc.,[34] were not very interested in milder prison discipline methods, they were convinced of the advantages which would accrue to the prisons by the removal of the more awkward characters from the general prison population in this way.

### NOTES TO CHAPTER XIII

1. *E.g.* Fox, Sir L., *English Prison and Borstal Systems*, 1952, p. 152. Compare the emphasis given here to "individualisation" with the much franker statement on pp. 129-30.

2. Teeters, N. K., "Prison System of England", *J. of Crim. Law and Criminology*, **41**: 5, 1951, p. 578.

3. Sec. 21.

4. Fox, *op. cit.*, p. 146.

5. Heckstall-Smith, Anthony, *Eighteen Months*, 1954.

6. For an interesting analysis of present English classification methods, see Mannheim, H., and Spencer, J. C., *Problems of Classification*, 1948.

7. Those not considered suitable are placed in special corrective training prisons, where maximum security conditions obtain. Here also, however, as far as possible, a full programme of training is maintained.

8. See Heckstall-Smith, A., *op. cit.*

9. For descriptions of the open prison for women at Askham Grange, consult Henry, Joan, *They Lie in Gaol*; and Kelley, Joanna, *Howard Journal*, **9**: 2, 1955, pp. 124 ff.

10. *Report of the Commissioners of Prisons*, 1954, Cmd. 9547, pp. 144 ff.

11. Quoted Fox, *op. cit.*, p. 136.

12. Leitch, A., "The Open Prison", *Brit. J. of Delinquency*, **2**: 1, 1951, p. 25. For even more favourable figures for other open institutions, refer to Fox, *op. cit.*, p. 153.

13. Morris, N., *The Habitual Criminal*, 1951, pp. 70 ff.

14. Fox, *op. cit.*, p. 320.

15. *Report of the Commissioners of Prisons*, 1953, Cmd. 9259, pp. 27 ff. Also *Report*, 1954, *loc. cit.*, pp. 32-3.

16. *Commissioners' Report*, 1954, *loc. cit.*, p. 9.

17. See Chapter VIII, above.

18. Fox, *op. cit.*, p. 147.

19. *Commissioners' Report*, *loc. cit.*, pp. 150-1.

20. Henry, Joan, *op. cit.*

21. Fox, *op. cit.*, pp. 147-8.

22. *Report of the Commissioners of Prisons*, 1952, Cmd. 8948. Also the *Report* for 1953, *loc. cit.*, p. 55.

23. The Mayflower Home at Plymouth, "Brentwood" in Cheshire, Spofforth Hall in Yorkshire, and Crowley House in Birmingham.

24. There is some mixing with other age groups for work at Wakefield.

25. *Commissioners' Report*, 1952, *loc. cit.*, p. 93.

26. Bagot, J. H., *Punitive Detention*, 1944. Radzinowicz, L., and Turner, J. W. C. (eds.), *Detention in Remand Homes*, 1952.

27. Grunhut, M., *British J. of Delinquency*, **5**: 3, 1955, pp. 191 ff.

28. More up-to-date information on admissions to detention centres will be found in the *Commissioners' Report*, 1953, *loc. cit.*, and for 1954, pp. 85 ff.

29. East, W. Norwood, and Hubert, W. H. de B., *Psychological Treatment of Crime*, 1939.

30. See *Lancet*, 1950, **258,** pp. 1123-6.

31. *Commissioners' Report*, 1954, pp. 100-1, which also contains a recent statement on the purpose of the new institution.

32. Mackwood, J. C., "Psychological Treatment of Offenders in Prison", *Brit. J. of Medical Psychology*, **40**: 5, 1949, pp. 5-22. Mackwood, J. C., and Roper, W. F., "Psychotherapy in Prisons and Correctional Institutions", *Proc. Royal Society of Medicine*, March 1954, pp. 220-3. Landers, J. J., MacPhail, D. S., and Simpson, R. C., "Group Therapy in H.M. Prison, Wormwood Scrubs", *J. of Mental Science*, **100**: 421, 1954, pp. 953 ff.

33. Some of the difficulties encountered are described in East and Hubert, *op. cit.*, Sec. II, and in the appendix prepared by H. T. P. Young. See also Mackwood and Roper, *loc. cit.*

34. *Report of Departmental Committee on Punishments in Prisons, Borstals, Approved Schools and Remand Homes*, 1951, *Cmd.* 8256, Part I, Paras 83-6.

# CHAPTER XIV

## FACTORS IN PRISON TRAINING

On a view of the prison as an institution for treatment not punishment, each sphere of prison activity—discipline, work, education, etc.—must be justified by its value in training. As might be expected, however, in view of the penal role which our prisons (whatever our protestations) are still expected to play, these various elements of prison life are very imperfectly adapted to a purely reformative function. They are too equivocal in their approach to training to be very successful at it.

We may be aware of the social roots from which these failures have stemmed, but we do not, therefore, have to condone them. We must examine what is done in our prisons strictly in the light of their avowed aim of changing the anti-social outlook of the prisoner, and bringing him into a more healthy frame of mind towards his fellow citizens.[1] Working with this yard-stick we shall find much to criticise.

### Training Methods

RECEPTION AND ORIENTATION. When an offender arrives in the reception block at the beginning of his term of imprisonment, great care is taken to see that he is clean and free from disease. Little or nothing is done to prepare him mentally for his training, so that he will have the right attitude to it.

There is usually great confusion in his mind about what he can and cannot do. A handful of cards hang on the wall of his cell which purport to tell him, but many of them are out of date, and they say nothing about the unwritten laws which derive from the ideas of the governor or the chief officer.[2] Moreover, as modern research on the psychology of communication has shown, notices are a very ineffective way of conveying information. They are either not read, or are read inaccurately, or they are misunderstood. Careful explanations, the opportunity to ask questions, and, above all, time to assimilate the *mores* of this strange new world, are required. If these are conceded many unnecessary disciplinary difficulties (especially early in a sentence) will be avoided, and a major cause of friction and hostility between prisoner and institution will have been removed.

Recent research on groups suggests that if new prisoners were allowed to examine the rules and their implications in discussion

groups, they might, through the interplay of ideas and their identification with the group, both understand and absorb them better.
They might also begin to see, in a shadowy way, how the prison is
seeking to help them, and to discover that it is in their own interest
to co-operate.[3] However it is achieved, some early opportunity
should be taken of eliciting the voluntary co-operation of the
prisoner. At present such co-operation is non-existent. Prison
life is a battle between prisoners and officers. On the surface,
prisoners are made to comply, but they fight back: with evasion
and obstruction, by taking immediate advantage of weakness, and
while making all the right motions, insulating themselves against
any reformative influences emanating from their captors.

DISCIPLINE AND REFORM. If there is one thing which tends to
confirm the prisoner in this attitude, it is the way in which discipline
is maintained. This is the responsibility of prison officers (formerly
known as warders) who are roughly equivalent in the prisons to
N.C.O.'s in the army. They are in daily contact with the prisoners,
and therefore *are* the prison to the inmates, much more than the
governor and his assistants

Without order no prison, indeed no social institution of any
kind, could achieve anything worth while. This is the justification
for the maintenance of firm standards of discipline in prison.
Nevertheless, if it has to be achieved at the cost of bullying, or at
least stony impersonality, as is unfortunately the case in most
prisons to-day,[4] then the price is too high.

Such an approach to the prisoner is to be put down in part to
the survival of retributive attitudes towards crime and punishment.
The criminal deserves no better treatment. But probably a more
important cause is fear: fear, if one relaxes, of losing face or losing
control. As a result, the prison officer's role has become purely
negative. One need not rely on the memoirs of ex-prisoners to
prove this: one need only examine the resolutions which are brought
forward at Prison Officers' Association Conferences, or the evidence
given on behalf of the officers before the Committee on Punishments
in Prisons and Borstals.[5]

Thus the reformative function which the officer might have
fulfilled is going by default. If he were able to listen sympathetically
to a man's troubles, to befriend him, and to give him advice, then
he would not only learn a good deal himself, but would really be
able to help his unwilling wards to make good. Nor, if such an
approach were carried out in a balanced way, would it necessarily

involve any real deterioration in the order of the prison, for such individualisation of treatment means dealing with disciplinary problems at their roots. A very experienced prison medical officer has made a similar plea.[6]

Some have suggested that social workers should be appointed to do such work with prisoners.[7] Social case-workers already exist in Belgian and French prisons,[8] but in no country will it be possible to provide enough of them to work intensively with the entire prison population. Nor is this necessary, although skilled case-workers should be available to deal with the more difficult cases, and to give general advice to other members of staff on case-work problems.

The crucial question is whether our prison officers are really competent to do this sort of thing, even with the advice and support of a professional worker. Certainly many of them would be (a few already do it[9]), and if not we should recruit those who can. We cannot evade this issue. Our prison officers are influencing the attitudes of prisoners every day, merely by supervising them or speaking to them, only at present they exercise their influence blindly, and with unfortunate results. We must accept this as a fact; when we do, we shall see the necessity for training them to assume such a responsibility.

Many, however, still object that there is not necessarily any conflict between reformation and the strictest discipline. The prisoners, it will be argued, acquire a habit of good behaviour in prison which will stand them in very good stead when they are discharged.

Ex-prisoners are unanimous in their view that this is not what happens. In summing-up the comments of conscientious objectors on their prison experiences during the war, Mark Benney writes: "Inevitably the warder soon loses any moral feelings he might start with about the men in his charge; they quickly become men who are either easy to handle or not easy to handle. He therefore has an occupational prejudice in favour of the old offender and against the new man . . . And since the smiles and frowns of the officer carry such weight, there is yet another strong incentive to emulate the 'big shots', to adopt wholeheartedly the furtive, shifty, dissimulating habits of the jailbird".[10]

In other words, prisoners comply so far as they must in order to be comfortable in prison, but they do not themselves identify with the institution and its rules. In themselves they remain untouched by it, building-up, below the surface, a community life of their own, essentially criminal in its ways, and anti-prison and anti-"screw" in its attitudes. In such a situation, the institution or its officers are hardly likely to exercise any sort of reformative influence. Deeper springs have to be tapped.

Dr Grunhut points out that in the Glueck follow-up studies of prisoners from the Massachussets State Reformatory, those who had good work records in the reformatory did not succeed much more frequently than those who were bad workers. He draws the inevitable conclusion: "Enforced habits slacken as soon as the situation from which they arose no longer exists . . . Habits acquired in unusual circumstances have a chance of persisting only if they are supported by strong motives which apply also to normal situations".[11] It should be the duty of our prison staffs to try to cultivate such motives in the men under their charge.

PUNISHMENTS. Closely connected with the question of discipline is that of punishments. From what has gone before, it would seem that punishments in prison have little long-term training value, though they have a short-term value in deterring the non-conformist and asserting, as it were, the standards of behaviour which the administration are determined to maintain. They include loss of remission or privileges, restriction of diet (to bread and water if necessary), and cellular confinement. Only for mutiny or gross violence to an officer can corporal punishment be imposed.

The governor's powers to impose punishments are rigorously limited by regulation; only the Visiting Committee (consisting largely of magistrates) can impose the severer penalties.

Punishments have, of course, always played an important part in the maintenance of prison discipline, and they are milder now than in the past; but it is none the less true that the purely negative system outlined above has replaced a more positive procedure under the old progressive stage system, in which marks towards privileges and remission had to be earned by good behaviour.

This marks-system was very cumbersome. Moreover, many of the privileges, such as library books, attendance at lectures, the privilege of association, and the right to receive earnings, are considered to have training value in themselves. It was, therefore, decided that all prisoners, after a short initial period, should receive the full quota of privileges and be credited with the full amount of remission. These could then be docked if a prisoner misbehaved himself. This is a much simpler scheme to operate than the marks-system, but there will be much disagreement as to whether a negative system imposing punishments is better in principle than a positive system providing incentives.   It is difficult to see how a punitive relationship of staff to prisoners can lead to the mutual trust which is a precondition for any kind of case-work.

PRISON LABOUR.   It is regrettable but true that, in spite of the progress made in developing constructive work programmes in the training prisons, the picture of prison labour in this country is still dominated by the mail-bag shop.   In 1953-4 a daily average population of 5,110 were engaged on mail-bag repair or manufacture, out of a total of 18,092 effectives.   Of the rest, the only group which reached four figures were the "cleaners, jobbers, and labourers" with 2,233.[12]   Mail-bag work is dull and monotonous, and together with the restrictions which are imposed on talking at work,[13] is well designed to encourage the day-dreaming and inability to concentrate which remain the mark of a prison sentence in spite of the abolition of separate confinement.

Work in prison should form part of a carefully designed programme of training, and aim to attain as many as possible of the following objectives:—

(a) To enlist the prisoner's spontaneous interest, and give him a sense of purpose, so that he may begin to develop through it.

(b) To give him confidence in his ability to work and to achieve things.

(c) To give him an opportunity to exercise and develop his skills.

(d) To inculcate in him good working habits.

There are many occupations in use which have high training value,[14] and these are predominant in the training prisons, but in the local prisons conditions are still very unsatisfactory.   However, there are many obstacles to the general introduction of a satisfactory work programme, and no purpose is served by not facing up to these. The obsolete buildings and the shortage of staff have already been mentioned.   The calibre of the prisoners is also often cited in extenuation of the present work position:  they are said to be inferior in intelligence, skill, and industriousness to most workers outside. Many of them may be fit for little but mail-bag work.   The labour force, also, is constantly changing, especially in the local prisons, and there are many short-term prisoners who are hardly in prison long enough to learn a skilled task.

More could be done, however.   Dull people, it is true, seem to be happiest at monotonous, repetitive tasks, like mail-bag work, but many intelligent prisoners are also put to this work.   Training, moreover, in both skills and diligence, is the job for which our correctional institutions exist, and they are not entitled to put forward the prisoners' shortcomings in these respects as an excuse for doing nothing about them.

The difficulties of coping with a transient labour force are real, but the exercise of a little organisational ingenuity should provide the answer. As far as short-term prisoners are concerned, it should be remembered that the modern industrial concern teaches its unskilled operatives to do their jobs in a couple of days. Many private firms have been faced with the problem of a constantly changing labour force in the years of full employment since the war, and have been able to deal with it.

More difficult to cope with is the actual shortage of work available for prisoners. The Committee on the Employment of Prisoners saw this as the root of the whole problem.[15] This "work-famine" is due to the opposition which private enterprise, and even more, the trade unions, offer to any proposals that prisoners should produce goods for the open market. All the skeletons of the scarcity years are taken from their cupboards and dusted on such occasions—"unfair competition" and "sweated labour", and so forth. There is an urgent need for some joint body, including the Prison Commissioners and both sides of industry, to work out and control a prison labour scheme. Nothing short of this will reassure industry, and give it the understanding which it needs if it is going to abandon its present hostile attitude towards the extension of prison work programmes.

The Commissioners might also make more use than they do of the opportunities offered by the building of new institutions. We need new and better prison buildings and could use prisoners to construct them. It might even be possible to draw upon the pioneering spirit which made the building of Lowdham Grange and North Sea Camp Borstals so very worth while from the correctional point of view. Certainly if the dull and apathetic type of boy at present sent to Lowdham Grange can participate in the Lowdham building project, many prisoners could do likewise.

There is probably also more scope for seasonal work, at least, in agriculture. Farms are still short of help at haymaking, harvesting and threshing times. Something is being done under this head, but it amounts in total to less than 4 per cent. of the whole work programme.

The chief obstacle to the extension of such activities as building and agricultural work is probably that of maintaining security. We do not want an extension of outside work if it is going to mean, as it did until very recently, the use of armed officers as at Dartmoor, or of irons as in some southern states of the U.S.A.[16] The record of the open prisons should encourage us, for it shows that all prisoners do not run away immediately the prison doors are thrown open. Prudence would no doubt have to be exercised in selecting prisoners for outside work, but most of those incarcerated in local prisons at any rate would probably be suitable. Many who might not be trustworthy enough for the minimum security camp might, nevertheless, be able to sustain the limited freedom involved in working under supervision outside the prison walls.

In spite of all these difficulties, British prisons had, before the war, a very high proportion of prisoners engaged on productive work. This amounted to 74·2 per cent. as compared with 43·5 per cent. in the United States.[17] This proportion had fallen to 64 per cent. in 1953, and much of this was only half-time work, so there is much leeway to be made up before even the pre-war position has been restored.[18]

Payment is now made to prisoners for the work they do. Wherever possible this payment is based on a piecework system, in order to add interest to the work and to give the prisoner an incentive to work hard. The money is very little, but appears to be much appreciated by the men. The Twelfth International Penal and Penitentiary Congress at the Hague,[19] recommended that such schemes of payment should be amended so that the prisoner could receive a wage from which he would himself make the necessary appropriations for his board, for the maintenance of his family, and perhaps for making restitution to the victim of his crime. Superficially this is a very attractive scheme, but the administrative complications are likely to be very great,[20] and as far as this country is concerned, such a plan will probably have to wait until prison industries have been rationalised and made more productive. The sum which could be paid at the present *per capita* level of productivity would be too small for the purpose.

EDUCATION. Vocational training provides a bridge between the labour and the educational schemes. There are always a number of excellent courses available in such trades as bricklaying, carpentry, and shoemaking.[21] Unfortunately it is not often that men who complete these courses can actually obtain jobs in the trade. Apprenticeship regulations and prejudice together often present an insuperable obstacle. There is room here also for consultation with industry.

Other courses range from instruction for illiterates to corre-spondence courses for the external degrees of London University, and include also many cultural and "hobby" classes. It appears that the amount of provision varies considerably between one prison and another. Dendrickson and Thomas paint a very gloomy picture of the educational provision at Dartmoor.[22] But where it is good it will not only improve the personal equipment of the prisoners, but will add to the constructiveness of the atmosphere, and may also provide interests and points of contact with other people after discharge.

RELIGION. For some prisoners, especially those with a religious faith, the chaplain may be able to do a great deal. For others it may be that any religious approach which lays emphasis upon the "rightness" and "wrongness" of actions is too simple and direct.

No one would suggest that a religious faith can be forced on a person. Any form of compulsory religious observance is therefore undesirable. There is no actual compulsion upon prisoners in British prisons to attend church services, but they must opt out on a permanent basis if they wish to be excused. They will be reluctant to do that if they feel it might earn them the disapproval of the authorities. Other prisoners, it seems, go to church merely to escape from their cells for an hour or so.

The motives for going to church, then, are rarely concerned with religion as such. This does not give the chaplain a chance to do the job he could do, for instead of being a matter of sincere conviction, religious observance in the prison generally becomes merely a means to an end, and falls into disrepute accordingly.

Various welfare services, education, and recreation, fall formally within the range of the chaplain's duties. This is an anachronism in these days of professionalism in education and social work. Education is therefore, in practice, directed nowadays by tutor-organisers, seconded to the prisons by local education authorities, and assistant governors are often appointed to perform welfare functions.

PHYSICAL WELFARE. In no sphere does the modern English prison lag so far behind its pretensions as in the sphere of physical welfare. The constant complaints by ex-prisoners about the diet and the conditions under which food is served,[23] for instance, never seem to receive the attention which they appear to deserve.[24]

The exercise yard is another burning topic. Although in some prisons "physical jerks" and recreational games are being used more, many prisoners still are to be seen at some time of the day shuffling around the concentric rings of the exercise yard, just as they did in Pentonville a century ago. Two prisoners may walk abreast now, and talking is allowed,[25] but the purposelessness of the whole procedure should have condemned it long ago. No prisoner may merely stand and talk. Exercise it is, and exercise it must be. But it is the mechanised soulless exercise of the ant heap.

The same lack of respect for the individual is to be seen in the refusal of the Commissioners to abolish the revolting and unhygienic chamber-pots, and the early morning penance of "slopping" them out. They claim that most prisoners do not mind;[26] whether they do or not at first, they learn not to do so. Such sordid features of the prison environment bring down the standards of all prisoners to the level of the worst.[27]

## Relationships with the Outside World

No matter how good the regime inside a prison may be it will fail in its task of social rehabilitation unless pains are taken to keep the prisoner in touch with the outside world; to preserve any place he may already have in it so far as this is possible; and as his sentence nears its end, to increase the number of points at which he can have experience of it so that he can once more become adept in its ways.[28]

Our prisons, by limiting the number of letters which a prisoner may write and receive, fly in the face of this requirement. No security considerations are involved, for all letters are read and censored, and as far as cost is concerned, prisoners could be required to pay for all letters in excess of a stipulated maximum.

Visits from relatives and friends are in rather a different category, for if these were irregular and too frequent they would upset the routine of the institution. Something should be done, however, to make the conditions in which the prisoner receives his visitors more natural. At present (except in the open prisons) he talks to them either in a cubicle with a wire mesh and a sheet of glass between, or, together with other prisoners, across a long table, with officers supervising from the ends.

All these precautions are designed to prevent the passage of contraband between visitor and prisoner, but they are not very successful in this. It should not be beyond the power of human ingenuity to find a more natural setting for visits without noticeably increasing the amount of contraband which evades capture. If visits are to bring a breath of normal society into the prisoner's life they should be as unrestricted and natural, as little dominated by the tone of the institution, as possible.

Homosexuality is widespread in prison, but regular visits from his wife or sweetheart are probably the best antidote which a man could receive. It would probably be considered dangerously advanced, perhaps even immoral, to suggest that he should be allowed to kiss her; in fact, much more than this could be justified. In the prisons of various Central and South American countries, prisoners are allowed to receive "conjugal visits" from their wives.[29] Where this is permitted, the man's ties with his wife are preserved, and he is armed against the temptation to indulge in homosexual practices. It may also reduce tension in the institution where this is the result of sexual frustration.

In addition to their personal visitors, prisoners may be visited by official "prison visitors". They are voluntary workers, appointed by the Commissioners on the recommendation of the governor, and have a group of about ten prisoners each allocated to them by the governor. Elizabeth Fry's "Ladies' Prison Committees" were an early example of this, but the practice fell into disuse until the 'nineties of the last century, when it was revived and placed on an official basis. It was not extended to men's prisons until 1922.

The prison visitor can bring the prisoner news of a wider world than that of his family circle, and being usually an educated and intelligent person, can do it more deliberately. By making the prisoner feel that someone at least is interested in him, he may also help in another way, reinforcing his will to make good.[30]

### After-care

There are two quite separate systems of after-care for prisoners in this country: statutory after-care, for certain special classes of prisoners, administered by the Central After-care Association, and voluntary after-care for the rest, this being the responsibility of the Discharged Prisoners' Aid Societies.

The C.A.C.A., the council of which consists of representatives of voluntary bodies and various government departments (including the Prison Commission) interested in the problem, is responsible for the after-care of all persons discharged from Borstal, corrective training and preventive detention, for "lifers", and for any prisoners under the age of twenty-one whose sentence exceeds three months.[31] All these classes of prisoners are required as a condition of their licences to report to the Association and carry out its instructions until the period of the licence has expired. An ex-prisoner who fails to do so may find that his licence has been cancelled and he has been recalled to the institution. The Association's own representatives keep in touch with him while he is serving his sentence, but after his discharge, when after-care proper begins, the work is carried through (for the C.A.C.A.) by probation officers.

Probation and after-care supervision have much in common, but the practice of combining the two functions has its drawbacks. One is clearly that of criminal contamination.[32] Also the after-care duties of the probation officer may be treated as "extras" rather than as an integral part of his work, competing for priority with the probation and matrimonial work which he does directly for the Bench employing him.

Much sound after-care work is undoubtedly being done by probation officers throughout the country. The next step (if the parochial basis of the probation service does not prevent it) must be for the officer who is to supervise a prisoner to make early contact with him in prison. He can then get to know him well, and begin to prepare him (and his family) for what is to come. After-care work thus begins as a form of social case-work in prison long before the prisoner is freed.

The voluntary system deals with the vast majority of the prisoners discharged. Discharges from local prisons are the responsibility of the local Discharged Prisoners' Aid Society, and from training prisons of the National Association of Discharged Prisoners' Aid Societies. The work done by these bodies is still very unsatisfactory in spite of very pertinent criticisms from two government committees in the last twenty years.[33] Too little real social work help is given. In many cases the societies are content to dole out material help, to hand the man a few shillings, usually too small a sum, anyway, to be really helpful to him.

Although most of them now have at least part-time paid welfare officers, few of these are trained social workers, and the work many of them do is not of a very high standard. However, they do make early contact in prison with cases which they are going to follow up, and in this respect are ahead of the statutory system. It is a pity that all this is done to so little effect.

Of course, not all prisoners desire after-care help. Many of them want to forget all about their imprisonment when they finally regain their freedom. In spite of this there would seem to be a good case for compulsory after-care in all cases, at least until the period of remission has expired. But if compulsory supervision is to work, it will have to be given teeth, in the shape of the power to recall those who fail to comply. This would transform our remission system into a general licence-system—a change of some magnitude which will not be brought about in a day. Meanwhile it is urgently necessary that the D.P.A.'s should be made more effective.

Much more money and much more attention needs to be devoted to this question of after-care, for it deals with the problem of treatment at its most vital point, when the ex-prisoner is about to take up the threads of his life again. He may have made all sorts of resolutions while he was in prison, but now he is confronted with practical situations. Now he really is exposed to the temptations and stresses which overcame him before. And as a " gaol-bird " the dice are more heavily loaded against him than ever, especially when he sets out to find a job.

Whether he succumbs once more will depend to a very large extent upon the relationship which the social worker responsible for his after-care is able to establish with him, and the skill with which the worker helps him to find a new niche for himself in the world. A good after-care officer may be able to repair even the damage done by a bad prison system, but there is nobody to put matters right if he fails.

### The Effect of a Term of Imprisonment

When the administrators of our prison system are as dubious as they are about the effect of a term of imprisonment, the criminologist cannot but be apprehensive.[34]

What do the figures show? About 20 per cent. of first offenders return to prison,[35] but a much higher proportion of that 20 per cent. return again and again. The actual proportion is not known, but we do know that in 1953, for example, 46 per cent. of the total male "receptions under sentence" had been in prison at least once previously.[36] The position is even graver than these figures suggest, for continual recidivism means longer sentences, causing reception statistics to understate its incidence. Moreover, it does not follow that those who have not returned to prison have committed no further offences; other penalties might have been imposed in a few cases, or they might not have been caught.

It is not possible to say just how many people are deterred or reformed by their stay in prison. Apart from the statistical considerations already referred to, many first offenders might not have committed another offence in any case. But it is clear that there is a group of no mean size who do not respond to the sort of training which they receive there. There is plenty of evidence from ex-prisoners, on the other hand (which prison officials will hardly deny), to suggest that many are positively corrupted by their prison experiences. It is for such reasons that well-known American criminologists such as Tannenbaum,[37] and Barnes and Teeters,[38] call for the abolition of prisons and their replacement by more rational training establishments.

In this country we are more inclined to transform our social institutions gradually, without making a complete break with tradition. This is what seems to have been happening slowly (too slowly) to our prisons in the course of the last hundred years. It remains to be seen whether such evolutionary methods will have the effect required, or whether (as in the case of the old Poor Law) the weight of tradition and the stigma of the past will prove too strong for new attitudes to correction really to take root in our institutions without a completely new start.

We might also make more use of non-institutional forms of treatment; short sentences especially, can have little reformative value. There is much room for experiment here. Mannheim has suggested the adoption of some form of compulsory labour without loss of liberty, which could be the adult counterpart to the attendance centres for juveniles, set up under the Criminal Justice Act 1948.[39] But probation is bound to be the core of our non-institutional provision, and it is, therefore, disturbing to find that it is being used less than before the war.[40]

## NOTES TO CHAPTER XIV

1. The Prison Rules state that "The purposes of training and treatment of convicted prisoners shall be to establish in them the will to lead a good and useful life on discharge, and to fit them to do so".

2. Benney, M., *Gaol Delivery*, 1948, pp. 45-7. Heckstall-Smith, A., *Eighteen Months*, 1954, p. 23.

3. The application of group discussion methods to the correctional institution is discussed at length in Chapter XVII.

4. See the writings of ex-prisoners, *e.g.* Benney, Heckstall-Smith, Henry, Dendrickson and Thomas, etc. For American prisons consult Barnes, H. E., and Teeters, N. K., *New Horizons in Criminology*, 1945, pp. 590 ff.

5. *Cmd.* 8256, 1951.

6. Roper, W. F., in *Howard Journal*, **9**: 2, 1955, pp. 91 ff.

7. Symposium by Klare, H. J., Tilley, M., and Morton, H. M., in *Howard Journal*, **9**: 1, 1954, pp. 36-51; Spencer, J. C., *Howard Journal*, **8**: 3, 1951, pp. 87 ff.

8. For the French system consult Hertevent, J., "Social Service in French Prisons", *Howard Journal*, **8**: 3, 1952, pp. 181 ff.

9. Ex-prisoners, in spite of their anti-prison bias, often write gratefully of the understanding and support they received from some of the officers who had charge of them.

10. Benney, M., *op. cit.*, pp. 89-90.
11. Grunhut, M., *Penal Reform*, 1948, p. 215.
12. *Report of the Commissioners of Prisons*, 1954, *Cmd.* 9547, pp. 162 ff.
13. Fox, *op. cit.*, p. 160.
14. *Commissioners' Report*, *loc. cit.*
15. *Departmental Committee on Employment of Prisoners*, *Cmd.* 4462, 1933.
16. American chain-gangs are described in Barnes and Teeters, *op. cit.*, pp. 624 ff.
17. Grunhut, *op. cit.*, p. 200.
18. Calculated from *Commissioners' Report*, *loc. cit.*
19. Fox, *op. cit.*, Appendix F. This recommendation was reaffirmed by the United Nations Congress on the Treatment of Offenders, held in Geneva in 1955.
20. *Ibid.*, pp. 461-2.
21. The six-months' courses of the Ministry of Labour are used.
22. Dendrickson, G., and Thomas, F., *Truth About Dartmoor*, 1954.
23. Such complaints are universal. See, for example, Dendrickson and Thomas, *ibid.*
24. Fox, *op. cit.*, pp. 231 ff. It is not sufficient for the prison administrator merely to recognise that the problem exists.
25. *Ibid.*, pp. 229-30.
26. For example, *ibid.*, p. 229.
27. Their impact upon the fastidious mind may be seen in Heckstall-Smith, A., *op. cit.*, pp. 19-24.
28. See above, p. 136.
29. Barnes and Teeters, *op. cit.*, p. 751.
30. Descriptions by prison visitors of this work, include Earl, Honor, *Prison Once a Week*, 1948; and Watson, J. A. F., *Meet the Prisoner*, 1939.
31. Prison Act 1952, Sec. 25.
32. See p. 237.
33. *Departmental Committee on Discharged Prisoners' Aid Societies*, 1952 (The Maxwell Committee), *Cmd.* 8879, 1953. *Departmental Committee on the Employment of Prisoners*, Part II, 1935 (Salmon Committee), *Cmd.* 4897.
34. See, for instance, Fox, *op. cit.*, p. 135.
35. *Ibid.*, p. 279.
36. *Commissioners' Report*, *loc. cit.*, pp. 13-14.
37. Tannenbaum, F., *Wall Shadows*, 1922, p. 141.
38. Barnes and Teeters, *op. cit.*, p. 949.
39. Mannheim, H., *Dilemma of Penal Reform*, 1939, pp. 134 ff.
40. See the figures given below, p. 240.

# CHAPTER XV

## BORSTAL

The English Borstal system has been praised by the penologists of many countries, Americans especially have shown great interest in it, and have argued for the adoption of a similar approach to the delinquent adolescent in the United States.[1]

There is, however, little room for complacency about our Borstal institutions, as the reconviction figures show:—

TABLE X

PERCENTAGES OF MALES RECONVICTED WITHIN SEVEN YEARS OF DISCHARGE FROM BORSTAL (OR BY 31 DECEMBER 1954, IF DISCHARGED SINCE 1947).[2]

| Year of Discharge | Number Discharged | Percentage Not Reconvicted | Percentage Reconvicted Once Only | Percentage Reconvicted Twice or More |
|---|---|---|---|---|
| 1937-8 | 1,741 | 59·5 | 19·5 | 21 |
| 1940-42 | 3,238 | 50·7 | 21·3 | 28 |
| 1943-5 | 3,929 | 41·9 | 23·3 | 34·8 |
| 1946-8 | 5,369 | 38·8 | 25·9 | 35·3 |
| 1949-51 | 5,358 | 43·4 | 28·5 | 28·1 |

The Commissioners are inclined to try to focus attention upon the last column of this table,[3] but these figures are probably not very relevant to Borstal, as the first reconviction after discharge would result in another sentence, in many cases prison. The results shown in column five are more likely to be the result of that second sentence than of the original period of Borstal training. All convictions must count, therefore, in any estimate of the effectiveness of Borstal.

The percentage of failure (bearing in mind that reconviction figures are almost certainly an underestimate of this)[4] was therefore rather less than 50 per cent. before the war, and rather more than 50 per cent. since.[5] George Benson[6] has compared the results for recent years with those for adolescent males discharged from prison:—

TABLE XI

DISCHARGES TO AFTER-CARE FROM BORSTAL AND PRISON IN 1949, 1950, AND 1951, AND NOT RECONVICTED BY 31 DECEMBER 1953

| | Number Discharged | Not Reconvicted | Percentage |
|---|---|---|---|
| Boys' Borstal | 5,358 | 2,523 | 47 |
| Prison .. | 1,256 | 864 | 68 |

The administrators of our Borstal system, one feels, should be more disquieted than they appear to be, and it behoves them to examine the methods of training used very narrowly, to see how they can be improved.

## Influence of Paterson

Although the Borstal system was founded by Ruggles Brise, the spirit which now animates it is the work of Alexander Paterson. The difference between the two men is quite clear from their writings. Wrote Ruggles Brise: "Experience showed that the (Borstal) system should be one of stern and exact discipline, tempered only by such rewards and privileges as good conduct, with industry, might earn: and resting on its physical side on the basis of hard manual labour and skilled trades, and on its moral and intellectual side on the combined efforts of the Chaplain and the Schoolmaster".[7]

Paterson, on the other hand, preferred to regard a lad in Borstal as "a living organism, having its own secret of life and motive power within, adapting itself in external conduct to the surroundings of the moment, but undergoing no permanent organic change as a result of outside pressure . . . The task is not to break or knead him into shape, but to stimulate some power within to regulate conduct aright, to insinuate a preference for the good and the clean, to make him want to use his life well, so that he himself and not others will save him from waste".[8]

In carrying out those principles, Paterson infused a creative spirit into the Borstals which still distinguishes them, and which led to the famous experiments with Open Borstals in the 'thirties.

## The Open Borstals

Under the leadership of a talented Borstal governor, W. W. Llewellin, a group of boys with their Housemasters and their officers marched in 1930 all the way from Feltham Borstal in Middlesex to the village of Lowdham in Nottinghamshire, and camped there while they set about the task of building their own institution. There were no bolts and bars, and no close supervision, and when Lowdham Grange Borstal Institution rose among the meadows, it was natural that it should become our first open Borstal.[9]

Lowdham was also the first and remains the only Borstal built for its purpose. Most of the others were converted prisons, in which it must have been heartbreaking to try to realise the vision of Paterson. Lowdham provided, for the first time, a setting within which it could be aimed at.

Five years later, Llewellin led twenty new Borstal entrants across England from Stafford to the Wash to establish the North Sea Camp Borstal.[10]   Living in huts on a site near Boston, about a hundred boys now work side by side with the staff, at the task of reclaiming rich agricultural land from the marshes and cultivating it.   Here, as at Lowdham, was a constructive task which could appeal to their social instincts, and to their admiration for such manly traits as strength and endurance.   Pioneering camps for delinquent adolescents in America (especially those run by the California Youth Authority) have learned much from these two classical experiments.

Other open Borstals followed, with Llewellin as the architect of two of them.   Out of a total of thirteen training Borstals for boys (up to May 1955) no fewer than nine are now open institutions.

The rate of absconsion from Borstal is high (one in every five boys in 1954[11]), but the Prison Commission have not allowed this, or the uproar about crimes committed by absconders, to panic them into reducing the number of open institutions or imposing more restrictions on the boys.   (Persistent absconders are, however, removed to a closed Borstal.)   It remains doubtful if the authorities are really dealing with the more fundamental problems of the Borstals, of which absconding is merely a symptom.

### The Borstal System

A sentence of Borstal Training can be imposed only on a person aged 16-21, who has committed an offence punishable with imprisonment.   The court must also be satisfied that "having regard to his character and previous conduct, and to the circumstances of the offence, that it is expedient for his reformation and the prevention of crime that he should go to Borstal".   Before passing such a sentence, the court must consider any report submitted by the Prison Commissioners on the offender's suitability for Borstal.   In general, Borstal sentences may not be imposed by Courts of Summary Jurisdiction; this is the prerogative of the superior courts.[12]

Reports to the court on "suitability" are, as in the case of corrective trainees, prepared by the governor of the local prison in which the boy is temporarily lodged, and the procedure is as open to criticism as in the case of corrective training.   There is no justification for imposing such a sentence after only a hasty appraisal of the facts by a lay person, but afterwards drawing upon all the skills of the psychologist, psychiatrist, doctor, and social worker to decide to which institution he shall be committed, as does in fact happen.

TYPE OF INMATE. Whether it is due to the inadequacy of the advice offered to the court on this score, or to the frequent failure of the court to accept advice, many inmates of Borstal certainly should not be there. The governor of a girls' Borstal reported: "We used to have a certain number of girls of average intelligence, though the majority were mentally subnormal and educationally backward. Now they are all like this".[13]

And from the governor of the boys' institution at Feltham: "It is scarcely hyperbole to say that some groups of Feltham receptions would beggar Hogarth's imagination. There is usually no lack of diversity except in the Terman mental age, and the tale of mental and physical disabilities. In size they range from the squeaky-voiced infant of four feet eight inches and eighteen years, to a shambling six feet five inches of over-grown weediness. In any dozen receptions one lad, as a rule, is so deaf that he has to stand by my chair to hear what he can of my reception talk. Another appears to be taken with an epileptic seizure when I address my first question to him, and I have to postpone the interview until I have time to deal patiently with a bad stammer".[14]

Rev. D. B. Kittermaster, a very experienced Borstal chaplain, has described cases of boys in Borstal who were suffering from obvious mental illnesses.[15] Homosexuality[16] also seems to be as widespread in Borstal as in the days of Mark Benney. It is deplorable that genuine inverts like the "queenies" described by Benney[17] should be robbed of the treatment they so desperately need, and be sent instead to live in a frustrated all-male community where their influence cannot be other than corrupting.

Better selection is obviously required, and research is being carried out on the problems involved. Ogden has completed a clinical study of the types of boy at Camp Hill Borstal, and the response of the different types to training.[18] An investigation has also been carried out into the value of prediction tables in selection,[19] but these cannot provide more than a statistical measure of the probability of success with whole groups of cases. Whether particular cases are likely to succeed must still be decided by a subjective judgment, and all possible steps have not yet been taken to ensure that the persons who make this judgment are those best qualified to do so.[20]

ALLOCATION. Classification after committal is carried out for boys at two Borstal reception centres, one in a wing of Wormwood Scrubs Prison, and one in another cellular institution at Latchmere

House, near Richmond in Surrey.   As the main aim of Borstal from the beginning was to provide a constructive alternative to prison for adolescents, it is obviously wrong that many Borstal boys should commence their Borstal careers at Wormwood Scrubs.   There is at present no proper classification procedure for girls; Sir Lionel Fox rather naively doubts if one is required, as the only decision to be made is whether they are suitable for the one open Borstal at East Sutton.[21]   This question is left to the staff of the closed Borstal for girls at Aylesbury.

The allocation of the boys, by contrast, is carried out very carefully by a full staff of specialist workers.   The criteria are fairly flexible, and include, besides criminal records, the boys' personal maturity, their vocational aptitudes,[22] and even the personalities of particular staff members at the Borstals to which they are going.   The older and more recalcitrant boys are sent to the closed institutions.

THE HOUSE SYSTEM.   To describe the boys' institutions (the girls' Borstals follow a similar pattern): Paterson made the House system, borrowed from the public schools, the hub of Borstal training.   The total population of the institution is broken up into Houses, so that the Housemaster, a man of intelligence and character, may get to know his charges and exercise some personal influence over them.   The House spirit means less than it did, but inter-House competitions of all sorts may be arranged, and selected boys are sometimes appointed as leaders to give them a taste of responsibility.

The attempt to transfer the public school House system intact to the Borstals has, in the main, been a failure.   Kittermaster, from personal experience as a chaplain, says that the "House spirit", in the closed institution where he worked, was largely a sham, and that leaders were often bullies, and usually looked upon as the House-masters' spies.[23]   The general atmosphere of the Borstals, as described by various former inmates,[24] only confirms this.   They are said to be training schools for criminals, in which tips are passed on and future crimes plotted.   Homosexuality is believed to be widespread.

Yet the spirit of Alexander Paterson fights its way through in spite of everything.   If the House system is a failure, the House-masters have been a great success.   Dr Leitch, a Borstal medical officer, has shown that the personal influence of Housemasters and officers is the main reformative element in Borstal training.[25]

Anything which can be done to increase the impact of this positive factor in training will be worth while. It is good, for example, to hear that the Prison Commission have smaller institutions in mind.[26] More than this, however, will be necessary if the influence of Borstal is to be made more wholesome. The most valuable single step would probably be to sever the present close relationship between prison and Borstal.

THE PRISON TAINT. Both building and staff bring with them the taint of prison. A number of the buildings are old cellular prisons, and are no more likely to realise the progressive aims of the modern Borstal than they were when Lowdham was founded. Borstal and prison staffs belong to the same service, and are freely interchangeable between the two branches. Their attitudes are bound to be affected by the ethos and practices of the older and more extensive system; Housemasters alone, having acquired their traditions in Borstal, are free from this danger.

There is also the same thraldom to rules and standing orders. It is much to the credit of some Borstals that they have declined to hibernate in spite of the cocoon of red-tape in which they are enmeshed, but the opportunities for experimentation are very few. And, above all, the rules and regulations which prescribe so minutely what they must and must not do, are rules and regulations made by an administration which is prison-minded in many ways.

Not surprisingly, the boys feel themselves to be prisoners. They ape the behaviour and the jargon of the old lag—the officer, although he doffs his prison uniform in Borstal, is still called a "screw", and boys talk glibly of "doing their time". The models before them are the fully fledged adult prisoners, and to these they inevitably look for their heroes and exemplars. And like the adult prisoner, many of them are apt to treat the authorities as their enemies, to be outwitted whenever possible: an attitude which it is easier to understand in punitive institutions such as most of our prisons are, than in the non-punitive, training institutions which our Borstals ought to be.

HOMOSEXUALITY. The sex problem in Borstal calls for special measures. If it is difficult for the adult prisoner to adapt himself to the monastic life of a one-sex institution, how much more so must it not be for the adolescent, who is having to cope with the first onset of the sexual impulse. Even outside, where he can sublimate his needs through the various outlets for coquetry which society has licensed, adolescence is often a difficult time for him.

There is a case to be made out for more female members of staff in our Borstals, and for more opportunities for meeting girls in organised social activities. As co-educational boarding schools have shown, homosexuality does not loom nearly as large where such opportunities exist. The need also to remove genuine inverts to an institution where they can receive treatment goes almost without saying.

THE WORK PROGRAMME. The work programme in Borstal has been universally praised. It is generally agreed that Borstal teaches boys to work, removing "the superstition common among thieves that hard work is something to be ashamed of".[27] This is a very substantial achievement. It is only to be regretted that it is not followed up by courses of trade training which will equip the boy for a job when he leaves Borstal. Vocational courses exist, but they are, like those organised in prison, six-month Ministry of Labour courses, not apprenticeships, and the same trade union resistance to subsequent employment in the trade is encountered.

PROGRESSIVE STAGES. There is a progressive stage system in Borstal. The details may vary from one institution to another, but the general framework is always the same. For the first few months, a boy is in the beginner's grade, the preliminary stage of classification and observation. He is then promoted to the training grade, when he is allowed to join certain clubs or to go out under escort. Finally, when at last he is showing evidence that he can be trusted, he enters the special grade and immediately acquires many new privileges. He is eligible to become a leader, and can take part in the activities of any of the clubs. He may even go out for walks, or to the cinema or the local youth club unaccompanied, or go out to tea with his parents when they visit. He becomes eligible also for home leave.[28]

The idea behind this system is not the classical one of providing incentives for good behaviour, but that of testing out the boys in the handling of more and more responsibility. To the same end the boy receives five days' home leave some-time during his training. Governors report on the value of home leave, referring to the salutary effect which trusting them in this way has upon the attitude of the boys, and also to the importance of home leave in bringing them face to face with the hard facts of their home situations while there is still time to discuss them with their Housemasters.[29] When the boy is almost ready to leave, he attends discharge classes, to discuss the problems of life outside.

AFTER-CARE. While the boys are being thus imperceptibly slid back into the stream of normal life, the Borstal Division of the Central After-care Association, which is responsible for their welfare when they leave, has not been idle. A representative of the Division makes contact with the boy while he is still in the reception grade, and talks over his circumstances and his future with him. A Borstal Associate in his home-town (usually a probation officer, though sometimes a voluntary worker) will visit his home to explore the situation, and perhaps try to solve any problems which he finds there. The Associate is also encouraged to visit the boy in the institution, though this is not often possible.

A Borstal sentence is now always for three years, but a boy may be licensed at any time after the expiration of nine months, if he is considered ready for release. The sentence is thus indeterminate between the prescribed limits. The average duration of training in the years 1951-3 was a little over nineteen months, so it is clear that the power to license is used very liberally.

After his release, a boy remains under the supervision of the C.A.C.A. for a year longer than the period of his sentence, *i.e.* for four years from the date of his committal, and if he fails to comply with the condition of his licence he may be recalled. If so, he is placed in the Recall Centre at Portsmouth, not in a training Borstal, in order to insulate other boys from his influence.

The actual work of after-care is done in most cases by probation officers, in their capacity as Borstal Associates, but some voluntary workers are also used. The use of voluntary workers in this way is part of a long tradition, for at one time all Borstal Associates were volunteers—the very first Borstal after-care was carried out by personal friends of Ruggles Brise himself. However, they do only a very small part of the work now; the C.A.C.A. claim that suitable voluntary workers are hard to find. The value of the continuous support and unofficial relationship which the voluntary Associate can offer is such that the Borstal Division should go on trying to find suitable recruits.[30]

### Need for More Experimentation

The Borstal system has much of great merit in it, and yet it is not succeeding. Can the reason be that we have not followed the principles laid down by Paterson to their logical conclusion? Or to put it in another way, can those principles really be realised so long as Borstal training is tied to the prison system?

Our Borstals also have been standing still since the heroic period of the nineteen-thirties. No student of the writings of Paterson would suggest that the creation of Lowdham and North Sea Camp exhausted all that Paterson had to teach us, and if it did, must we assume that illumination ceased when he died? What about the use of self-government in Borstal? Only one timid experiment has been carried out,[31] but with very satisfactory results. Modern group psychology gives us good reason to believe that this one device could transform our Borstal institutions for the better.[32]

What we must eschew is the reactionary road of increased discipline and heavier punishments, advocated by the Departmental Committee on Punishments in Prisons and Borstals.[33] That would be a denial of the very spirit of Borstal, and would place the emphasis still further upon hypocrisy. The face and the hands may comply, but the heart will not be touched.

## NOTES TO CHAPTER XV

1. Healy, W., and Alper, B. S., *Criminal Youth and the Borstal System*, 1941. Teeters, N. K., and Reineman, J. O., *Challenge of Delinquency*, 1950, pp. 539 ff.

2. *Report of the Commissioners of Prisons*, 1954, *Cmd.* 9547, p. 77. It will be noted that a full seven-year follow-up is only possible for discharges up to 1947. Results for discharges in subsequent years are not strictly comparable; other failures will have occurred by the time the seven-year period has expired.

3. Fox, Sir L., *English Prison and Borstal Systems*, 1952, p. 400.

4. Few will be returned to Borstal. (See Fox, *ibid.*, p. 397.)

5. Rose, A. G., *Five Hundred Borstal Boys*, a detailed follow-up study of individual cases, fills out this picture in a number of ways, but does not materially alter it.

6. Benson, G., *Howard Journal*, **9**: 2, 1955, p. 142.

7. Ruggles Brise, Sir E., *The English Prison System*, 1921, p. 93.

8. *Principles of the Borstal System*, 1932, pp. 13-14.

9. Llewellin, W. W., in *Howard Journal*, **3**: 4, 1933, pp. 36 ff.

10. Llewellin, W. W., "The North Sea Camp—a Fresh Borstal Experiment", *Howard Journal*, **4**: 3, 1936, pp. 250 ff.

11. *Commissioners' Report*, *loc. cit.*, p. 71.

12. But see the next chapter, p. 210.

13. *Report of the Prison Commissioners*, 1951, *Cmd.* 8692, p. 109.

14. *Report of the Prison Commissioners*, 1935, p. 66.

15. Elkin, W. A., and Kittermaster, D. B., *Borstal, a Critical Survey*, p. 39.

16. Heckstall Smith, Anthony, *Eighteen Months*, 1954, p. 133. Elkin and Kittermaster, *op. cit.*, pp. 39-40.

17. Benney, M., *Low Company*, 1936, Chapter VII.

18. Ogden, D. A., "A Borstal Typological Survey", *Brit. J. of Delinquency*, **5**: 2, 1954, pp. 99 ff.

19. Mannheim, H., and Wilkins, L. T., *Prediction Methods in relation to Borstal Training*, 1955.

20. See above, pp. 156 ff.

21. Fox, *op. cit.*, p. 360.

22. The value of vocational guidance in Borstal was demonstrated in: Rodger, A., *A Borstal Experiment in Vocational Guidance*, 1937.

23. Elkin and Kittermaster, *op. cit.*, p. 37.

24. Edward, Louis, *Borstal Lives*; Benney, M., *op. cit.*

25. Leitch, A., *Brit. J. of Medical Psychology*, **20**, 1946, pp. 77 ff.

26. *Report*, 1953, *loc. cit.*, p. 72.

27. Benney, *op. cit.*, p. 240.

28. Fox, *op. cit.*, pp. 369 ff.

29. *Report of the Prison Commissioners*, 1948, *Cmd.* 7777, pp. 86-7.

30. A description of the work of the Borstal Division of the C.A.C.A. will be found in Foster, F., "Borstal After-Care", *Howard Journal*, **9**: 2, 1955, pp. 136 ff.

31. Kenyon, H., "Concept of Shared Responsibility in Borstal", *Howard Journal*, **8**: 3, 1952, pp. 189 ff.

32. See Chapter XVII.

33. *Report of the Departmental Committee on Punishments in Prisons and Borstals*, 1951, *Cmd.* 8256, Part II.

# CHAPTER XVI

## THE APPROVED SCHOOLS

Schools for delinquent children in this country ante-dated the Borstals by half a century. At a time, in the middle of the last century, when it was still considered right and proper to imprison adolescents, most thoughtful people were won over to the view that it was quite wrong for children to be kept in prison. This was the belief which had led, in 1838, to the building of Parkhurst to house and train delinquent children awaiting transportation: no more than a children's prison certainly, but intended to be a "reformatory asylum"[1]; and it was followed in 1857 by the first Reformatory Schools Act.

### The First Reformatory Schools

These changes had been in gestation for a long time. In 1788, the Philanthropic Society had been formed for "the protection of poor children and the offspring of convicted felons, and the reformation of children who have themselves been engaged in criminal practices".[1] The latter would be received from time to time on conditional pardon from transportation or prison. The children were looked after in three or four cottage homes.

Then, in 1818, the Farm Colony was founded at Stretton-on-Dunsmore in Warwickshire. The common gaols had power to hire out prisoners as labourers, and the Farm Colony took advantage of this to rescue some twelve to twenty children from prison. These they cared for and trained, using methods which must have been very progressive for their time. Mary Carpenter described the aims of the Colony as the "placing them (the children) under a certain degree of restraint; making them feel the advantages and comfort of a well-ordered family; inspiring them with the hopes and fears of religion and principle of obedience to the will of God. Endeavouring to keep up a preponderating moral influence in the institution in favour of virtue and religion".[3]

THE RAUHE HAUS. On to this native stock (the significance of which seems to have been underestimated by historians of the reformatory school movement) were grafted powerful influences from the Continent. In 1833, J. H. Wichern opened the *Rauhe Haus* in a cottage in the middle of a wood near Hamburg. In twenty years, the number of young offenders under his care had increased from three to 300. Wichern emphasised, above all things, the value of small family groups in which personal influence could become effective, and so divided the children into families of about fifteen, each living in its own cottage. Each family was supervised by a Brother, a missionary or social worker in training. Personal suasion was used instead of force, and sincere and strong religious feeling dominated all the work done.

Seven years later, a French judge, F. A. De Metz, set up a *Colonie Agricole* at Mettray, near Tours, which gave the type of training pioneered by Wichern a wide audience throughout Europe. It has sometimes been suggested that Mettray was more artificial than the *Rauhe Haus*, that family feeling became esprit de corps, and that there was much repression;[4] but through the publicity which it received, Wichern's own influence was much increased. The Philanthropic Society moved its school to Red Hill in Surrey in 1949, and under the influence of the Warden, Sidney Turner, who had visited Mettray, adopted a family cottage pattern which has lasted there to this day.

MARY CARPENTER AND THE REFORMATORY SCHOOL MOVEMENT. There was, then, much ferment in this country; more and more philanthropists were becoming interested in the plight of children in prison, Mary Carpenter was the leader of this movement. In 1851, she wrote a book demanding government aid for reformatories and similar institutions, and setting out the principles on which they should be based. She chose for her book a title which made a shrewd appeal to the fears of the governing classes: *Reformatory Schools for the Children of the Perishing and Dangerous Classes, and for Juvenile Offenders*. An institution which later became the Norton Training School was founded at Birmingham by Joseph Sturge in 1850, and in 1852, Barwick Lloyd Baker, one of Mary Carpenter's friends, set up the Hardwicke Reformatory for boys, near Gloucester. A few months later came Mary Carpenter's own Kingswood School at Bristol, then a mixed institution but now a famous boys' approved school. By the end of 1851, there was enough general interest for a successful conference of those engaged in the work to be held in Birmingham.

STATUTORY RECOGNITION. The position of all these schools was, however, a somewhat precarious one. They had little official standing, and the courts could not commit children to them. They had to obtain their children either by conditional pardon, or by adopting some such stratagem as that used by the Stretton Farm Colony.

At last, in 1854, the State went part of the way towards accepting its responsibilities in this matter, with the Youthful Offenders Act, which provided that children could be committed to the reformatories by the courts. The retributive principle was, however, well maintained by the further provision that a child must first serve the sentence passed as a punishment for his offence, which must be at least fourteen days' imprisonment. Not until the 'nineties[5] were the courts permitted to send children to reformatories without a prior term of imprisonment, and not until 1899 were they required to do so.[6] In 1857, the first Reformatory Schools Act placed the new institutions on a sound legal and financial footing.

The new legislation, in spite of its obvious limitations, proved a great success. The number of institutions available rapidly increased: forty-four had been registered under the Act of 1854 by the end of 1857. According to Mayhew and Binny, 11,453 boys and girls between the ages of five and seventeen passed through the prisons of England in 1853,[7] but on 31 March 1894, the prisons contained only 100 under the age of sixteen.[8]

Industrial schools, which were first authorised in 1857,[9] were originally intended for children who were found begging or homeless, or were beyond control, but they were permitted in 1861 to admit the younger delinquents.[10]

### The Sterile Period

The progressive ideals of the Stretton colony have already been described, and Mary Carpenter spoke of drawing upon "the power of love and of a sound mind" rather than "the spirit of fear",[11] but these were the exceptions. Much nearer the normal view were Sidney Turner's ideas about punishment at Red Hill. "Confinement in a cell," he writes, "with a bread and water diet, for periods varying from a few hours to a few days, will be found in general a sufficient punishment, provided always that the cell is not warmed and fitted up as comfortably as a fashionable boudoir, but gives the inmate just as much cold and privation and discomfort as proper regard for health, cleanliness and the making a kindly impression on the offender, will allow for. Cases may arise when the cell fails or is inappropriate, and in which a whipping will do far more good; faults of indecency and cruelty come under this head, so does anything like insolence, or defiance of the master."[12]

These were the ideas which the Rev. Sidney Turner was able to propagate from a position of great influence, when in 1857 he became an Inspector of Prisons, and the first inspector to be appointed especially to devote his time to the new reformatories.[13] It is easy to see that he owed more to De Metz than to Wichern.

Over the years the system grew in rigour and impersonality. The children were dressed in drab uniforms, and the school door and gates were always locked. They were marched about the school in crocodile formation, often with their hands folded behind their backs. They were fed, and kept clean and healthy, but little was done to stimulate their minds or capture their interest, and their opportunities for showing initiative or assuming responsibility were almost nil.[14] The attitude of the schools towards the children in their care became increasingly patronising: they were receiving charity, and should be duly grateful.

## Emergence of the Modern Approved School

Progress became possible when, after the passing into law of the Children's Act 1908, the supervision of reformatory and industrial schools was transferred to a new department of the Home Office known as the Children's Branch. In 1913, Charles Russell, a pioneer boys' club leader, was appointed Chief Inspector of the Children's Branch, and under his enlightened leadership, the schools were gradually transformed.

Such changes are more difficult to effect in the approved schools than in the prisons, for the Children's Branch (now the Children's Department) have less power than the Prison Commission. The latter administer the prisons, and the governors are their servants. The former, however, have only supervisory powers over the approved schools, which are run and owned by local authorities and voluntary organisations throughout the country. It has recently been estimated that while about two-thirds of the schools are run by voluntary societies (like the Philanthropic Society, which still exists), 99 per cent. of their expenditure is met from public funds by grants of one sort or another.[15] Some disquiet was expressed about this position in the *Eighteenth Report of the Select Committee on Estimates*, 1949, which accordingly recommended that the representation of local authorities on the governing bodies of the schools should be increased.[16]

Nevertheless, by constant pressure, and only very rarely the threat to withdraw the Home Office certificate of approval (which has given the schools their present title) and the grants which go with it, the inspectors of the Children's Branch have had their way. In so doing, they have not only improved the work of the schools, but have also achieved a degree of uniformity which is only slightly less striking than that to be found in our prisons and Borstals. There is, in our approved schools, none of the variety of provision and methods described in the periodical surveys of American correctional schools conducted by the Osborne Association of New York.[17] We may very appropriately speak of an English approved school *system*.[18]

DISCIPLINE AND PUNISHMENT. One of the main ingredients of the system is discipline, a kindly discipline often imposed with a twinkle in the eye, but firm, nevertheless. The view that the forcible maintenance of good standards will necessarily lead to their perpetuation afterwards, when the disciplinary measures are withdrawn, has already been discussed, and found to be fallacious.[19]

Discipline and obedience are accompanied by rewards and punishments, with their implication that the child is primarily motivated by such external incentives. In so far as his delinquency springs from inner emotional conflicts, however, this is a very doubtful assumption. Thus it is often found that a child who is unloved at home will misbehave in order to attract attention, even if it is only in the form of punishment.[20] The psychopathic or affectionless child to whom punishment means nothing must also be considered, as must the criminal with an unconscious sense of guilt who is actually seeking punishment.

Even in other cases in which deep-rooted conflicts do not exist, it is fairly certain that personal relationships are more important to the child than material rewards. In so far as they are really effective in changing a child's behaviour, it is probably because of what they imply about the feelings of the teacher or headmaster towards him.

It is difficult to understand the opposition to such ideas as these for they are commonplaces of daily observation. All of us know how little, as children, we learned from school-teachers whom we disliked, and how readily we identified ourselves with our childhood heroes. Any mother, moreover, knows that when she slaps her erring offspring, the tears are often disproportionate to the physical punishment imposed. What has upset him is the discovery that she really is cross with him. At the clinical level, every psychotherapist recognises the importance of this personal factor and makes potent use of it in treatment.

Unfortunately, close and intimate relationships are considered in approved schools to be subversive of discipline. The children, it is said, would "take advantage" of any undue familiarity on the part of the staff. The approved school worker is, therefore, always a little detached and stiff in his dealings with his charges, and freezes up immediately at the first signs of real spontaneity on the part of the children.

But even if this were not so, the frequency with which the staff have to assume a punitive role would make it very difficult for them to capture the affection of the children.[21] A comparative study by the present writer has shown clearly that children living under a punitive regime are much more likely to avoid and reject the staff than in schools with a more affectionate approach.[22]

This does not mean that order need not be maintained, or that the development of good habits is a waste of time. Some degree of order is necessary, for instance, in the interests of administration as well as for the peace of mind and comfort of the staff. Even the child can gain from it, for if he is to learn from this experience in the institution, it must be a reasonably intelligible experience. But the discipline imposed should not be such as to make personal work impossible, for this must be the heart of any really reformative process.

COTTAGE SYSTEM. Wichern recognised the importance of the personal approach, and found in his cottage system the ideal framework for it. In spite of the *Rauhe Haus*, Mettray and Red Hill, however, very few of our schools have adopted the cottage pattern. This, according to the Home Office, is because of the expense involved.[23] The Reynolds Committee on the Remuneration and Conditions of Service of Approved School and Remand Home Staffs strongly urged the appointment of Housemasters on the Borstal pattern to do personal work with children,[24] but where these have been appointed, it has rarely been possible to divide the children into House groups who can live any sort of communal life apart from the rest of the school, or to provide enough Housemasters to reduce House groups to a manageable size.

EDUCATION IN THE APPROVED SCHOOL. The educational facilities in junior and intermediate schools, and work programmes among intermediates and seniors, form the third pillar of the edifice. Approved school children in general are of lower intelligence than children in the normal population,[25] and many will have truanted or been difficult in school. The approved schools, therefore, contain many children who are educationally backward, and not a few who are quite illiterate. In many of the schools, particularly junior schools, this problem is being tackled imaginatively, and by up-to-date methods, including the use of a good deal of practical activity. Work programmes are also varied and constructive; an outstanding achievement was the building of an entire classifying school by the boys of Red Bank Intermediate School in Lancashire.[26]

The approved schools have been a little more successful in securing trade recognition for their vocational training work than the prisons or the Borstals. Building-trade training in the approved schools is now accepted as counting towards the period of apprenticeship, and it is hoped that similar arrangements will be possible also in other skilled trades.[27]

ABSCONDING. Most approved schools are completely open (the exceptions are a few in which the children are locked up in their dormitories at night), and from time to time there are waves of absconding in different schools, often accompanied by the stealing of clothes or money in the neighbourhood. The number of absconders in 1950 was 1,407,[28] nearly one out of every six children in the schools.

The Children and Young Persons Act 1933, provides that a child who runs away may have his period of stay in the school increased by as much as six months, or if he is sixteen or over be sent to Borstal. (This or misconduct in an approved school are the only circumstances in which a court of summary jurisdiction may commit to Borstal.)[29] These sanctions have not proved much of a deterrent. The provision for committal to Borstal is also undesirable on other grounds. Approved schools receive, as well as delinquents, children found to be "in need of care and protection". If such children, who may never have committed any other offence, run away from the school, they are as liable to be sent to Borstal as the most confirmed offender. In May 1949, there were twenty-three "care and protection" cases in the girls' Borstals alone: about 10-15 per cent. of the total number in those institutions.[30] It is both unjust and imprudent to allow this to go on.

The Children's Department of the Home Office are attempting to deal with the problem of absconding by setting up, in an existing boys' school, a "closed block" for persistent runaways. This is probably better than an entirely closed school, with the restricted and rather grim air which this would have. On the other hand, absconding is extremely contagious, and it remains to be seen whether the stability of the rest of the school will be affected by the behaviour of the runaways.

A closed block is in any case a negative approach to the problem. Absconding may be due to many things: anxiety about home, temporary resentment about something which happened in the school, or in more serious cases, fundamental instability in the child or serious defects in the way the school is run. A positive approach would require careful diagnosis, and then measures aimed at eliminating the real causes. It is, therefore, good to know that experiments along these lines are being attempted in one of the classifying schools, close supervision of persistent absconders being combined with psychiatric study.[31]

## Selection of Cases

There is only one limitation upon the power of the courts to send children to approved schools: children under the age of ten can be committed only in exceptional circumstances.[32] There are various other ways in which delinquents can be dealt with. They can be fined, or placed on probation, or be committed to the care of a "fit person". In deciding which of these alternatives to choose, the juvenile court is faced with a difficult decision, which ought to be based upon a careful study of the child and his situation.

OBSERVATION CENTRES. As lay magistrates (or professional judges) are not equipped to make this sort of decision, observation centres have been set up in some countries to give skilled advice to the court. The centre at Moll in Belgium was one of the first and most famous of these. In America and Scandinavia, the determination of treatment has been taken out of the hands of the courts altogether. They are limited to deciding upon the guilt of the child, his treatment afterwards being prescribed by a Youth Authority or a Child Welfare Council consisting of specialists in social welfare.[33]

The Curtis Committee on the Care of Children urged that observation centres like that at Moll should be set up in remand homes in this country,[34] but only one or two small observation units have been brought into existence. Our juvenile court magistrates are still left to their own unaided judgment, with perhaps (but by no means always) a report from the probation officer to help them

In such circumstances it would be hopeless to try to trace any uniform principle behind committal to approved schools. Different magistrates have very different ideas. Some try to proportion the severity of the punishment to the heinousness of the crime, and so send the persistent offenders or those who commit what they consider to be the worst crimes to approved schools. This is probably the commonest ground for committal. In other cases a child is removed from home because his home is unsatisfactory, either physically or morally, or because he is getting into bad company.

It is possible that if treatment were more scientifically planned, fewer children would find their way into approved schools. Bowlby has shown that in many cases the maladjusted child is really only a symptom of a maladjusted family.[35] By the same token, the more stable child, whose social standards only are at fault, is really the product of a family with defective standards. To remove either from home is not to solve the underlying problem, but to evade it. Even if such a child did improve in the schools, he would be a very unusual person indeed if he did not relapse when he returned to his former environment.

Treatment needs to be directed towards the family rather than the child; and where, for good reasons, the child is removed from his home, work to improve his family circumstances should continue all the time he is away.

The courts might also make more use of their powers to commit delinquents to "fit persons"[36] than they do at present; they are much more ready to do this in "care and protection" than in delinquency cases. If a child were committed thus to the care of a local authority, acting as a "fit person", it would be possible for him to be boarded out with foster parents. This is not only much cheaper than keeping him in an approved school, but would also provide some children with the closer relationships which they need, and which not even the best school could hope to give them. The boarding-out of delinquents has been developed on an extensive scale by, for example, the Boston Juvenile Court, in U.S.A., and in spite of Home Office doubts, foster parents could be found for the purpose in this country too. Various voluntary organisations who board out difficult children (*e.g.* the Birmingham Society in Aid of Invalid and Nervous Children) have proved that.

THE CLASSIFYING SCHOOLS. The approved school classifying system, which has been developed since the war, has been attacked on the grounds that the diagnostic services which it provides should be available to decide whether a child should go to an approved school, as well as what school he should be sent to. It is suggested, in other words, that they should operate as pre-sentence observation centres of the sort discussed above.

Bowlby has also argued that to send a child temporarily to a classifying school after he has already been lodged temporarily in a remand home, is undesirable because of the feeling of rootlessness and insecurity which it must give him to be passed on from hand to hand in this way.[37]  If, as Bowlby maintains, many of our persistent offenders are so because they have been deprived of a continuous personal relationship with parental figures,[38] it can only exacerbate their condition to treat them thus.

To meet this criticism, the classifying schools have reduced the time spent on classification: from eight weeks to about two.  It is hoped that this period will be too short to make any mark upon the child; he will not have time to build up any sentiments towards the staff which he afterwards has to break.  Failing observation centres, this appears to be a sensible compromise, for sound classification is certainly necessary.

The training schools themselves are, in the main, classified only on a formal basis: according to age, sex, and religion, with a school here and there which specialises in a particular form of vocational training, *e.g.* agriculture or nautical training.  There are only two schools for special types of delinquent: one for emotionally disturbed senior girls,[39] and one for highly intelligent boys.[40]

This means that there are few hard and fast criteria to which the classifying schools have to conform in allocating children.  They could, if they wished, take account of many factors, including the personality of the child and the more intangible aspects of life in the various schools, such as the personalities of the staff and the type of children already there.  It seems that the classifying schools are missing their chance here; a book by the principal of the original classifying school at Aycliffe in County Durham, shows that they are still aiming at objective criteria[41]—perhaps because they make the task of allocation so much easier.

More schools for special types of children would add even more to the formal character and inflexibility of the classification procedure, but some certainly are needed.  A school for emotionally disturbed boys should be a priority.  It would be a boon to the other schools who find these boys a great trial.  These children also should be receiving psychotherapy.  If they receive any treatment at all under present conditions, it can be only intermittent, *e.g.* a weekly session with a visiting psychiatrist or at a child-guidance clinic, and only too often not even these are available.

**After-care**

A child is committed to an approved school for a period of three years or until he has reached the age of fifteen, whichever is the greater, with the further proviso that he must not be detained after he has reached his nineteenth birthday.[42]   He may be released on licence at any time after the end of the first year, and even earlier if the Home Secretary agrees.[43]   He remains under the supervision of the managers (*i.e.* the committee which controls the school) for the period of the licence and for three years afterwards, though not beyond the age of twenty-one.   The managers can revoke the licence and "readmit" the child to the school if they think that desirable, and even after his licence has expired can "recall" him for a further stay of up to six months, so long as detention does not extend beyond the age of nineteen.   They have, therefore, very powerful sanctions to their hands.

Their after-care functions are carried out in a variety of ways. Some may be in the hands of the staff of the school, a housemaster perhaps, or the headmaster himself.   Probation officers and officers of a city or county Children's Department may also take a share. In addition, there is a full-time staff of regional welfare officers employed by certain schools but doing after-care work also for other schools which have children in the area.

Which method is most suitable depends upon the case.   A probation officer may be the best person if he already has a good relationship with a child who has been under his care before.   If the child lives within easy reach of the school, a member of the school staff, whom he knows and has learned to trust, or the regional welfare officer, may be better.   If the local Children's Department is already doing rehabilitative work with the family, it may be undesirable for any other agency to intervene, and in such cases approved school supervision should be the responsibility of the child-care officer. There is no reason to believe that managers do plan after-care as carefully as this, however, and the Home Office has recently issued a memorandum on the subject which is intended to improve the situation.[44]

RESULTS.   Results are difficult to assess, but two-thirds of the children discharged from approved schools do not come before the courts again.[45]

**Remand Homes**

Remand homes, as their name implies, are intended primarily to ensure that children who are to appear before the court are available when the court meets. Many of them will have been remanded for further enquiries, *e.g.* by a probation officer or a doctor. In addition, it is possible to send a child to a remand home for a month's detention as a punishment, or to place there as "a place of safety", a child who is in need of care and protection.

It is obviously wrong to mix such very different types of case. Children in need of care and protection who have not themselves displayed delinquent tendencies, should be kept apart from delinquents, both in approved schools and remand homes. Nor should a place which is mainly for remand purposes be used as a punitive institution. But its use in this way may decline now that detention centres provide an alternative.

### NOTES TO CHAPTER XVI

1. See the *Report of the House of Lords Committee on Juvenile Offenders and Transportation*, 1847.

2. Russell and Rigby, *The Making of the Criminal*, quoted Cadbury, G. S., *Young Offenders, Yesterday and Today*, 1938, pp. 23-4.

3. Carpenter, Mary, *Reformatory Schools for the Children of the Dangerous and Perishing Classes, and for Juvenile Offenders*, 1851.

4. Teeters, N. K., and Reineman, J. O., *Challenge of Delinquency*, 1950, pp. 61 ff.

5. Reformatory Schools Act, 1893.

6. Reformatory Schools Act, 1899.

7. Mayhew, H., and Binny, J., *Criminal Prisons of London*, 1862, p. 456.

8. Report of the Gladstone Committee, p. 29. The figures are not strictly comparable, but nevertheless give some idea of the progress made.

9. Industrial Schools Act, 1857.

10. *i.e.* under the age of twelve.

11. *Op. cit.*

12. Quoted Hinde, R. S. E., *British Penal System*, 1951, p. 108.

13. See his first Report as Inspector where he writes in almost identical terms.

14. Maxwell, Sir Alexander, *Institutional Treatment of Delinquents:* Ninth Clarke Hall Lecture, 1949, pp. 20-2.

15. *Eighteenth Report of the House of Commons Select Committee on Estimates*, 1949, H.C. 314, p. vi. According to the more recent *Seventh Report on the Work of the Children's Dept. of the Home Office*, 101 out of 127 are run by voluntary bodies, *i.e.* over three-quarters.

16. *Report, loc. cit.*, p. xiv.

17. The Osborne Association: *Handbooks of American Institutions for Delinquents*, Vols. I-IV, 1938-43.

18. Very few accounts have been written of the work of the approved schools, and such as exist are not very adequate. The following might be mentioned: Simmons, M. M., *Making Citizens*, 1946; Vardy, John, *Their Side of the Story*, 1942; Gittins, J., *Approved School Boys*, 1952. Much information will also be found in the various numbers of the *Approved Schools Gazette*.

19. See p. 182.

20. It has been suggested this may be the first step in an ominous trend towards masochism. (See Jackson, L., *Aggression and its Interpretation*, 1954, especially pp. 62-3.)

21. Where a punitive system is in use with difficult children, the inevitable infractions by the children must lead to frequent punishment, and make adult-child relationships very negative in character.

22. See Jones, Howard, Ph.D. Thesis, London University, 1953.

23. Select Committee on Estimates, *loc. cit.*, Appendix I, p. xvi.

24. *Report of the Departmental Committee on Remuneration and Conditions of Service in Approved Schools and Remand Homes*, 1946, pp. 8-9.

25. Gittins, *op. cit.*, Chapter 5.

26. In many of the girls' schools, the girls go out to school and to work.

27. *Howard Journal*, **9**: 2, 1955, p. 155.

28. *Report of the Departmental Committee on Punishments in Prisons, Borstal Institutions, Approved Schools and Remand Homes*, 1951, Part III, p. 21.

29. Children and Young Persons Act 1933, Sec. 82 and Schedule 4.

30. Elkin, W. A., and Kittermaster, D. B., *Borstal: a Critical Survey*, p. 22.

31. *Howard Journal*, *loc. cit.*, p. 155. See also the *Seventh Report on the Work of the Children's Dept.*, *loc. cit.*, pp. 57-8.

32. Children and Young Persons Act 1933, Sec. 44.

33. See above, pp. 156 ff.

34. *Report of the Care of Children Committee*, 1941, *Cmd.* 6922, pp. 172-3.

35. Bowlby, J., "Study and Resolution of Group Tensions in the Family", *Human Relations*, **2**: 2, 1949, pp. 123 ff.

36. This power is defined by the Children and Young Persons Act, Sec. 57.

37. Bowlby, J., *Maternal Care and Mental Health* (World Health Organisation), 1951.

38. See above, pp. 51 ff.

39. The consultant psychiatrist has written an account of his work in this school: Craike, W. H., "Psychiatric Treatment of Adolescent Delinquent Girls", *Howard Journal*, **8**: 4, 1953, pp. 258 ff.

40. Simmons, M. M., and Davis, R., "Experiment at Kneesworth Hall School", *Brit. J. of Delinquency*, **4**: 2, 1953, pp. 109 ff.

41. Gittins, *op. cit.*, Chapter 3.

42. Children and Young Persons Act 1933, Sec. 71, amended by the Criminal Justice Act 1948.

43. Children and Young Persons Act 1933. Fourth Schedule.

44. This memorandum provides a convenient summary of the present position in respect of licensing and after-care.

45. *Select Committee on Estimates, loc. cit.*, p. xiv.

# CHAPTER XVII

## TOWARDS THE CORRECTIONAL COMMUNITY

Although it is of great importance that such specific aspects of institutional training as the work and educational programmes should be reformative in character, they will be abortive if the general atmosphere of the institution is inimical to reform. Atmosphere in this context really means attitudes: the group attitudes of both inmates and staff. If these are unfavourable, the training programme must be ineffective for it has to battle against the powerful gregarious impulses of human beings. Only a very unusual, perhaps a very abnormal, person would fly in the face of the attitudes of his own social group, the public opinion of his own community, in order to accept such alien norms. The analogy with "delinquency areas" is very close. Here, also, it has been found that specific measures, such as clubs or probation were powerless, so long as the attitude of the local community remained hostile.[1]

In prisons, and to a lesser extent in Borstal institutions and reformatory schools, such obstructive group attitudes are taken very much for granted. But they are powerful and all-permeating, and so long as we allow them to continue we are condemning our institutions to impotence.

### The "Conflict Situation"

The prison may be taken as an example, as the process described is most marked there. The prison situation is, in the words of Hayner and Ash, "a conflict situation".[2] Although both prisoners and officials may pay lip service to the reformative function of the prison, neither really accept this. To the staff the prisoners are there to be feared and kept in order, and to "pay" for their crimes. To the inmates the staff are "screws": the representatives of a hostile society, and in themselves individuals who are constantly frustrating and humiliating them.

Both sides make their accommodation to this situation as they see it. The staff become stern and unrelenting, and only occasionally make genuine relationships with the prisoners. They reserve their favours for the prisoner who causes least trouble, even though he is apt usually to be either a confirmed old lag who knows the ropes or just a hypocrite. The emphasis, that is to say, is placed upon outward conformity rather than inner conviction. They make use of stool-pigeons from among the prisoners, and reward them: a practice which is not only destructive of all mutual trust and respect, but involves the encouragement of positively anti-social qualities.

The prisoner soon learns to accept the position. Even if he had been prepared to be frank and open, he will not now be so. He complies when he must, but is not himself in any way involved. His real spontaneous self he saves for the relationships built up under the surface with his fellow-prisoners. He needs genuine relationships, and with them at least he can be himself.

THE PRISONERS' UNDERWORLD. The prisoners' underworld which ensues has been described in many articles and books. It has its own laws, which are none the less powerful for being uncodified, of which one of the most important is: "No official is to be trusted or assisted". It has its own hierarchy of leaders, whose positions are secured by the fact that they truly represent the group and its needs. Against them the officially appointed "trusties" have little influence, in spite of the formal power they may wield. It has even its own economic system, with tobacco as the universal currency. Tobacco is as much sought after in the prisons of the world as is money in the great society, and in the same way as money, the desire for its possession leads men into rivalry, prostitution, and even crime.

The prisoner is thus shut off from any reformative contact with the staff and left instead to the influence of the inmate community. As this is a criminal community, its effects are bound to be deleterious. A formidable criminal record is the passport to respect. Crime and its techniques are the main topics of conversation. Criminal contacts are made in this highly specialised group which the beginner in crime could never have found for himself. The young prisoner with no confirmed criminal tendencies will be isolated with these corrupting influences throughout his sentence, and will be fortunate to remain unscathed.

COMMUNITY PROBLEMS IN THE CORRECTIONAL SCHOOL. In correctional schools, where the attitudes on both sides are less uncompromising, the rift between staff and inmates is not so wide, but even here it exists. The underlying hostility on the part of the children is shown by the ruthless way in which they persecute a weak member of the staff; and many a headmaster, when a deplorable tale of bullying, homosexuality, or planned absconding comes to light, discovers how little he knew of what was really going on between the children. The classical example was the murder of a teacher at the Standon Farm School in 1947. Here dangerous undercurrents had been building up for months, without any of the staff realising what was happening.[3]

## Classical Experiments in Self-government

It has been to counter this state of affairs that experiments in inmate self-government have been carried out from time to time in correctional institutions. This is not a new idea: Wichern made use of it at the *Rauhe Haus* with his Order of "Children of the Peace". However, the most celebrated of the pioneers was William R. George, who founded the first Junior Republic at Freeville, N.Y., in the 'nineties.[4]

THE GEORGE JUNIOR REPUBLIC. After attempting to tackle delinquency by means of clubs and summer camps, George eventually set up a permanent institution, and gradually worked out the twin principles of democracy and self-support on which it was to be based. A system of democracy was created which was modelled closely upon the American constitution, with an elected legislative body, a judge, a district attorney, and even a written constitution.

The economic structure of the Republic was derived from the same model. The pattern was one of private property and competitive free enterprise. Citizens were responsible for their own maintenance, and could either go into business themselves or obtain a job from someone else. They were paid in the Republic's own currency, and how much they were able to earn determined what their standards of life would be.

The aim seems to have been to provide an environment in which the children could learn by experience. If they showed faulty judgment in electing their representatives they paid for it with inefficient government. If they misbehaved, they suffered the penalties laid down by the laws of the Republic. If they were lazy or lacking in enterprise, they had to live in the Hotel, a cheap lodging house with few amenities, or seek temporary shelter, as paupers, in the jail. At no point could they blame others for their hardships as these were the result of their own acts.

MUTUAL WELFARE LEAGUES IN PRISON. Thomas Mott Osborne, an associate of George, adapted the latter's methods in the years 1914-15 for use with adult prisoners.[5] First at the historic Auburn prison, then as Warden of Sing Sing, he set up "Mutual Welfare Leagues" among the prisoners, which took over many disciplinary functions formerly exercised by the staff, such as the maintenance of order in the workshops, and the punishment of offences. Privileges, such as attendance at entertainments or classes, were restricted to members of the League, so that it could bring its more recalcitrant members to heel by suspending them from membership. A token currency and a canteen were introduced to supply the economic element.

The achievements of Osborne's Leagues were considerable. In Sing Sing disorder was reduced, there were fewer escapes, and the prisoners worked harder. However, official opposition to his ideas grew. He was accused of "coddling the prisoners", and eventually resigned his post. There is still a Mutual Welfare League at Sing Sing, but it is now little more than a prisoners' grievance committee.[6]

HOWARD GILL AND THE NORFOLK COLONY. The Junior Republic and the Mutual Welfare Leagues were sustained very largely by the powerful personalities of George and Osborne. It is probably for this reason that many who tried to follow their lead were unsuccessful. Howard Gill was probably as great a man as either, but he saw the danger, and when he created his Norfolk Penal Colony in Massachussets, took pains to ensure that it was not too dependent upon him for its success.

The Norfolk Colony was specially built for its purpose. The entire colony was surrounded by a closely guarded concrete wall, but peripheral security being thus guaranteed, it was possible to give the prisoners a high degree of freedom within it, and to institute a system of what Gill called "co-operative self-government", under which staff and prisoners together tackled the problems of the institution. All the staff except the guards shared in the administration of the system, so that it did not rest upon a single pillar. The participation of the staff also acted as a brake upon precipitate or unwise action by the inmates. It was essentially a "safety first" system.

The exclusion of guards from the system of joint responsibility was based upon the principle of separating custodial and reformative functions, which was embodied most impressively in the great wall. Security was to be unquestioned, but to remain peripheral.

Unlike the members of the Mutual Welfare Leagues, the inmates of the Norfolk Colony had no power to impose punishments on individuals, but together with the staff they made the rules. Joint committees were set up to deal with food, entertainments, the library, the canteen, and other activities of the prison.[7]

THE LITTLE COMMONWEALTH.   Homer Lane, the inspired creator, immediately before the First World War, of the Little Common-wealth, a reformatory school in Dorset, preceded both Osborne and Gill, but his methods showed definite advances over both of them. An American and a follower of George, he was, nevertheless, opposed to the imposition of systems of government upon the children from above. What he did in essence was to extend George's principle of "learning by experience" to the creation of the regime itself.   He felt that the children should learn by experience the need for good order and government, and so allowed them to find out for themselves how difficult and uncomfortable life could be if it was lacking.

After an initial period of disorder they gradually evolved a system of government, and as this was designed to meet their own felt needs, they could identify themselves with it as they would never have identified with one, no matter how benevolent, which had been worked out for them.   It was theirs, and commanded their loyalty and respect for that reason.

Lane also recognised the great importance of personal relation-ships.   In the Little Commonwealth the children did not live in "Hotels" and "boarding houses", but in "families".   Lane and his staff also developed the closest relationships with the children, aiming to cure them by love, and by intimate understanding of their problems.

He was also a brilliant, practical psychologist.   He knew that behaviour was not always what it seemed, that, for example, the defiant child was often only an insecure one.   He was not afraid to use the dynamics of personal relationship in an unorthodox way, abandoning the crude bludgeon of rewards and punishments in favour of more subtle and effective weapons.   In fact, with Lane self-government was becoming a "searching group analysis of family and community life",[8] and the essential role of the staff-member as the analyst was becoming apparent.[9]

## Group Therapy

This trend in the direction of the more deliberate and dis-criminating use of group processes has been carried further by post-war developments in what has been called "group therapy". The great increase in nervous illness as a result of the war led to attempts at treatment in groups.[10]   It was soon found that group therapy was more than a device for economising the services of psychologists and psychiatrists; it had definite advantages of its own, over and above those possessed by individual treatment.

Group therapy with adults usually took the form of group discussion. The patients might discuss the incidents of their daily lives, and by sharing experience, give each other greater understanding and the ability to cope better in future.[11] In more clinically oriented groups, they would seek to give each other insight at a much deeper level, discussing significant childhood experiences, and trying to elucidate unconscious motives.[12] The extent to which the psychotherapist participated himself would vary. Some therapists would assume a very active role, guiding the discussion along the most fruitful lines, or even preface the discussion with a lecture on some relevant principle of behaviour or psychology.[13] Those with a psycho-analytical background usually adopted a more passive role. They would leave the discussion to be steered by the needs of the group, and confine themselves to an occasional remark, clarifying some issue which had already been well discussed, or interpreting unconscious resistance when it arose within the group.[14]

Children do not respond very well to verbal methods of this sort. They are not very capable of analysing their motives and feelings, and in any case find verbal expression difficult. Group activity methods have, therefore, been developed for them, in which they play together under a trained leader. If the group is skilfully handled, they will be able to benefit from the healing effect of satisfying personal relationships, and also learn to handle social situations more competently.[15]

A near relation of activity-group therapy is the psychodrama: it also sets out to by-pass the stage of verbal discussion. In the psychodrama, the patient (who may be either an adult or a child) acts out his problems on a stage, either with other patients, or with assistants known as "auxiliary egos". Here, instead of aiming at a verbal understanding of a situation, he obtains the "feel" of it in actual experience. Thus in spite of the acting involved, it can be a more real experience than discussion therapy, but it does not lead to the clear insights of the latter.[16]

VALUE OF GROUP THERAPY. The most obvious gain from group therapy is insight, secured through the interplay of ideas and personalities, but there are others. Insight itself depends upon the identification of the individual with the therapy group, and this has further consequences. It causes the group member to identify with and accept as his own the norms and standards of the group. From the point of view of psychotherapy this is important because these norms are directed towards recovery, *i.e.* towards co-operating in treatment and trying to get better. Another gain is the opportunity to try oneself out in a sympathetic social group, and find one's niche there. There is also the mutual understanding and acceptance to be found, not only in the group itself, but also in one's relations with the therapist.

THE NORTHFIELD PROJECT. As life in a residential institution is a very intensive group experience, group therapy is obviously relevant to its problems, as a number of workers have seen. Thus when Bion and Rickman[17] were made responsible for the discharge wing of a military psychiatric hospital at Northfield, Birmingham, they found that morale in the wing was very low, and that very few men were recovering sufficiently to be returned to their units. They decided that they were confronted by a group illness, rather than a number of sick individuals, and that group methods of treatment were therefore called for. Patients' committees were set up under skilled guidance, to control various aspects of life in the wing. They discussed its daily problems and worked out solutions, and as, in such a hospital, many of the social problems of the group were bound to arise out of the personal problems of the inmates, these also were inevitably brought under review. As Bion put it: "The objective of the wing was the study of its own internal tensions with a view to laying bare the influence of neurotic behaviour in producing frustration, waste of effort, and unhappiness in a group".[18]

GROUP THERAPY AND THE CORRECTIONAL INSTITUTION. With the Northfield project, the fundamental identity between self-government and group therapy becomes clear, as does the application of both to penal problems. In our correctional institutions, as at Northfield, there is every sign of a group malaise which is preventing progress from being made in the rehabilitation of individuals—with the same indication of the need for an attack on the group situation as such.

### Pattern of a Correctional Community

If more responsibility for the control of an institution were placed in the hands of the inmates, there would be a real chance for the first time that they might begin to identify with it and its reformative purpose. And as the "conflict situation" between staff and inmates would no longer have a basis in the facts of institutional life, it would lose its force. Better relationships between staff and inmates would become possible. The way would then be open for intensive personal work with individuals.

Some sort of deliberative system would be required: general meetings perhaps, and representative councils. An inmate court would also be needed to deal with violations of the rules made. These would provide the opportunity for gaining insight which the therapy group provides in psychiatry. Inmates would be able to try out their ideas in the government and daily life of the institution, and as the results became apparent, would be able to sift their experience in their meetings and learn from it. As at Northfield, this could never rest at a purely administrative level. The short-comings and difficulties of individuals would constantly arise, and would have to be dealt with. (They would arise most frequently, of course, at the inmate court.)[19]

The staff would not be inactive in this situation. Certain spheres of activity in the institution would be entirely withheld from inmate control. In a prison one might expect many matters connected with security to fall at first into this class. But even in the spheres in which responsibility has been delegated to the inmates, they are not left to shoulder it alone. It would be a system of joint responsibility rather than self-government. The staff, or certain members of the staff, would participate in their meetings with them, and try, like the therapist in his group, to help them to understand themselves and their group problems.

This would be an important safeguard against imprudent decisions, but it would be important that the staff should not try to dictate to the group or to manage it and rig its meetings. If they did, the system would forfeit the respect and allegiance of the group members, who would feel that they were no longer making the decisions. The democratic machinery would be seen as merely another weapon in the staff armoury. Moreover, as David Wills, a distinguished follower of Homer Lane puts it: "This is living by doing in a very real sense and nothing is learned if no mistakes are made".[20]

### Current Experimental Work

A little experimental work has been done along these general lines in recent years. David Wills, already mentioned, ran a camp for difficult and delinquent boys of Borstal age at Hawkspur Green, Essex, in 1936, where the principles of shared responsibility were successfully applied.[21] Subsequently he used the same methods with younger boys in a residential school for maladjusted children.[22] At Chaigeley, a residential school for maladjusted children in Lancashire, a similar approach but with a greater affinity to group-therapy methods was adopted for a time.[23]

But these have all been institutions outside the official correctional system. Within that system, few advances have been made. One or two approved schools have clubs which are run by their members, but none of them have given the children any real share in the government of the school itself. Hugh Kenyon has operated a cautious shared responsibility scheme with great advantage in a Borstal institution,[24] but no other Borstal governor has been willing to follow his example, or the Prison Commission to encourage them to do so. This in spite of the evidence provided in governors' reports every year of the alacrity with which Borstal boys and girls accept such small responsibilities as are entrusted to them, and the conscientious way in which they carry them out.

IN PRISONS. In the prison service, such work as has been done has been confined to the prison hospitals at Wakefield and Wormwood Scrubs, where it could assume the character of medical treatment and so pass muster.

The first therapy groups were organised, on a psycho-analytical basis, by Dr J. C. Mackwood at Wormwood Scrubs, and were for prisoners referred for psychiatric treatment.[25] This has developed under Landers, Macphail, and Simpson into a form of community therapy. A small group of prisoner-patients live in a special ward within the prison hospital, and also work together in the bookbinding shop. They maintain discipline themselves, all officers having been withdrawn. As well as group discussions and individual psychotherapy, the psychodrama is used. The group has maintained a very high standard of discipline in spite of the absence of officers, and psychiatric results also seem to have been good.[26]

Roper's work at Wakefield (which is at present in abeyance) was also located in the hospital, but was not confined to psychiatric cases. Groups of selected prisoners were formed to discuss difficulties of daily life in the institution, and to try to develop more constructive attitudes towards them. It became possible eventually to increase the number of groups by recruiting prison-officers-in-training as group leaders. This, incidentally, shows that prison officers can do personal work if entrusted with it and given a little guidance.[27]

NEXT STEPS. No great risk need be taken when this sort of work is extended beyond the confines of the prison hospital. It could be restricted to special classes of prisoner, perhaps to the open prisons. Until more experience has been gained in using the techniques, it might also be limited in scope, perhaps to food, recreation, education, and personal disputes between prisoners. More use might also be made of the potentialities of the Verne at Portsmouth. The physical similarity between this prison and the Norfolk Colony is striking.

## NOTES TO CHAPTER XVII

1. Shaw, C. R., and McKay, H. D., *Juvenile Delinquency and Urban Areas*, 1942, especially Chapter VII. Hughes, E. W., *Brit. J. Educ. Psychol.*, **13**: 3, 1943, pp. 60-1.

2. Hayner, N. S., and Ash, E., "The Prison as a Community", *Am. Sociol. Rev.*, **5**: 4, 1940, pp. 577 ff. For a very thorough study of sociological aspects of prison life, see Clemmer, D., *The Prison Community*, 1940.

3. *Report of the Committee of Enquiry into the conduct of the Standon Farm School*, 1947, *Cmd.* 7150.

4. George, W. R., *The Junior Republic*, 1909. George, W. R., and Stowe, L. B., *Citizens Made and Remade*, 1913.

5. Osborne, T. M., *Prisons and Common-sense*, 1924. Tannenbaum, F., *Osborne of Sing Sing*, 1933.

6. *Paterson on Prisons* (ed. S. K. Ruck), 1951, Chapter 9.

7. Commins, W. H., Yahkub, T., Powers, E., and Doering, C. R., *The Development of Penological Treatment at Norfolk Colony in Massachussets*, 1940.

8. Bazeley, E. T., *Homer Lane and the Little Commonwealth*, 1948, p. 145.

9. *Ibid.*; Lane, Homer T., *Talks to Parents and Teachers*, 1930.

10. See Rees, J. R., *Shaping of Psychiatry by War*, 1945, for an account of the many important developments which occurred under the stimulus of war.

11. Much group therapy work is conducted at this level, and in particular forms of community therapy (such as the Northfield Experiment described below) in which stress is bound to be laid to some extent upon social adjustment, as against the deeper exploration of the individual's problems.

12. Foulkes, S. H., *Introduction to Group Analytic Psychotherapy*, 1948. Wolf, A., "Psycho-analysis of Groups", *Am. J. of Psychotherapy*, **3**: 4, 1947, and **4**: 1, 1950.

13. Klapman, J. W., *Group Psychotherapy*, 1948.

14. *E.g.* Wolf, *op. cit.*; Foulkes, *op. cit.*

15. Slavson, S. R., *Introduction to Group Therapy*, 1943.

16. Moreno, J. L., *Psychodrama*, 1946. Haas, R. B. (ed.), *Psychodrama and Sociodrama in American Education*, 1949.

17. Bion, W. R., and Rickman, J., *Lancet*, 27 November 1943, p. 678. For a more recent experiment in this kind of community therapy, consult Jones, Maxwell, *Social Psychiatry*.

18. Bion, W. R., "The Leaderless Group Project", *Bull. Menninger Clinic*, **10**: 3.

19. Post-war Chinese prisons seem to have discovered the value of group discussion. See Sprott, W. J. H., "Chinese Prisons", *Howard Journal*, **8**: 4, 1953, pp. 267 ff.

20. Wills, W. D., *Barns Experiment*, 1949, p. 59.

21. Wills, W. D., *Hawkspur Experiment*, 1941.

22. *Barns Experiment, op. cit.*

23. Jones, Howard, Ph.D. Thesis, London University, 1953.

24. Kenyon, Hugh, "Concept of Shared Responsibility in Borstal", *Howard Journal*, **8**: 3, 1952, pp. 189 ff.

25. Mackwood, J. C., "Group Therapy in Prisons", *Howard Journal*, **8**: 2, 1950-1, pp. 104 ff.

26. Landers, J. J., MacPhail, D. S., and Simpson, R. C., "Group Therapy in H.M. Prison, Wormwood Scrubs", *J. Mental Sci.*, **100**, 1954, p. 421, pp. 953 ff.

27. Writings by Roper are to be found in *Howard Journal*, **8**: 3, 1952, pp. 158 ff.; *Howard Journal*, **9**: 2, 1955, pp. 91 ff.; *Proc. Royal Soc. Medicine*, **47**: 3, 1954, pp. 221-3.

# CHAPTER XVIII

## PROBATION

There is still confusion in the minds of many as to what is meant when an offender is placed on probation. Some, for example, believe it to be a "let-off"—a second chance without strings attached. As will appear, this is very far from the truth. Before one can speak of probation in the modern sense, all of the following conditions must be present:—

(1) No punishment is imposed initially.

(2) The offender is given a fixed period to redeem himself.

(3) During this period he is placed under the supervision of a probation officer (*a*) in order to keep the court informed of his progress, (*b*) to help him to make the best of the opportunity given to him.

(4) If he makes good, the original crime is considered to have been purged, but if he fails to do so, he may be brought back into court and sentenced for this, as well as for any other crime he may have committed since.

It is not a "let-off" then, because the probationer must either make good or suffer punishment later. In fact, the duty of reporting to a probation officer and accounting for one's behaviour to him over a long period is much more onerous than some formal punishments such as a fine, especially if, as is often the case, additional duties and restrictions are also imposed under the terms of the probation order.[1] Whatever the theory, the probationer must often feel that to be placed on probation is itself a punishment.[2]

### Development of Probationary Supervision

The general misconception about its nature is due to the fact that it originated from the centuries-old English common-law practice of releasing offenders on their own recognisances (*i.e.* their promise, or "recognition") to be of good behaviour. Where other persons were also required to go bail for the offender before his release was permitted, it may be assumed that they would want to protect their own interests by keeping a watchful eye upon him, but where such sureties were not demanded, there would be no form of supervision at all. In strict law this remained the position even after the enaction of the first probation statutes, the Summary

Jurisdiction Act 1879, and the Probation of First Offenders Act 1887.

In the actual operation of the service, however, pioneers had already begun to experiment with different kinds of supervision. As early as 1820, the Warwickshire magistrates would sometimes sentence a young offender to only one day's imprisonment, on condition that "he returned to the care of his parent or master, to be by him more carefully watched and supervised in the future".[3] Matthew Davenport Hill, as Recorder of Birmingham, followed a similar procedure from about 1841, and also arranged for the police to make periodical enquiries into the offender's conduct.[4] In America, also in 1841, a Boston cobbler named John Augustus rose in court and offered to stand bail for and supervise a man charged with drunkenness. Encouraged by his success with this first case, Augustus continued with his work, and in the eighteen years of his life which were left, supervised nearly 2,000 persons who had been, as he himself termed it, "bailed on probation".[5]

In 1876, the Church of England Temperance Society set up its first Police Court Missions to try to reclaim drunkards appearing before the courts. This work was gradually extended to other types of offender. Meanwhile the magistrates co-operated by releasing offenders on bail to the missioners. The courts received statutory authority for this practice in the Acts of 1879 and 1887, but the supervision itself remained entirely unrecognised and unofficial. By contrast, Massachussets set up a state visiting agency for this purpose as early as 1869.[6]

Probation in the fullest sense was not explicitly recognised by statute in this country until the Probation of Offenders Act 1907, which referred to probation officers and supervision for the first time in an Act of Parliament. It is with good reason, therefore, that we look upon this Act as the real basis of our probation service. It has been modified since, notably in 1925 when what, in the 1907 Act, had been merely permission to appoint probation officer in our courts, became a duty; but its main provisions remain unaltered. The system is at present governed by the Criminal Justice Act 1948,[7] and by Statutory Rules made by the Home Secretary under that Act.[8]

### The Probation Order

Probation orders may be made for any period of from one to three years, and special requirements may be added to them as the court thinks fit. Thus an offender may be placed on probation on condition that he undertakes psychiatric treatment,[9] or goes to live in some place stated in the order, *e.g.* a hostel. Or he may be required to abstain from alcohol. There is some doubt about the wisdom of some of the additional conditions imposed by the courts. It is very difficult, for example, for a probation officer to know whether his probationer is abstaining from alcohol, and it must detract from the authority of both the order and the officer, if a probationer knows that he can get away with a breach of the order like this.

Unless an offender is under the age of fourteen, he must give his consent to being placed on probation, otherwise an order cannot be made. This is clearly derived from the older procedure under which the offender was bound over on his own recognisances, but it is more than a historical relic. It places the emphasis upon the willing co-operation of the offender himself. He, as it were, accepts the chance which the court is giving him. In this respect probation is able to start off on a better footing than ordinary punishments, which necessarily have to be imposed by the court.

### The Probation Service

Probation officers are appointed by Probation Committees set up by the Justices of each petty sessional division,[10] and the expenses of the service are met by the local authority in whose areas the division is situated.

This arrangement has sometimes been assailed on the ground that a centralised government service would be more efficient and uniform. There seems little justification for this, for the local administration of the service is already inspected and closely supervised by the Probation Branch of the Home Office.

Through its Training Board, the Probation Branch works constantly to raise standards of training and qualification among probation officers, and it is now very rare indeed for officers to be appointed who have not taken the Board's full-time courses in the theory and practice of the work. Most have also taken a preliminary training in general social work in a University School of Social Studies. This must not be taken as implying that training cannot be improved (something will be said about this later), but little is likely to be gained on this score by more centralisation.

What would be lost would be the opportunity of close and fruitful collaboration between magistrate and probation officer. It has already been argued in another chapter that one of the drawbacks of our present system of administering the criminal law is the gap between the court which sentences and those who administer the sentence.[11]  In our probation system this gap has been reduced to a minimum, especially now that all Probation Committees are required to set up Case Committees to consult with the probation officer on the progress of individual cases.  Local justices now have the chance, which a centralised system would take from them, of getting to know how the probation system really works, and of following the fortunes of those whom they have assigned to it.  In their turn they can contribute their local knowledge and influence to help the probation officer.  These, of course, remain opportunities only unless the Bench is a keen and active one, and there are still some (especially in rural areas) which are neither.

### Duties of the Probation Officer

The probation officer is nowadays much more than a probation officer alone.  He has become a general court social worker.  He has duties in connection with adoption and the care of neglected children.  He is required to do delicate and often distasteful work in the field of matrimonial conciliation.  He supervises those discharged from corrective training, preventive detention, and Borstal, and often does approved school after-care also.  He carries out any home visits or social enquiries which the court may require, including, for example, enquiries into the means of persons who have failed to pay their fines.

PRELIMINARY ENQUIRIES.  As probation officer proper, however, his duties should begin with the preparation of a report on a case, for the information of the court.  The Departmental Committee on Social Services in the Courts of Summary Jurisdiction, which reported in 1936, urged that no offender should be placed on probation without a full preliminary enquiry into the circumstances of his offence.[12]  One might go further and contend that such an enquiry is necessary whatever the form of treatment proposed.  Some Benches do call for reports, whenever there seems a need for it, and where this happens, the probation officer may be seen as the precursor of the Treatment Boards referred to earlier.[13]

Some difficulties do arise.  The probation officer must either make his enquiries before the accused has been found guilty, or the offender must be remanded after conviction while the probation officer prepares his report.  The latter is easier to arrange in a petty sessional court than in Assizes, and virtually impossible in Quarter Sessions because it meets so infrequently.

The necessary enquiries could, of course, be carried out before the trial, but some courts and probation officers take the view that this is an unwarranted interference with the private life of the individual. When it has been proved that he has committed an offence, and only then, should the court interest itself in his private affairs. Apart from such ethical objections, the probation officer has no legal right to demand information, and it will probably be withheld if the informant feels that it is harmful to the cause of the accused. Many courts do make use of the pre-trial enquiry, and in Scotland it is legally compulsory in all cases involving children and young persons,[4] but it places the probation officer in a very delicate situation. He will need all the interviewing skill he can muster to deal with it satisfactorily.

As a makeshift it seems unavoidable, but its deficiencies do underline the urgency of making better arrangements for planning and determination of treatment than our present judicial process provides.

CASE-WORK. Where probation is decided upon as the most appropriate form of treatment, the officer who carried out the preliminary investigation will already have made contact with the probationer. It is this relationship which he has now to deepen and utilise, for a firm and positive relationship is the basis of all constructive case-work. In some cases it need be no more than mutual understanding and respect, for often, all that the probation officer has to do is to provide support and occasionally advice, as the probationer passes through this difficult period in his life. In other cases, where great changes in the probationer's attitudes or way of life have to be achieved, the relationship must be a stronger one, for it will often be under strain.

Much of the resistance which the officer encounters in this connection arises from the deterrent element which must always be present in probation, by virtue of its nature as a suspension of sentence. The possibility of further punishment hangs over the probationer all the time. As, in such an event, it is the officer who will be reporting him to the court, their relationship is bound to be affected. The probationer may be suspicious of his officer, unwilling to confide in him, and dubious about his motives. This is very likely to be the case where an officer lays great stress upon his client's precarious position, as a short-cut to securing obedience and a trouble-free period of supervision.

The good officer is able to avoid this pitfall. He cannot neglect or minimise the deterrent aspects, and they must tend to colour the attitudes of the probationer to some extent, but he has more positive aims in view and sets out to capitalise the more positive reactions of his client to having been placed on probation. The probationer will, for example, probably be relieved that nothing worse has befallen him, and in some degree grateful to both the court and the probation officer for this. If the officer shows clearly that his intention is to help him, not to catch him out, he will usually respond.

Subsequent treatment will then depend upon the probation officer's diagnosis of the situation. Some cases call for no more than an occasional reassuring and supportive interview with the officer. In others, some adjustment of the offender's material environment may be required: the finding of a job, or of a house, or of help with furnishing.

Sometimes, however, it involves going much further, and helping him to disentangle his personal relationships, and to modify deeply ingrained attitudes. This means that he will have to learn not only to understand his situation better, but (what is more difficult) to understand himself also. Such insight is very hard to accept; we usually see ourselves as we would like to be rather than as we really are. Nevertheless, it is, except in the simplest cases, the only basis on which a real cure can be achieved. If we confine ourselves to reducing the environmental stresses impinging upon a probationer, we may make him law-abiding for the time being, but can have no certainty that he will remain so when life once more becomes difficult. Indeed, as he is no better equipped for dealing with his problems, has no better understanding of them than he had before, the chances that he will break down again are considerable.

Need for Better Case-work Training. It must be admitted quite frankly that the practical training of probation officers does not really equip them to deal with this sort of problem. The more talented officers can do it, and the more perceptive among the officers of long experience, but most do not know enough about the handling of relationships and the sort of resistances which are encountered in social case-work to make it possible for them. As a result, many cases which ought to be carried on to the point at which insight is achieved are halted at the earlier stages of support and environmental adjustment.

Practical training is at present given on the job, by practising probation officers. This prevents preciousness, but as inbreeding, is bound to slow up the absorption of new ideas. In recent years there has been great progress in the field of social case-work, but the probation service has not gained as much from this new knowledge as some other case-work professions, such as, for example, psychiatric social work. There are signs that the Probation Training Board is at last waking up to this important fact.[16]

## Other Handicaps to Intensive Work

One other obstacle to really intensive work is lack of time. Case-loads are quite large; the average is about sixty for men officers, though it has been reduced to around forty for women.[17] There is also administrative work to be done; and the officers spend many hours in court awaiting the pleasure of the Bench. Then there are all the other functions enumerated above, which the officer has to perform, and which are not concerned with probation at all.

There is always the obvious solution, of course, but many other social services might make the same claim for more staff. Any large increase in probation staffs is bound to be ruled out by the economic situation.

Two further avenues remain for exploration. One is the better utilisation of the officer's time. In most courts, probation officers spend much time sitting in court which should be devoted to case-work. An officer should certainly be present when a case in which he is concerned is being discussed, and he should be "on call" at other times, so that the Bench may obtain his advice if they need it, but that does not mean that he must be present all the time the court is sitting.

USE OF VOLUNTARY HELPERS. The other answer is to make more use of voluntary helpers. They are at present little used in the probation service in this country. This is a very controversial matter, and many issues of principle arise in connection with it. Many are also wary of it because it has been difficult to obtain approval for full-time appointments in some areas, and to return to the use of voluntary workers seems a little like "tempting the gods". However, in the light of experience on the Continent, where voluntary systems are well established,[18] the proposal does seem to merit further consideration.

The probation service of the Netherlands provides an example. In the Netherlands, probationers are placed directly under the supervision of philanthropic societies, several of which are connected with the various religious denominations (the most important of all the societies is the Roman Catholic Rehabilitation Society). The actual case-work is carried out by voluntary workers, acting under the general direction of full-time, salaried officers employed by the societies. Local co-ordination between the different societies in the same district is effected by means of Rehabilitation Councils, on which they are all represented, together with judges and other official members, and these in turn are co-ordinated by a National Council.

The Swedish system (which applies only to adults, children being dealt with by the Child Welfare Councils already described) differs in that the voluntary supervisors are appointed in person by the courts. As in Holland, they are superintended by professional workers, who in this case are full-time employees of the Swedish prison administration. In neither country does a voluntary worker take on more than one, or possibly two cases.

Such arrangements obviously enable supervisors to devote much more time to individual cases than any British probation officer could spare. Nevertheless, this would not solve the problem of the complicated cases requiring intensive case-work, for untrained voluntary workers cannot have the necessary skill for dealing with these. It seems that these more difficult cases must be carried by fully trained officers, who presumably would also maintain a general oversight on the work of the volunteers. They would, however, have much more time for their "problem cases" if they could be relieved of the burden of the large number of "support cases" in this way.

High standards would have to be demanded of the volunteers if such a system was to be workable. The Select Committee on Social Services in the Courts of Summary Jurisdiction, who favoured the wider use of voluntary supervisors, emphasised the importance of selecting them carefully, and of removing a probationer from the supervision of a voluntary helper if the progress made was not satisfactory.[19] It would be important also to insist upon the regular and full performance of duties; the voluntary worker must not be allowed to think (as some voluntary workers are wont to do) that he can work when the spirit moves him, be unpunctual, or be slack about administrative matters such as sending in reports. They ought also to receive some training. The full-time Dutch rehabilitation officers receive only one day's training a fortnight over one or two years; the voluntary workers themselves probably need as much as this. Apart from its effect upon the quality of their work, their willingness to accept such an onerous responsibility would be a valuable test of their interest.

In addition it has been claimed that the use of volunteers in the Netherlands has made for wider understanding of probation among the general public.[20]  Many opportunities which would otherwise not have been so readily available to probationers may also be opened up for them, for the voluntary workers will all have their own contacts in the community, which they can make use of in the interests of their wards.  Thus some may have industrial contacts which will help to solve problems of employment, and others may be in touch with recreational organisations, youth clubs, etc.

The value of thus enlisting the active co-operation of the community in which remedial work is being done would seem to be indisputable, particularly in view of the conclusions to be drawn from local studies about the importance of local standards and the local public opinion in determining the level of crimes in a neighbourhood.  Some of the most hopeful, practical attempts to control juvenile delinquency in particular areas have taken precisely this form.[21]

## Specialisation in the Probation Service

Among other questions which have a bearing upon the effectiveness of the case-work which the probation officer carries out, is that of specialisation of function within the service.  It is laid down that a man and a woman officer must be appointed in each probation area, and that all female probationers must be placed under the woman officer,[22] but no further specialisation is required by law.  Specialisation does, however, go a little further than this in most areas, and much further in some.  It is usual, for example, for younger boys also to be under the care of the woman officer.

A good case can be made out for specialisation up to this point. Some services, however, allocate certain officers to deal exclusively with matrimonial cases, or to concentrate on court work and enquiries.  Against such a policy it is argued that these different functions are really part of the same problem.  For instance, matrimonial troubles are frequently at the root of cases of delinquency.  Preliminary enquiries also, should, if possible, be carried out by the officer who will have to handle the case if it becomes a matter for probation, for he will already have begun to build up a relationship with the offender, and will also know the real situation in the case, which the words of his report can convey only very inadequately.

A more general point is that specialisation according to function cuts across the present principle of assigning officers to local areas.

If the specialist principle did displace the geographical basis of allocation, the intimate knowledge which officers are able at present to build up about social conditions in their areas would be lost, and this would greatly reduce their effectiveness.

There are, however, other difficulties, which, if they do not point to a need for specialisation, do suggest that some separation between different kinds of case should be achieved in some other way. There would seem to be a clear need to prevent young first-offenders on probation from encountering old lags, who are receiving after-care supervision from the same officer. It must also be very embarrassing to the parties in a matrimonial case to have to call at the same address as, and perhaps share a waiting-room with, offenders of all sorts. Such a prospect is bound to make them more reluctant to call on the officer and make use of his services. Specialisation would solve such problems as these, but they could be solved also (as they are in some areas) by setting aside different premises for different functions, or even to some extent by arranging appointment for different types of client.

## Group-work in Probation

But if the probation officer's function should not be restricted by specialisation, what are we to say about proposals which are sometimes made for extending it? In America, probation officers often do not confine themselves to case-work, but also work with groups, in clubs for instance.

PROBATION HOMES AND HOSTELS. Little group-work is done by the probation service in this country. Apart from very occasional experiments with play-groups, our experience with groups has been limited to probation hostels and homes. These have been set up to provide a more stable home background for juvenile offenders of over school age whose homes are unsatisfactory. In such cases a "condition of residence" would be included in the probation order.

Approved homes and hostels are run by both public and voluntary agencies, but probation officers play a considerable part in the running of many of them. On occasion the Warden has himself been a probation officer, and officers help with activities organised there. A boy placed in a home or hostel, moreover, would still maintain his contact with his own probation officer, though if placement had meant removal to another area, he would be transferred to an officer in his new area.

The use of institutions by the probation service, in this way, was challenged by the Departmental Committee on the Treatment of Young Offenders in 1927, on the grounds that probation is a service for offenders who can be left in their own homes, and that committal to an institution is quite a different form of treatment, involving a different approach.[23]   This criticism is more applicable to probation homes than hostels, for the young people work and receive education and training in the former, much as they would in an approved school.   The hostel, on the other hand, functions more like an ordinary home, and the youngsters, while living there, go out to classes or work, or even for recreation.   But even in connection with probation homes, too doctrinal an approach would be a mistake; if lines of demarcation are maintained too rigidly many fruitful, if theoretically illegitimate, developments may be prevented. The dangers are slight so long as reasonable discrimination is used.[24]

INDIVIDUALISATION VERSUS GROUP-WORK?   Another objection which might be made is that the probation officer should confine himself to individual case-work.   That he is in a position to do case-work is the great advantage which he has over the institutional worker.   For him to concern himself with groups, is to abandon his position as the one worker in the correctional services who really has a chance to individualise treatment.

CLUBS FOR DELINQUENTS.   This objection would also apply to the suggestion that probation officers should do club work with groups of delinquents.   Many probation officers do this sort of thing in the United States: a very good example is the Citizenship Training Department run by the probation staff of the Boston Juvenile Court.   All boys placed on probation who are between the ages of twelve and seventeen attend the Department for two hours a day for twelve weeks, and take part in recreational and physical activities, discussion groups, and educational classes.   The Department also aims to serve as a bridge to membership of the ordinary youth organisations.[25]

The nearest approach to a formal programme like that of the Boston court, are the attendance centres set up under the Criminal Justice Act 1948.[26]   Offenders aged seventeen to twenty-one may be required to attend in their own time for up to a total of twelve hours.   Most of the existing centres are run by the police, and discipline is very strict.   Programmes also tend to be rather narrow and superficial, with physical training predominating.[27]   They do not make any use at all of the opportunities given to us by modern group psychology, or of providing a therapeutic and socialising group-milieu for the group members. If therapeutic groups are to be set up they will have to be in more skilful and enlightened hands than those which at present control the operations of the attendance centres.

THE NEED FOR GROUP-WORK. There is good reason for asserting that the probation officer cannot tackle his job really effectively unless he is prepared to take some responsibility for work with groups. Many delinquents are neither anti-social nor maladjusted, but normal youngsters who get into trouble because they are members of a delinquent gang.[28] The real problem lies in the group itself, and it is there that it has to be tackled.

It is a misconception to believe that group-work is necessarily a retreat from the principle of individualisation. At one time it would have been fair to have seen group-work as the application of standard patterns of treatment to whole groups, but we now know much more about individual interaction in groups, and can use group experience in a very specific way in the interests of the individual member. In addition, there are certain opportunities for influencing offenders which exist only in the group situation—in the form of mutual interaction and stimulation within the group, and the exploitation of the influence of the public opinion of the group over its members.[29]

## Use of Probation by the Courts

Between 1907 and 1938 there was a steady growth in the use of probation:—

TABLE XII (a)

PERSONS PUT ON PROBATION, EXPRESSED AS A PERCENTAGE OF ALL COURT DISPOSITIONS IN ENGLAND AND WALES (INDICTABLE OFFENCES)[30]

| Year | Courts of Summary Jurisdiction | | Courts of Quarter Sessions | Assize Courts |
| | Excluding Juvenile Courts | Juvenile Courts | | |
|---|---|---|---|---|
| 1910 | 11·3 | 25·7 | 7·3 | 0·2 |
| 1913 | 12·2 | 27·4 | 9·6 | 0·2 |
| 1919 | 11·7 | 27·4 | 16·9 | 0·2 |
| 1925 | 18·4 | 47·7 | 15·9 | 1·0 |
| 1928 | 20·1 | 53·4 | 14·2 | 1·9 |
| 1930 | 21·1 | 55·3 | 16·3 | 3·2 |
| 1933 | 19·1 | 53·9 | 15·9 | 4·4 |
| 1938 | 22·2 | 50·8 | 23·6 | 10·5 |

Not unnaturally, in view of the close connection between the probation service and the petty sessions, the largest proportion are reported by the petty sessional courts, especially the juvenile court. The fact that the less serious offences are dealt with in petty sessions tends to the same result. It is a striking fact, however, that the *proportionate* increase since 1910 has been greatest in the superior courts in spite of all the difficulties under which they labour. The percentage of probation cases has trebled in Quarter Sessions and increased fiftyfold in Assizes, as compared with a twofold increase in courts of summary jurisdiction. Since the war there has been a slight setback.

TABLE XII (*b*)

| Year | Courts of Summary Jurisdiction | | Quarter Sessions and Assizes |
|------|------|------|------|
| | Excluding Juvenile Courts | Juvenile Courts | |
| 1946 | 11·0 | 41·9 | 14·8 |
| 1947 | 10·4 | 41·9 | 14·5 |
| 1948 | 12·3 | 41·7 | 15·3 |
| 1949 | 13·1 | 41·8 | 16·6 |
| 1950 | 11·8 | 40·8 | 17·2 |
| 1951 | 10·9 | 40·6 | 17·9 |
| 1952 | 11·7 | 40·4 | 17·2 |
| 1953 | 12·5 | 40·0 | 17·1 |
| 1954 | 13·3 | 40·6 | 16·7 |

The decline has been most marked in the adult petty sessions, where the absolute number placed on probation has diminished, although the total number of cases disposed of has greatly increased. In all the other courts, numbers placed on probation have tended to increase, but the percentage has been reduced by the much larger total number of committals.

LOCAL DIFFERENCES. The general picture shows an increasing awareness of the value of probation as a means of treatment in all grades of court, but the average percentages quoted conceal considerable variability as between one court and another. This is borne out by figures for the year 1933 given by the Departmental Committee on Social Services in Courts of Summary Jurisdiction. "In courts of summary jurisdiction the percentage of cases put on probation ranged from 5 per cent. to 43·8 per cent.; in juvenile courts from 29·4 per cent. to 78·1 per cent.; in courts of quarter sessions from nil per cent. to 35·9 per cent.; and in courts of assize from nil per cent. to 7·7 per cent."[32] A similar variability is shown by post-war returns.[33]

This may, in part, be the result of local differences in conditions, but the Departmental Committee were unwilling to allow that this was sufficient to account entirely for such wide divergencies.[34] Probation officers also find that probation is treated with much more understanding and sympathy in some courts than others. There is no doubt that it is the responsibility of the probation officer, as the expert in this form of treatment, to help the court to understand how probation should be used, but before he can do this with any confidence, he needs to know more himself about the kind of cases in which it is likely to be successful.

## Choice of Suitable Cases for Probation

"Probation used wisely," writes Leo Page, "is merciful and efficient; the same system used unskilfully brings the administration of the Criminal Law into public derision."[35] There is little except unsystematised experience, or prejudice masquerading as experience, to go on in deciding which cases are most likely to respond to supervision. If research on this question is to be carried out, some of it should be by probation officers, who know their own cases so much better than any outsider can ever hope to do.

One point of departure might be from the principle that probation is essentially a form of domiciliary treatment, *i.e.* as compared with placement in an institution. The home and the family must themselves be remediable. Some authorities believe that a bad home is in itself a contra-indication for the success of probation,[36] but this is perhaps going too far. The probation officer must accept the responsibility for doing some work with the family. In fact he does; it is remarkable how frequently a probation officer's preliminary report to the court is a report on the family rather than on the offender himself. What we need to know, and what only further research can tell us, is what features in a home make the prognosis doubtful.

Sutherland, summarising the results of three studies in America, concludes that the most important factors determining success or failure on probation are "previous criminal records, previous records of irregular work, low economic status, low occupational level, residence in deteriorated neighbourhoods, families with records of crime and vice, immoral associates, great mobility in residences, and few or irregular contacts with schools or churches".[37] These criteria are biased on the side of sociological factors, and in themselves cry out for more refined analysis.

The significance of psychopathy would seem to be undoubted. Other less extreme personality difficulties such as "plausibility, unreliability, sulkiness, cunning" were found by Hughes, in his Coventry study, to affect outcome adversely.[38]   Hughes found age also to be a significant factor: the older probationers are the more likely to be successful.[39]

There are, however, certain defects in this procedure of listing specific traits as favourable or unfavourable in themselves: defects which are serious enough to invalidate any conclusions that may be drawn from it. It was argued in an earlier chapter that the importance of a given causal factor depends upon its place in the total personal equation formed by the interaction of the offender with his environment. The same must be true of factors operative in probation—with the addition of elements derived from the personality and techniques of the probation officer himself.

Other investigators have worked out prediction tables which purport to forecast, by an actuarial analysis of previous experience, which kinds of case are likely to succeed on probation.[40]   But given the probability ratio which can be drawn from a carefully worked out prediction table, we still do not know which particular cases are likely to succeed, for the tables are statistical devices based on the trends shown in large numbers of cases. They have their value, but are no substitute for the careful study of the individual case in all its ramifications.[41]

### Its Effectiveness

Various studies have been made of the effectiveness of probation in this country. In a Home Office survey carried out just before the war,[42] the histories of 2,311 probationers from fifteen petty sessional areas were studied over a period extending for three years after the expiration of their probation order, and gave the following results:—

| Age | Percentage of Success | |
|---|---|---|
| Under 14 .. .. | 65·3 | |
| 14 and under 17 .. | 68·2 | Average for all ages: 70 per cent. |
| 17 and under 21 .. | 73·3 | |
| 21 and over .. .. | 81·8 | |

These correspond fairly well with the results obtained in studies of probation in particular areas. Hughes followed up 330 male cases in Coventry for five years after their period of probation ended, and found that 245 (or 74 per cent.) had not been in further trouble.[43] A careful investigation of Cardiff cases placed on probation in 1928 and 1929 over a period of five years from the making of the order gave 64 per cent. and 68 per cent. successes respectively.[44]

Local results are necessarily going to be affected by the policy of the local court in choosing cases for probation. A high rate of success may merely mean that a court uses probation very little, and only with the safer cases. Results obtained should, therefore, always be compared with the percentage of probation orders made. Nor is it possible to attribute all the successful cases to the ministrations of the probation officer, for probation cases, in the main, consist of the less serious offenders, less confirmed in their criminality. Some of them probably would not have offended again in any case.[45]

The probation service is now an integral part of our social service structure. It is recognised and used in all our courts. It is achieving a commendable amount of success. It would, however, be short-sighted to assume that its period of development is at an end, and that the present pattern will not ever need drastic overhaul.

There is reason to believe that a further period of vigorous development is needed, in which techniques of case-work will be refined, and the new discipline of social group-work will be exploited. The era of probationary supervision has very largely fulfilled itself, and should now be succeeded by a period in which a more active process of "therapy" will begin to develop. And as a constant check on the effectiveness of their work, and a guide to the selection of suitable cases for probation, Probation Committees should keep records which will enable them to say, not only which probationers have failed during their period of supervision, but which of them have failed during a subsequent follow-up period of at least three years. For the real test of the skill of any social worker is whether his clients can ultimately be left to manage without him.

## NOTES TO CHAPTER XVIII

1. See below, pp. 229-30.
2. Harris, S. W., former Assistant Secretary of State, argues that it is a punishment—see his, *Probation and other Social Work of the Courts: Third Clarke Hall Lecture*, 1937, pp. 24-5.
3. *Report of the Departmental Committee on the Treatment of Young Offenders*, 1927, *Cmd.* 2831, p. 10.
4. Hill, Matthew Davenport, *Suggestions for the Repression of Crime*, 1857.
5. National Probation Association (of America): *John Augustus, First Probation Officer*, 1939.
6. This was the result of the success achieved by John Augustus, and other voluntary workers who succeeded him. This Act applied only to children.
7. Sections 3-12, and the First and Fifth Schedules.

8. Probation Rules, 1949.

9. This was specifically provided for for the first time by the Act of 1948, Section 4.

10. Sometimes two or more petty sessional divisions combine to form a single Probation Area. (Criminal Justice Act 1948, Fifth Schedule.)

11. See above, pp. 158-9.

12. *Cmd.* 5122, Para. 64.

13. See pp. 156 ff.

14. Criminal Justice (Scotland) Act 1949, Eleventh Schedule.

15. A useful study of probation from the practical point of view will be found in Glover, E., *Probation and Re-education*, 1949. Also Minn, W. G., "Probation Work", in Morris, C. (ed.), *Social Casework in Great Britain*, 1950.

16. A few probation trainees are being enrolled in generic casework courses at various Universities, where they will receive their training at a fairly advanced level, in company with members of other casework professions.

17. *Howard Journal*, **9**: 2, 1955, p. 156.

18. See *Probation and Related Measures* (United Nations Dept. of Social Affairs), 1951, Chapter 10 for details.

19. *Cmd.* 5122, Para. 142.

20. Muller, N., quoted *Probation and Related Measures*, p. 169.

21. See Chapter XX below.

22. Criminal Justice Act 1948. Fifth Schedule, paras. 3-4.

23. *Loc. cit.*, p. 54.

24. For a general discussion of the role of the hostel, consult Spencer, J. C., and Grygier, T., *The Probation Hostel in England*, 1952.

25. Connelly, Judge J. J., *Citizenship Training Department of the Boston Juvenile Court*, 1950.

26. Section 19.

27. *Seventh Report on the Work of the Children's Department of the Home Office*, 1955, pp. 41-2. Spencer, J. C., "The Attendance Centre in England: the First Year's Work", *Howard Journal*, **8**: 3, 1952, p. 146.

28. See pp. 82 ff., above.

29. On group methods generally, see Chapters XVII and XX.

30. Adapted from *Probation and Related Measures*, p. 127.

31. *Ibid.*, and *Criminal Statistics*, 1950-3.

32. *Probation and Related Measures*, p. 125.

33. See the *Supplementary Criminal Statistics*, issued annually by the Home Office, and available to all libraries and research workers.

34. p. 40.

35. Page, L., *The Young Lag*, 1950, p. 292.

36. *Probation and Related Measures*, p. 238.

37. Sutherland, E. H., *Principles of Criminology*, 1947, pp. 404-5.

38. Hughes, E. W., *Brit. J. Educ. Psychol.*, **13**: 3, 1943, pp. 113-25.

39. This is almost certainly not true without qualification; *e.g.* middle-aged habitual offenders are hardly likely to succeed more frequently than juveniles who are before the court for the first time.

40. For instance, Monachesi, E. D., *Prediction Factors in Probation*, 1932.

41. Prediction tables are examined above, pp. 161 ff.

42. *The Probation Service* (Home Office), 1938, p. 13.

43. Hughes, *loc. cit.*

44. "Report of the Cardiff Probation Committee for the year 1933", summarised in the *Handbook of Probation* (ed. Mesurier, Mrs L. le), 1935, pp. 48-50.

45. A recent examination of the effectiveness of probation is: Grunhut, M., *Practical Results and Financial Aspects of Adult Probation in Selected Countries* (United Nations), 1954.

# CHAPTER XIX

## PREVENTION: EUGENICS AND CHILD-CARE

Although the expression "prevention of crime" is being used here in a narrower sense than in the classical theories of "individual and general prevention",[1] it remains an enormous topic. Possible preventive measures are as numerous as possible causal factors. So prophylactic nostrums in great variety are continually being advanced by different groups. Education is the answer to rising crime figures according to one school of thought, the censorship of newspapers and films according to another. Some argue that more police are needed, and others more social workers. Religion and temperance have powerful advocates. Better housing conditions, or measures to prevent or relieve large-scale unemployment, raise wider issues. In America, enthusiasts have even put forward the claims of better dentistry, more lights at street corners, more piano playing, or fewer juke boxes.[2]

Three areas of possible preventive activity do stand out, however, as being crucial to the problem. The possibility offered by social work in and with communities will be discussed in the next chapter. Here we shall confine ourselves to the contribution which might be made by eugenic measures, or by improvements in our methods of child-care and training.

### The Eugenic Solution

Selective breeding is the only solution for those who contend that crime is due to inherited traits of temperament, or to lack of intelligence. W. A. Sheldon puts their point of view with brutal frankness: "Prepare for drastically reduced and for selective reproduction," he writes, and continues, "The basic change will no doubt rest on reproduction as a kind of licensed and subsidised specialty instead of a laissez-faire competition".[3]

Eugenists put forward both a negative and a positive policy. The former is concerned with preventing procreation by the biologically inferior. This could be achieved by requiring all those desiring to marry to obtain a medical certificate of their biological fitness, or by institutional segregation of a sort which is already a fact in many countries including our own. If mental defectives, the chronically insane, or persistent offenders, spend many years of their lives shut off from the opposite sex in this way, their rate of reproduction is bound to be reduced. The segregation of mental defectives is often lifelong.

STERILISATION. Such measures as those above escape notice very easily, but not so the proposal which is often made for the sterilisation of the unfit. This arouses very strong feelings, especially among religious people. But it is opposed not only on religious grounds; many object that it shows too little respect for human personality and human rights as such. Such objections are not met by permitting only voluntary sterilisation, as mental defectives and the insane, for example, are in no state to make such a decision for themselves.

The question of criteria also arises: what kinds of disability are to justify such drastic action? In criminology this largely resolves itself into the question of what crimogenic characteristics can be shown to be hereditary.

It will be obvious by now that very little is definitely known about the contribution of inheritance to the causation of crime. Certain forms of mental deficiency are almost certainly hereditary, but mental deficiency has been shown to be of little importance as a crime-producing factor. The inheritance of psychopathy, once widely accepted, is now more and more questioned, and even if it were established it might prove dysgenic rather than eugenic to eliminate psychopathic stock by sterilisation. As Henderson has shown, many of the world's greatest and most creative figures have been "odd men out", displaying distinctly psychopathic characteristics.[4] If there is any doubt at all about the hereditary character of an undesirable trait, it would seem to be quite unjustifiable to take such a drastic and irrevocable step as the sterilisation of those possessing it.

Closely related to sterilisation in its effects would be personal counselling, and education in birth-control methods, intended to encourage the inferior individuals to have smaller families.

In the Latin countries, sterilisation has made no headway, mainly because the Roman Catholic Church is obdurately opposed to it. In this country also, in spite of a favourable report by a Departmental Committee (the Brock Committee) twenty years ago,[5] it is not permitted except on a purely voluntary basis, where the health of the individual imperatively calls for it. In Scandinavia, sterilisation laws exist, and in Nazi Germany they were applied on a vast scale, even to the congenitally deaf and blind, and to alcoholics.

Sterilisation laws in the United States got off to a bad start with an early Act, passed in Indiana, which provided, among other things, for the sterilisation of criminal recidivists. This was speedily held to be unconstitutional by the federal courts, but many states now have similar laws directed mainly against mental deficiency, though only in California have they been used at all widely.

CASTRATION. Although sterilisation does not nowadays take the form of castration, and does not cause the same loss of sexual desire as the latter, it is convenient to discuss legal castration at this point, for it does, of course, result in sterility.

It is not, however, adopted for this purpose, but to solve the problem of the incorrigible sex offender. Castration laws exist in certain states of the U.S.A., but little use has been made of them. In Denmark and Sweden the persistent sex-criminal is committed to prison on an indeterminate sentence, and later offered his release on condition that he submits to castration. As a result of the operation his sex-drive disappears, and he is no longer impelled to acts of rape or indecency. It is claimed that his physique and personality are impaired in no other way by the operation.[6] The name of Dr George K. Stürup of the Herstevester institution for psychopaths in Denmark is well known in connection with these developments.

Legal castration is defended by an eminent Swedish psychiatrist on the ground that it is "more humane to give an habitual sexual criminal the chance to live in society as a free citizen without sexual drive than to force him to spend years in prison, tortured by his abnormal desires".[7] There is force in this argument, but it tramples a little too heedlessly over the question of relative values. Religion and ethics alike might prompt many to reject it.[8]

But the most important objection to both sterilisation and castration is the fatalistic attitude which they embody. They assume that any sort of adjustment at the social or psychological level is impossible. But defectives can be trained, and some believe that psychopaths can be treated.[9] Progress, moreover, will continue so long as we go on trying. So long, that is, that we do not give up attempting constructive action in favour of a surgical short-cut.

POSITIVE EUGENICS. On the positive side the eugenics movement is concerned to encourage biologically well-endowed types of person to produce more children. According to Burt, the present trend is in the opposite direction as far as intelligence is concerned: the largest families are being produced by the least intelligent sections of the population. If current tendencies continue, Burt estimates that, between the years 1950 and 2000, the number of children of scholarship ability in this country will be approximately halved, and the number of feeble-minded children almost doubled.[10]

Recent studies of the actual trend of national intelligence have cast some doubt upon this conclusion,[11] but if it is shown to be well founded, positive measures to halt such an ominous trend might include family allowances of the sort already provided under the British national insurance scheme. Even general children's allowances such as these will probably give a special boost to the birth rates of the better endowed, as they are probably more prudent than the rest of the population in their calculations of what size of family they can afford. Special family allowances for the well endowed would probably be more certain in their action. Such special allowances already exist in certain professions, e.g. among the academic staffs of British Universities. In so far, however, as those who are biologically favoured already belong to the better-paid professions, any allowance scheme which discriminated to their advantage would be opposed to modern ideas of social justice.

It may be, in any case, that such economic motives have been overrated, and that more important are general attitudes of optimism or pessimism about the future. Education and propaganda also have a part to play. The Nazis showed us how much could be done by propaganda to encourage selective mating—though it does not follow that the romantic Englishman would respond to such an appeal as readily as the serious and conscientious German.[12]

Positive eugenics is at least voluntary, and unlike sterilisation, can be gone back upon later. In these respects, it is unexceptionable. But it suffers from the same basic weakness as the negative methods: fatalism, and the lack of certain knowledge about the inherited component in such social problems as crime.

## Improvements in Methods of Child-care and Training

It is probably more to the point to direct attention to the family environment, and in particular to methods of child rearing. The work of Burt, Healy and Bronner, Bowlby, and many others has shown the decisive role which emotional experiences within the family play in creating young delinquents of the most serious and persistent sort.[13] The prevention of emotional deprivation in early infancy is probably the most constructive single step which could at present be taken to prevent serious criminality in later years.

EDUCATION OF THE MEDICAL PROFESSIONS. Education will help, and it is unfortunately true that it is as much needed by the medical professions as by the mothers themselves. Doctors, midwives, and health visitors, to whom mothers naturally turn for advice about their children's health problems, are well equipped to deal with problems of physical health, but know very little about mental health, and are apt in any case to be very resistive to psychological ideas. As a result, they place all the emphasis upon physical hygiene and rigid habit training; and the child, in order to conform with such standards, is faced with the task of suppressing some of his most vital inner impulses. The error is not in aiming at such standards, but in trying to achieve them too early and too speedily.

There is a related tendency to decide that a home is unsatisfactory and to remove a child from it because material standards are low, irrespective of the quality of the emotional environment which the family provides. Many sluttish families, nevertheless, love each other dearly. It may be difficult to train indolent and dirty parents in better ways, but it is easier than curing the affectionless child who may result if he is deprived of his relationship with his mother at an early age.

Doctors nowadays do receive more psychological training than they did before the war. Nurses, whether in their basic training, or when they qualify, later, as midwives and then as health visitors, have very little. But it is the midwife at the infant welfare centre, and the health visitor who calls at the house, who have the greatest influence upon the methods of training which a mother uses. Their training urgently needs revision, so that they may be able to help raise standards of mental hygiene in the community as much as they have already helped to raise our standards of physical hygiene.

HELPING THE DISTURBED MOTHER. Sometimes, however, the education of parents is more than a matter of learning facts and acquiring ideas; their own emotions may be deeply involved in the methods of child-training which they adopt. For example, a mother's own sense of anxiety and insecurity may cause her to be inconsistent, or fussy and demanding, with her offspring. Or the mother who is (probably unwittingly) at the mercy of strong aggressive feelings, may continually give expression to them when she is handling her child. The child, who was herself unloved at home, also peeps out in the defensively impersonal attitude of the mother who is now incapable of giving love to her own child.

Any attempt to change parental attitudes in such cases will be a long-term business, involving case-work skills bordering on the psychotherapeutic. General workers such as midwives and health visitors cannot be expected to specialise in this way. This is the task of the psychiatric social worker.

Many psychiatric social workers are at present employed in child-guidance clinics where many problems of the sort described are already being tackled. The child-guidance service, however, only comes into the picture when, as a result of the prolongation of family tensions, the child is already showing signs of psychological disturbance. The child-guidance team of psychiatrist, psychologist, and psychiatric social worker then work together on the case. Intelligence and personality tests are administered by the psychologist, the child receives psychotherapy from the psychiatrist or the psychologist, and the social worker tackles the parental attitudes which have given rise to the problem.[14] There are also hostels or schools for maladjusted children to which children who need full-time residential treatment can be transferred.[15]

But some way needs to be found of bringing influence to bear at an earlier stage, when mothers are encountering the earliest storms and crises of infant-rearing and are making their first mistakes. In some places the experiment has been tried of posting a psychiatric social worker in an infant welfare centre, and has been found very well worth while.[16] Another approach is through discussion groups with the mothers of young children. These may begin at the factual level, but, as a form of group therapy, can eventually be utilised to give reassurance and insight at very deep levels indeed.

AVOIDANCE OF SEPARATION. Steps also need to be taken to ensure that the very young child is not deprived of the love and attention he needs from his mother, by being physically separated from her. This is a real danger in those parts of the country where women supply a large part of the industrial labour force. In the textile areas of the north, for instance, it is traditional for married women to go to work, leaving their children with a "grannie"— either a real grandmother or a professional "minder". This may not be too harmful if the child is always looked after by the same woman, as is usual under the traditional system. The greatest harm is likely to be done, paradoxically enough, by modern day nurseries, which can provide trained staff, and cleaner and more hygienic conditions, for here the frequent use of nursery-nurses-in-training, whose stay is bound to be temporary, and the adoption of shift systems, make it almost impossible for a child to adopt any particular person as a "mother substitute".

Dorothy Burlingham and Anna Freud have given a revealing picture of the deprivations from which children in a residential nursery suffer.[17] These are common also to many children placed in a day nursery, for they are taken to the nursery almost before they are awake, and when their mothers collect them in the evening, it is time for bed again.

The illness of the mother is an unavoidable contingency, but frequent changes in foster mother should be avoided at all costs. A few hospitals are now aware of the importance of preserving the mother-child relationship when the child himself has to be taken in for treatment. The late Professor J. C. Spence, in his work at Newcastle-on-Tyne, tried to arrange for treatment at home whenever this was at all possible, but if the child had to be admitted to hospital, the mother was taken in too, slept in the child's room, and tended it. At Rotherham, a specially organised Children's Nursing Unit, run since 1949 by the local authority, has made it possible to keep large numbers of children out of hospital.[18] Other hospitals allow the mother to come in each day to feed and bathe the child, and play with him a little. In many others, visiting restrictions have been greatly relaxed.

THE UNSTABLE FAMILY. Temporary disturbances, like this, in the child's family background are bad enough, but what if his home is about to be permanently destroyed by the separation of his parents, or by his removal from their care because he is considered to be neglected?

In itself, the prevention of separation or divorce may not be the best way of ensuring that a child grows up in a psychologically healthy atmosphere. This is the fallacy of those who lay such stress on the broken home as a cause of juvenile delinquency. Probation officers and marriage guidance councils, who are now doing much valuable work in the field of matrimonial conciliation, recognise this, and aim not merely at keeping the partners together, but at trying to help them to sympathise with and understand each other more. It is not the legal bond uniting the family which is important to the young child, but the emotional bond.

Where a child is being neglected at home, it may be that social work or timely material help will make it unnecessary to take the child away. Many local authorities have set up co-ordinating committees of the social agencies which are concerned with children. Sitting, often, under the chairmanship of the Medical Officer of Health, they discuss cases from their different points of view and try to mobilise all their resources in the interests of the children. And the wide range of professional viewpoints which they represent has meant that more attention is given to the possibility of keeping the children in their own homes.[19]  A joint circular from the Home Office and the Education and Health Ministries in 1950, strongly urged the setting up of such committees in all county and county borough areas.[20]  The general rehabilitative work done by such bodies as the Family Welfare Association or the Family Service Units, must also prevent many children from being taken into the care of the local authorities.

SUBSTITUTE HOMES.  If it is imperative that a child should be taken away from his parents, then the principles of sound child-care demand that he should be found an environment which is going to be stable, and also intimate enough to give him the emotional satisfactions which he needs for healthy psychological growth.  A good foster home, if its permanence can be assured, is the best solution.  Foster parents are likely to be more natural as parental figures than professional child-care workers, and also to provide the child with a more natural home-setting in which to grow up.  The Curtis Committee came down heavily on the side of foster homes.[21]  Pressure on local authorities from the Home Office followed, and between 1946 and 1949 the proportion of the children taken into care who were boarded out increased from 23 per cent. to 34 per cent.[22]  By 1954 the proportion had risen further, to 44 per cent.[23]

However, the superiority of the foster home must not be automatically assumed.  In some cases, a children's home placement may be preferable for special reasons, and a good small children's home is always preferable to a series of unsuccessful foster home placements.

In dealing with crime at its infantile roots in this way we may hope to reduce the number of those whose offences are due to deeply-lying hostility or insecurity, to inner conflicts, or to a psychopathic or affectionless disposition.  Many obviously pathological crimes, sex crimes, for instance, may also be prevented.  There will remain a large number of normal criminals, for an explanation of whose predatory activity we must look, not to methods of child-care, but to the wider social environment in which they have grown to maturity, and from which their standards of behaviour have very largely been acquired.

## NOTES TO CHAPTER XIX

1. See Chapter IX.

2. Tappan, P. W., *Comparative Survey of Juvenile Delinquency, Part I, North America*, 1952 (United Nations, Dept. of Social Affairs), p. 84.

3. Sheldon, W. H., *Varieties of Delinquent Youth*, 1949, p. 888.

4. Henderson, D. K., *Psychopathic States*, 1939.

5. *Report of the Departmental Committee on Sterilisation*, 1933, Cmd. 4485.

6. Rylander, G., "Treatment of Mental Abnormal Offenders in Sweden", *Brit. J. of Delinquency*, 5: 4, 1955, p. 266.

7. *Ibid.*

8. A valuable discussion of sterilisation and castration laws will be found in Mannheim, H., *Criminal Justice and Social Reconstruction*, 1946, Chapter 2.

9. Abrahams, J., and McCorkle, L., "Group Psychotherapy at an Army Rehabilitation Centre", *Diseases of the Nervous System*, 8: 2, 1947; Franklin, M. E., *Use and Misuse of Planned Environmental Therapy*, 1945 (especially p. 8); Lindner, R. M., *Rebel Without a Cause*, 1944; Jones, Howard, *Group Methods in the Institutional Treatment of Delinquent and Problem Children* (London Ph.D. Thesis, 1953), Chapter V. See also the reference to the work of Jonnson in Sweden, in Bowlby, J., *Maternal Care and Mental Health* (World Health Organisation), 1951, pp. 50-1.

10. Burt, Cyril, *Intelligence and Fertility*, 1946, p. 32.

11. Emmett, W. G., "The Trend of Intelligence in Certain Districts of England" *Population Studies*, 3: 1950, pp. 324-7; Scottish Council for Research in Education: *Trend of Scottish Intelligence*, 1949.

12. On the whole question refer to the *Report of the Royal Commission on Population*, 1949, Cmd. 7695.

13. See above, Chapter IV.

14. A concise account of the work of the child guidance clinic will be found in Burbury, W. M., Balint, E. A., and Yapp, B. J., *An Introduction to Child Guidance*, 1947.

15. Wills, W. D., *The Barns Experiment*, 1949, is an account of one such school.

16. Joseph, B., "A Psychiatric Social Worker in a Maternity and Child Welfare Centre", *Brit. J. of Psychiatric Social Work*, No. 2, August 1948, pp. 30 ff.

17. Burlingham, D., and Freud, A., *Young Children in Wartime*, 1942, and *Infants Without Families*, 1943.

18. Spence, J. C., "Care of Children in Hospital", *Brit. Medical J.*, 1: 125, 1947. Gillet, J. A., "Children's Nursing Unit at Rotherham", *Mother and Child*, 26: 8, 1955, pp. 194 ff.

19. The Co-ordinating Committee at Salford, Lancs., is described in Donnison, D. V., *The Neglected Child and the Social Services*, 1954, Appendix II, pp. 144-6.

20. *Sixth Report of the Work of the Children's Dept. of the Home Office*, 1951, Appendix IX, pp. 138-9.

21. *Report of the Care of Children Committee*, 1946, Cmd. 6922, pp. 152 ff.

22. *Sixth Report of the Work of the Children's Dept. of the Home Office*, pp. 11-12.

23. *Children in the Care of Local Authorities*, 1954, Cmd. 9488.

# CHAPTER XX

## PREVENTION THROUGH COMMUNITY WORK

Although changes, and often improvements, in social amenities are continually taking place, it is not often possible to measure what effect they have had upon the amount of criminal activity in the community. So many changes are always taking place simultaneously that the effect of any given factor is hopelessly obscured. But as regards the effect of the improvement in housing conditions which we have witnessed in this country over the last thirty years, some tentative conclusions can be drawn.

### Failure of Rehousing

Social reformers have always hoped that if environmental conditions could be improved, especially by a general rehousing programme, improvements in behaviour would follow. As far as crime is concerned, this has not so far been borne out by the evidence.

The "delinquency area" studies pioneered by C. R. Shaw and his collaborators, established that most criminals lived in the overcrowded and decaying slums near the centres of cities. Various British studies[1] have shown, however, that as the slum areas have been cleared and their inhabitants transferred to the new municipal housing estates, the centres of delinquency have shifted with them. The new estates have begun to surpass even the old central areas in the number of crimes committed by those who live in them.

It is probable that over a longer period the more wholesome conditions in the estates will make themselves felt. Delinquency figures do seem to fall a little when an estate has been occupied for a few years[2]—though there are many other possible reasons for this. But one thing remains clear: improvements in the material environment do not, in themselves, result in any reduction in crime in the short run. For quicker results, the emphasis will have to be placed upon trying to influence individuals directly, rather than more remotely, through changes in their material background.

### Difficulties Confronting Social-work Agencies

Social work seems to be the obvious answer, but much of the work that social agencies have tried to do in some areas has been rendered nugatory by forces arising from within the community itself. W. F. Whyte, in his Chicago investigations, found that the agencies were treated as alien intruders, and that the local residents would have little or nothing to do with them.[3] E. W. Hughes gained the impression that in certain areas of Coventry, membership of a boys' club gave rise to comment: "a sort of 'marked man' outlook".[4] In a delinquency area near Nottingham the young people regarded youth clubs as "too classy ('they are for the top end of town'); too strict; too like school; or tied to a church, 'which would put some off'".[5] The natural result of such attitudes as these was, as W. F. Whyte found, that lads tend to prefer their own "street-corner group" to anything which the settlement house provides.[6]

All this evidence, however, is based upon subjective observation: observation carried out, it is true, by skilled investigators or experienced social workers, but involving all the time a process of generalisation and interpretation which is full of possibilities for misunderstanding. For this reason, the attempt at an objective measure of the value of social work in the Cambridge-Somerville Youth Study is of special interest.[7]

THE CAMBRIDGE-SOMERVILLE YOUTH PROJECT. This was a ten-year project begun in 1937 by Richard Clark Cabot, Professor of Social Ethics and of Clinical Medicine (*sic*) at Harvard. Two groups of matched individuals were to be constituted: a treatment group (the "T" group), consisting of boys who were to receive the attention of counsellors, and a control group (the "C" group), who were to be left to their own resources. Over the period of the study the membership of both groups totalled 650 boys, though of course only 325 of these received preventive care.

Counsellors were expected to establish an intimate and friendly relationship with their clients, but beyond this they were entirely free to use whatever methods they thought best. While some adopted the techniques of the trained case-worker, others inclined to an approach through personal friendship, emphasising "inspiration, practical help, and persuasion".[8] Counsellors were not confined to the case-work relationship in their attempts to help the boys. They could place them with foster-parents. Educational and medical services were available. And although counsellors were not permitted to undertake club-work themselves, they often sent boys away to camp or encouraged them to join existing youth clubs.

· The result of all this lavish expenditure of dollars and effort on behalf of the treatment group was disappointing. While there was practically no difference between the frequency of committal to a correctional institution in this group as compared with the controls, the total number committing offences was actually less in the control group. Between 1938 and 1945, 267 "T" boys committed offences of all types, but only 246 "C" boys. If only the more serious offences are included, the number of "T" boys concerned was 76, as compared with only 67 "C" boys.

The design of this study as a social experiment has been much criticised. The lack of any sort of clear definition of the methods of treatment to be used is one obvious defect. Also treatment itself was adversely affected by the war, which caused a number of the boys to lose the counsellor to whom they had become accustomed, and removed a number of the older boys from treatment altogether. Much also hinges upon how well the "C" and "T" groups were matched; there is reason for doubting if this was as accurate as it might have been.[9] But in spite of all these reservations, the negative conclusions drawn by the investigators from their study are well substantiated. As they put it: "The special work of the counsellors was no more effective than the usual forces in the community in preventing boys from committing delinquent acts".[10]

### Community Organisation

This is a very significant statement, implying as it does that there are natural recuperative forces within the community upon which the counsellors did not draw. Taken together with the observations already made about the resistance which the community offers to the efforts of social agencies from outside, it suggests very strongly that preventive work should be carried out through the public opinion and institutions of the delinquent community itself.

· CHICAGO AREA PROJECT. Preventive work of this sort has been one outcome of the "delinquency area" investigations in Chicago. In 1934, the Chicago Area Project was set up under the direction of C. R. Shaw to encourage the community itself, through its own natural leaders, to tackle its delinquency problems. Existing agencies have been very largely by-passed, the local residents being encouraged to set up their own neighbourhood committees. With the aid of an organiser supplied by the Project, but without any obligation (or any undue inclination) to accept his advice, these committees examine their problems, work out solutions, and to a very large extent find their own funds.

Indigenous leaders have had to be sought out and made aware of the problems confronting their community. Some of those who came forward were professional men, like doctors or lawyers, and others were factory workers or housewives. Some were even ex-criminals themselves, and where this is so their experience has proved invaluable. But the impact of the Project has not been limited to the leaders, the select few serving on committees. Many other residents have been drawn in as volunteer probation or truancy officers, or to help with fund-raising campaigns. Still larger numbers share in the work by contributing to the funds. It is, in fact, a mobilisation of the community in the face of a common threat.[11]

MECHANISMS AT WORK. It is illuminating to compare this method of attack upon the problem of delinquency with group therapy,[12] and with the experimental work which Kurt Lewin and others have been doing in recent years in the field of group dynamics. Lewin found that desirable changes in the dietary habits of a group of families could be most effectively achieved by allowing mothers to discuss the pros and cons of the case quite freely, and then come to group decision about what they would give their families to eat in future.[13] In the language of group therapy, it appears that they had secured insight through their discussions, and that their identification with the group and its decisions provided them with a further powerful motive to change, *i.e.* through their desire to conform with the norms of their own social group.

The same mechanisms can be seen in operation in the Chicago Area Project, and if they are used skilfully their effect should be not only to increase the effectiveness of the measures of treatment and prevention adopted, and thus reduce the amount of delinquency in the area, but also to change local attitudes towards crime. Area projects may thus operate as preventive measures at two levels: as a means for the working out of locally acceptable and effective programmes of social work, and at a more fundamental level, in the slow transformation of the folk-ways and ideals of the group.

ACHIEVEMENTS. No figures have been published by which the success of the Project might be judged. Neighbourhood committees have been very active, both on their own account and in drawing upon the facilities provided by other agencies. They have sponsored clubs, camps, and playgrounds, and have encouraged educational developments. They have done work in the field of housing, and have provided employment exchanges. They have also done direct social work of all sorts with delinquents, in which they appear to the offender not as "outsiders, offering him a pseudo-fellowship as charity, but responsible citizens of his own neighbour-hood, speaking his own language, and whom he knows".[14]  It is still not possible, however, to say whether any appreciable reduction in delinquency has resulted from all this activity.[15]

On the other hand, the internal chemistry of the community has been stimulated into greater activity, and into activity which is obviously sound and constructive.  The developments in the very submerged areas "back of the yards", where Alinsky worked with rather more unorthodox and drastic methods than those used elsewhere,[16] has been generally agreed to be remarkable.

BRISTOL SOCIAL PROJECT.  No work of any account along these lines has yet been carried to completion in this country, though it seems likely that the current Bristol Social Project under J. C. Spencer will develop along similar lines.  As this is primarily research, we may perhaps hope that it will include an attempt at the sort of evaluation of these methods which we have so far lacked.[17]

SOME OBJECTIONS.  There are certain misgivings to which the critical observer will want to give expression.  The most important is whether the inhabitants of such areas, where standards are very low, can be expected to feel that delinquency matters, or that they need to do anything about it.  It may be particularly difficult to start the necessary leaven working if the area is very small and delinquent attitudes almost universal.  As Sprott and his collabo-rators have pointed out, the process of discussion and insight-gaining will then have to loom very large in the programme.[18]

Competent native leaders may also be difficult to find under such circumstances, though experience in Chicago has shown that this difficulty can be exaggerated.  Leadership ability is not the prerogative of one class in society; it is simply that we do not recognise it for what it is when it embodies aims and standards which are different from and, perhaps, opposed to our own.  It does not need to be created, but merely to be informed.[19]

Mays has wondered if the cultural inbreeding which Area Projects appear to encourage may not lead to aesthetic impoverish-ment.[20]  It certainly may do if the work is being carried on behind an "iron curtain".  As it is, there will always be many points of contact with neighbouring communities, and many opportunities for fruitful comparison with them.  The aim of the Area Project is not to isolate the delinquent community from its neighbours, but to make it more self-conscious as a community, so that it will be impelled to seek for itself a happier and more comfortable place in the great society.

## Group-work with Gangs

The juvenile gang needs special consideration, for it is a miniature community in its own right, shaping the behaviour and ideas of its members to a considerable extent. It will often reflect the lax *mores* of the community in a delinquency area, but may also embark upon delinquent acts because of the lack of other outlets for energy and the spirit of adventure. The gang may often be a haven, in this way, from the adult ideas which prevail elsewhere, and a means to securing satisfactions which the adult world denies.

In particular, the existence of the gang may be seen as evidence of the failure of the ordinary youth organisations to satisfy the needs of the gang members. There is plenty of evidence to show that the type of child who becomes delinquent will not stay in youth clubs.[21] This may be partly due to the general attitude of the neighbourhood towards the clubs, but it is certain that their inflexibility and their relatively high standards also make them unattractive to these restless, aggressive, and adventurous children. When such children do make contact with the club, it is often to attack it, as club leaders in tough areas often find out to their cost. The gang emerges to fill the vacuum which the failure of the youth club has left.

THE NORMALITY OF THE GANG. The older approach to the gang saw it as an unhealthy growth in the body social for which the only remedy was immediate excision. Even Cyril Burt, who was well aware of the gregarious needs which gangs subserve, could see no other solution than to disperse them.[22] To hope, as many courts and some probation officers seem to do, to keep a child away from the "bad influence" of a gang, is to deny his gregarious nature. He may pay lip-service to the prohibition, but he will rarely keep to it. And this is in itself a hopeful sign, for it shows that he has social needs and respects social norms even though they are the atypical ones of a delinquent group. The psychopathic or affectionless offender is ominously indifferent to such group influences.

Those who acknowledge the normality and, indeed, the desirability of gang formation will turn their attention to its activities, and the needs which these satisfy. They will try to find for it what the psycho-analysts call "sublimations", so that these needs may be met without delinquency.[23] An early venture along these lines was made by William George, before he founded the first Junior Republic.

GEORGE'S "LAW AND ORDER" GANGS. He made contact with a large gang of delinquents on the East-side of New York, and became its leader by defeating the previous leader in a fight. He then set out to show his followers that they could obtain as much fun and excitement out of helping to keep the peace, as in breaking it. The gang was re-formed into a body of police auxiliaries, and helped the regular force to track down, trap and round-up the more elusive types of offender, who had previously escaped scot-free.[24]

SHERBORNE ROAD YOUTH CENTRE. The great increase in delinquency in this country during the war led to a number of interesting innovations in youth-work methods, which had a similar general rationale to George's "law and order gangs". The Sherborne Road Youth Centre, which was located in a City of Birmingham Evening Institute, provided a club for those who were not willing to satisfy the more stringent demands of the ordinary youth club.

The staff made their contacts with young people about the streets of the city, and brought them into the club. Only the tougher element was admitted. Standards of discipline were relaxed, though all members were required to join at least one serious educational or hobby class. At first there was much disorder, but gradually the centre became tidier, more settled and better mannered. After a while, however, the flow of new members ceased; the club had become too orderly for them. The leader concluded that at this point a second centre was really needed for new members, and from which they could be promoted as their standards improved.

It was claimed that gang-members who joined the Sherborne Road Centre soon transferred their loyalties from the gang to the club. Less than two years after it was opened, there were only two active street gangs left within a half-mile radius of the centre.[25]

THE BARGE CLUB. In 1948, the Barge Boys' Club was started in Wapping. This was intended to appeal to "unclubbable boys", *i.e.* those who would not join the ordinary youth club, or were rejected by it because of their behaviour. The club was to be located on a Thames barge floating at anchor. It was hoped that such an unusual club room would be a special attraction, as would also be the adventurous activity on the river which it would provide.

A local and very unruly gang became the core of the club. Unlike the local youth clubs, the Barge was able to hold their interest, and after an initial period of aimlessness they entered upon a phase of constructive activity in which they repaired and adorned their floating club room, and set about learning the skills of the waterman under the friendly tutelage of the river police. The club's esprit de corps reached a high level, and led them into victory in various contests on the river against apprentice watermen and pre-service cadets, in spite of their relative indiscipline and lack of technique.[26]

CENTRAL HARLEM STREET CLUBS PROJECT. The Central Harlem Street Clubs Project in New York was set up in 1947, to study methods of handling anti-social gangs of adolescents.[27] Warfare between gangs, resulting in many casualties, had brought the matter into public notice. Further investigation by project workers showed that many offences of all sorts were committed or inspired by these gangs: rape, stealing, and damage, as well as violence.

Nevertheless, as the replacement of the pejorative word "gang" by "street club" implies, the project adopted a constructive attitude towards the problem. In the words of G. Howland Shaw, it reacted against "the sensationally and essentially negative view of the street club and its potentialities which from time to time has been widely publicised".[28]

The workers made informal contacts with the gangs, and gradually became accepted by them. They made no attempt to usurp the leadership of the groups, but through the relationships they had made, tried to get them to consider the implications of their behaviour, and to seek their ends through more socially acceptable channels. The aim in fact here, unlike that of the other projects described, was not to convert the gang into a youth club, but to put the gang itself on the right lines.

## Fundamental Importance of Social Attitudes

The causes of crime, it has been emphasised, are multiple, the process of causation, complex. Social attitudes seem, however, to be the most fundamental of them all. They are reflected in our child-rearing methods, and even in group-differences in the birth rate. Many social changes and measures of reform may contribute to reducing the amount of crime, but their success in this and, indeed, their very existence, depends upon the existence of favourable social attitudes.

It is, then, to the gradual growth in social relationships and social insight within the general community that we must look as the ultimate preventive.   This, it is true, means no more than that crime will diminish as the quality of our social life improves, but it is more than the truism which it seems at first sight.   It does at least provide clear and intelligible criteria towards which we can work.

## NOTES TO CHAPTER XX

1. See pp. 79-80 above.

2. This is one of the conclusions to be drawn from the Leicester study described on p. 79.

3. Whyte, W. F., *Street Corner Society*, 1943.

4. *J. Educ. Psychology*, **13**: Part III, 1943, pp. 60-1.

5. Sprott, W. J. H., *et al.*, *Social Background of Delinquency*, 1954 (limited circulation by Nottingham University), p. 116; also p. 140.

6. *Op. cit.*

7. Powers, E., and Witmer, H., *An Experiment in the Prevention of Delinquency*, 1951.

8. Powers, E., in the *Annals of the American Academy of Political and Social Science*, 1949, p. 82.

9. Powers and Witmer, *op. cit.*   Also Mannheim, H.: Review in *Brit. J. of Delinquency*, **3**: 3, 1953, p. 211.

10. Powers and Witmer, *ibid.*, p. 327.

11. Shaw, C. R., and McKay, H. D., *Juvenile Delinquency and Urban Areas*, 1942, p. 442-6.   Also: *A Program for the Prevention of Delinquency*, 1954 (pub. Chicago Area Project).   Witmer, H. L., and Tufts, E., *Effectiveness of Delinquency Prevention Programs* (U.S. Social Security Admin., Children's Bureau Pubn. No. 350), 1954.

12. See Chapter XVII above.

13. Lewin, K., "Group Decision and Social Change", in Swanson, G. E., *et. al.*, *Readings in Social Psychology*, 1954,

14. Ellingston, J. R., *Protecting our Children from Criminal Careers*, 1948, p. 334.

15. Such information as is available about the results of the work will be found in: *A Program for the Prevention of Delinquency*, *op. cit.*   See also Witmer and Tufts, *op. cit.*

16. Alinsky, S., *Reveille for Radicals*.

17. Carnegie United Kingdom Trust, *Annual Reports* for 1953 and 1954. Spencer, J. C., "Planning of a Social Project in Bristol", *Case Conference*, **1**: 3, 1954.

18. *Op. cit.*, pp. 290-1.

19. See Shaw and McKay, *op. cit.*, p. 445.

20. Mays, J. B., *Growing Up in the City*, 1954, p. 135.

21. Reed, B. H., *Eighty-thousand Adolescents*, 1950, pp. 132-4; Bagot, J. H., *Juvenile Delinquency*, 1941, pp. 53-5; Henshaw, E. M., *Report on Juvenile Delinquency* (Bradford Education Committee), 1942, p. 16, etc.

22. Burt, Cyril, *Young Delinquent*, 1944, pp. 502 ff.

23. For a further discussion of this question, see: Jones, Howard, "Group Sentiment and Delinquency", *Mental Health*, **8**, 1948, pp. 41 ff.

24. George, W. R., and Stowe, L. B., *Citizens Made and Remade*, 1913, pp. 6 ff.

25. *Youth in a City*, 1943.   Board of Education Pamphlet, No. 117.

26. Turner, M. S., *Ship Without Sails*; Spencer, J. C., "The Unclubbable Adolescent", *Brit. J. of Delinquency*, **1**: 2, 1950, pp. 113 ff.

27. Crawford, P. L., Malamud, D. I., and Dumpson, J. R., *Working with Teen-age Gangs*, 1950.

28. *Ibid.*: Foreword by G. Howland Shaw, p. vi.

# INDEX

Mettray Colony, 205, 209
Michael, J., 22 *n*
Millbank Prison, 131, 138
Milner, K. O., 32
Minn, W. G., 244 *n*
Missioners, police-court, 143-4, 229
Moll, 21
Moloccans, 77
Monachesi, E. D., 166 *n*, 244 *n*
Monthly variations, 112-13
Moral imbecile, 37
— insanity, 36
Moreno, Jacob L., 226 *n*
Morris, Norval, 178 *n*
Morrison, Herbert, 168
— W. D., 115 *n*
Morton, H. M., 192 *n*
Muller, N., 81, 244 *n*
Mullins, Claud, 158
Mutual Welfare Leagues, 219-20

NATIONAL Association of Discharged Prisoners' Aid Societies, 190
Natural crime, 4
Neglectful mothers, 175-6
Negroes, 86
Neurosis and crime, 41, 92
Neurotic character, 50
Newgate Prison, 132
Newman, H. H., 40 *n*
Newspapers, 67-8
Norfolk Island, 135
— Penal Colony, Mass., 220, 226
Northfield Project, 223, 224, 226 *n*
North Sea Camp Borstal, 147, 185, 196, 202

OBSERVATION centres, 157, 211
Ogden, D. A., 197
Open institutions, 147, 172-3, 176, 188, 195-6, 198
Ordinaries, 170, 171, 172
Osborne Association, 208
— Thomas Mott, 219-20, 221

PAGE, Leo, 165 *n*, 241
Panopticon, 131
Park, R. E., 75
Parker, Judge F., 160-1
Parkhurst Prison, 145, 173, 204
Paterson, Sir Alexander, 146-7, 195, 198, 202, 226 *n*
Paul, Sir George Onesiphorus, 131, 138
Peak-age, 106-7

Penal servitude, 134-5, 136, 142, 148
*Penchant au crime*, 99-101
Penitentiary movement, 136
Pennsylvania system, 136-9
Penology, 10
Penrose, L. S., 39 *n*
Pentonville Prison, 138, 188
Persistent offenders, 94-5, 109, 162, 177, 191
— — treatment of, 142-3, 147-8, 160, 170, 173, 191, 245-6, 247
Personal responsibility, 8-9, 118, 119, 124-5
Philanthropic Society, 145, 204, 205, 207, 209
Phillip, Arthur, 133-4
Polansky, N., 19
Police, 6, 16-18, 102, 103, 122-3, 238-9
Pollak, O., 115 *n*
Popham Acts, 130-1
Poverty, 58-65
Powdermaker, Florence, 53
Powers, Edwin, 165 *n*, 226 *n*, 262 *n*
Precipitating factors, 93-5
Prediction tables, 89-90, 161-4, 197, 242
Predisposition, 93-5, 101
Pre-trial enquiries, 232
Prevention, 126, 245-62
Preventive detention, 119, 142-3, 147, 148, 170, 176-7, 189, 215
Prichard, J. C., 36
Prison system, English, 167-78, 217-18
Probation, 143-4, 145, 158, 211, 226-43
— officers, 144, 190, 201, 211, 214, 226, 229, 230-9, 251, 259
Professional thief, 91-2, 96-7
Progressive stage systems, 129-30, 134, 135-6, 173-4, 183-4, 200
Psychiatric social workers, 234, 250
— treatment, 95, 177-8, 197, 211, 213, 250
Psycho-analysis, 44-7, 78, 121, 123
Psychodrama, 222, 225
Psychosis, 41
Punishment, 116-26, 128, 130, 131, 133, 138-9, 143, 146, 147, 150, 151, 155, 160-1, 180, 199, 206, 208
Punitive detention, 176-7, 215

QUETELET, A., 99-101

RADIO, 67, 70
Radzinowicz, L., 9, 10, 111, 114 *n*, 126 *n*, 178 *n*

PRINTED IN GREAT BRITAIN BY UNIVERSITY TUTORIAL PRESS LTD, FOXTON
NEAR CAMBRIDGE